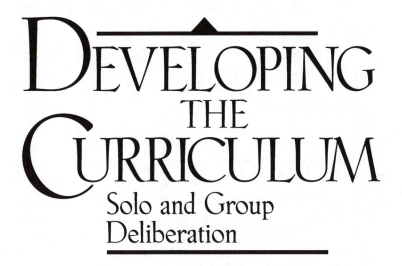

DEVELOPING THE CURRICULUM

Solo and Group Deliberation

Gail McCutcheon

The Ohio State University

D0022359

Longman *Publishers USA*

Pn

Developing the Curriculum:
Solo and Group Deliberation

Longman, 10 Bank Street, White Plains, N.Y. 10606

Associated companies:
Longman Group Ltd., London
Longman Cheshire Pty., Melbourne
Longman Paul Pty., Auckland
Copp Clark Longman Ltd., Toronto

Senior acquisitions editor: Laura McKenna
Production editor: Linda Moser/Professional Book Center
Cover design: Parise Design
Back cover author photo: Bill Tijerina
Production supervisor: Richard Bretan

Library of Congress Cataloging-in-Publication Data
McCutcheon, Gail, 1941–
    Developing the curriculum : solo and group deliberation / Gail
McCutcheon.
         p.   cm.
    Includes bibliographical references and index.
    ISBN 0-8013-0949-2
    1. Curriculum planning—Decision making.   2. Curriculum planning—
Decision making—Case studies.   I. Title.
LB2806.15.M3   1995
375'.001—dc20   94-8965
                                                                   CIP

1 2 3 4 5 6 7 8 9 10-VMA-9897969594   FTW
                                      AHH9294

I dedicate this book to the educators who helped me learn about deliberation as I did the research for this book. It is always an aesthetic and somewhat awe-inspiring experience to be in the presence of genuinely dedicated, magnificent teachers. It is neither magical nor mysterious, but it is moving. I hope this book helps to demystify what these excellent teachers do and how they think about the curriculum. They were generous, patient, and thorough in teaching me about their deliberations. For that I am truly grateful.

Contents

v

Foreword

America's "love affair" with efficiency and effectiveness expresses itself in virtually every walk of American life—education is no exception. We have tried in this country to think about schooling in forms that echo the organization of factories and mobilization of armies. We have wanted for years to create a theory of education and an array of educational practices that would ensure the achievement of our educational aspirations. Indeed, rationality itself has been conceived of as the ability to efficiently relate means and ends.

In some ways, such aspirations are understandable. Developing efficient and effective systems reduces effort and increases both precision and probability. In American education, we have historically been on the hunt for the one best method. We have tried to work out systems—expressed most acutely during the efficiency movement in education—that lead to curricula that are "teacher proof" and whose consequences can be measured with such clarity and certainty that the American public would, at last, know whether it was getting its money's worth.

It was in the late 1960s, largely through the initial insights of Joseph Schwab, that another view of educational practice emerged, particularly with respect to the planning of curricula. Schwab's orientation acknowledged the importance of deliberation and the inherent incompleteness of existing theory or any combination of theories. Schwab's approach celebrated, in a sense, a democratic planning process in which individuals guided by curriculum specialists would bring their own specialties to bear on the complex and often contentious task of deciding what to teach, to whom, when, and under what conditions. Gail McCutcheon's book, *Developing the Curriculum: Solo and Group Deliberation*, participates in the tradition that Schwab and others initiated, but its roots go back to Aristotle's distinction between theoretical and practical reasoning. Theoretical

ix

reasoning has to do with subject matters whose behavior was of necessity. Practical reasoning pertains to the contingent, that is, to situations that could be other than the way in which they were.

The field of curriculum development within the broader field of education has not had a rich literature addressing the ongoing deliberations of practitioners. To be sure, there are some works published, but in the main books on curriculum planning tend to describe normative conceptions of what it is that schools ought to teach or analytic categories that are intended to enable those making curriculum decisions to address matters that count. What Gail McCutcheon has done is to examine the nuances of group and solo deliberation in making curriculum decisions. In this effort she draws not only from the Aristotelian and Schwabian traditions, but from the work of a wide range of scholars both in and outside of education who have concerned themselves with various forms of reasoning and with the conditions that motivate or inhibit people from adequately addressing the complexities involved in complex decision making. Because so much of the book relates directly to the thought processes and articulations of practitioners, *Developing the Curriculum* has a kind of practical authenticity that is usually absent from most of the theoretical books on curriculum. How teachers feel, what they have to say, the matters they attend to, and those that they neglect are a part of the educational dialogues that the book makes available. In doing this, it gives the prospective teacher and student of education a more or less first-hand glimpse of what teachers and curriculum planners think about when making curriculum decisions. Such an orientation is quite consistent with the tradition in which McCutcheon is working. That tradition acknowledges that deliberative processes are seldom linear in character, that they address problems that have no single correct solution, and that it is not uncommon for deliberators to find themselves dealing with multiple attractive alternatives. In some sense, practical reasoning represents the apotheosis of human rationality. Deliberation is a process through which individuals or groups can come to some temporary resolution in order to make a decision on how to act.

From this perspective, theory in curriculum, as in education, has an important but limited role. It cannot be used deductively to prescribe specific courses of action in local circumstances. Local circumstances always have a richness and a specificity that theory, which is idealized, can never encompass. Theory is about the general; teachers work with the particular. Hence, the role of theory is not to direct teachers but to give teachers intellectual tools that they can shape and employ when addressing the situations in which they teach. Some of these situations can be planned for in advance, but many of the most critical decisions are made "on the fly." Thus, even the distinction between curriculum and teaching blurs when one considers that teachers are always in the process of shaping the conditions within which students learn.

Because of the richness of the case studies included in this volume, case studies that reflect McCutcheon's sensitive eye and rich experience as a former elementary school teacher, the volume has the ring of a writer who knows of what she speaks. *Developing the Curriculum: Solo and Group Deliberation* is not a second-hand theoretical treatise written by someone who's never really been in a classroom. On the contrary, it is written by someone who knows educational practice at the elementary school level intimately and that intimacy is reflected on virtually every page.

I am particularly pleased to see this volume appear in the educational literature. It will give prospective teachers, in particular, a genuine sense of what teachers do in making decisions about their own curricular practices and pedagogy. It will reassure prospective teachers that some of the prescriptions that emanate from government offices concerning how to plan are as misguided as they seem to be. What McCutcheon has done is to provide a basis for understanding why high-level specificity in preplanning programs does not work and why flexible purposing—to use Dewey's phrase—is a necessity. McCutcheon has further demonstrated that complex decisions affecting the lives of groups of people benefit from *genuine* deliberation. Efficiency is not a virtue when it reduces the phenomena that need to be addressed and oversimplifies and under-appreciates the conditions within which teachers work. Gail McCutcheon has given us a volume that makes the reality of schools, teaching, and planning vivid. It makes an important contribution to the literature of education and will be an important tool for those seeking to understand at a deeper level what genuine curriculum deliberation consists of.

Elliot W. Eisner
Stanford University

Preface

PURPOSES AND CONCERNS OF THIS BOOK

My purpose in this book to educate people about the processes of curriculum development teachers use both in planning alone and in department, schoolwide, and systemwide groups. I employ concepts about deliberation in theoretical and in case study chapters because deliberation seems very powerful for understanding what occurs in curriculum development. Many individuals and groups already use elements of deliberation when developing the curriculum; a fuller understanding of deliberation may help enrich their work as they strive to develop an optimum curriculum for their particular students. By understanding the nature of curriculum deliberation, I believe people can create more specific processes to facilitate curriculum development in their unique settings.

For most of my professional life I have been concerned about curriculum development. As a classroom teacher, I made countless interrelated curriculum decisions each day. I chaired a curriculum committee in one school system where we solicited and reviewed teachers' proposals for curriculum reform and funded some of them. Later, as a doctoral student and professor, I continued to recognize that learning how people make curriculum decisions—alone and in groups—is central to the field of curriculum. Moreover, I believe that curriculum is the center of education because decisions about what to teach are the most important ones that educators make. It has also become clear to me that many people have difficulties making good curriculum decisions. Without understanding the processes involved, they make flawed decisions that later necessitate revisions. Revisions are also continually needed because as society changes the curriculum must be changed. Whether due to these societal changes or previous flaws, curriculum development is ongoing and never ending.

I've designed this book to bring to light the nature of processes of curriculum development and to discuss and raise issues about its improvement. In this book I reveal and examine how people make curriculum decisions alone and in groups. I've based some of this discussion on other scholars' work because it is useful. However, the literature in curriculum development is scattered in numerous journals, books, and conference presentations and thus is often difficult to locate. In this book I synthesize these scholars' major contributions. In addition to curriculum literature, I have drawn on literature about teacher planning, thinking, and theorizing and about the social construction of knowledge because these areas are also fundamental to understanding educators' curriculum development. I encourage people to read these scholars' works in their original form.

In addition to this theoretical work, I present examples of cases of curriculum development to provide detailed illustrations of processes at work, what influences them, and what actions result from the decisions. I also discuss these illustrations in light of the literature included here. In short, the book focuses upon how people make curriculum decisions, a fundamental and important process in education.

I include several qualitative case studies and many examples in this book for several reasons. The most important reason concerns how such case studies inform readers and inform the theory. In a sense, such case studies comprise nonfiction "stories" that engage readers or listeners, provide information to them, and invite them to think about that information in a manner that is different from other kinds of discourse, a point Carse (1986:133–134) makes very well. In his view, narrative prose such as stories engages readers or listeners in thinking because it *shows* something to them rather than by *telling* them through discursive prose. Stories aim less at persuasion, conversion, or control than at engagement in thinking: "The stories they [storytellers] tell touch us. What we thought was an accidental sequence of experiences suddenly takes the dramatic shape of unresolved narrative." Stories invite readers and listeners to think about the lack of resolution and patterns inherent in an enterprise as they exist in parables, fables, motion pictures, novels, and myths. The cases in this book reveal how *real* people in *real* settings make *real* curriculum decisions alone and in groups. These nonfiction "stories" enable readers to "see" themselves in the cases as they watch people in similar situations treating similar curriculum problems. By seeing how others make curriculum decisions, readers place themselves in the text when they recognize their own experiences. Readers then reflect upon themselves, their curriculum problems, their setting, thought processes, and the patterns inherent in making curriculum decisions.

It is crucial to recognize that this form of generalizability between the cases and readers occurs through *readers'* active thinking and involvement in the cases, not merely by *my* explaining potential generalizability. That idea is called "transferability."

I have also included the cases and a research appendix in order to permit readers to decide whether contentions in explanatory chapters are warranted and whether the cases are trustworthy. Finally, the cases also constitute points of discussion about alternatives, reasons why some people made particular curriculum decisions, and the nature of and reasons for the lack of resolution when it occurs. In short, discursive prose *tells* readers but does not *show* what deliberation looks like. Both explanatory and narrative prose are needed here to develop a full understanding of curriculum deliberation, which is complicated unless one can "see" it in action or, better yet, participate in it. Perhaps curriculum theory, like other kinds of theories about people, should consist of a series of parables so readers can have access to the ideas in a human manner.

CURRICULUM: A DEFINITION

It is only reasonable before proceeding to stipulate what I mean by "curriculum" in this book. By "curriculum" I mean what students have opportunities to learn under the auspices of schools: the content that schools offer.[1] Broadly speaking, curriculum concerns *what* should be taught. However, this is more complicated than it seems because several kinds of curricula are available in schools.

The Explicit Curriculum

Teachers teach the explicit curriculum overtly because it is the publicly advertised fare of schooling, is intended, and is taught openly. School systems typically list the overt curriculum in documents and policies such as graded courses of study, curriculum guides, scope and sequence charts, and report cards. Some examples here are knowledge, attitudes, and skills.

The Implicit Curriculum

Students also have access to *implicit* learning, which may be intended or unintended but arises out of and is inherent in the everyday nature of classroom life or life in a school. Because schools, classrooms, and educational materials have particular qualities, students have opportunities to learn things emanating from the nature of those schools, classrooms, and materials. For instance, Jackson (1968) believes students learn to live in crowds, to postpone their personal desire to talk with a busy teacher, to disregard interruptions, to wait until someone has finished using a needed object (such as a book or tube of paint), to tolerate boredom and passivity, to accept other people's evaluations, and to compete with both teachers and fellow students in order to obtain rewards. Implicit learning is the result of a generalized effect of schooling, one that seems to happen without planning and prior knowledge. It comprises an unacknowledged set of learnings available because of the nature of schools, educational materials, and individual teachers. For example, I recently heard a teacher say:

Lois, keep your eyes on your own work.
Mark, let's get busy here. Get your work done on time.

Nancy, I know you can do better. Sit down and recopy this so it's neater. You need to do work you can be proud of, not this messy trash.

Alexander, you simply *have* to be more responsible. You can't leave your homework at home every night like this. Now, grow up. If you can remember your baseball glove every day, you can remember to bring your homework, too.

In these instances and in some of those that Jackson lists the teacher seems to intend the learnings. The implicit curriculum evolves out of the everyday goings-on at school and has not been planned in any formal sense.

Teachers do not bear sole responsibility for the nature of the implicit curriculum. For example, many states mandate saying the Pledge of Allegiance every morning. This recitation may result in students' learning a sense of patriotism or ritual whether educators intend it or not. Indeed, teachers may take this simple ritual for granted. A curriculum is also implicit in curriculum materials. In the following example, the stated purpose (its overt curriculum) seems to be at odds with its implicit curriculum, and I encourage readers to consider this discrepancy while reading it.

> ### *Puppet Activity[2]*
> ### *Ginny and Jerry*
> PURPOSE: To help children accept themselves as they are unique individuals.
>
> MATERIALS: Hand puppets (one boy, one girl)/Tree (Prop 7)/Scarf to be worn by girl puppet*/Two *bats* (pencils or appropriate substitutes)*/Two beanies (cut two 1 × 8-inch strips of paper, loop around puppets' heads and hook)*/Newspapers*. [Starred items are not included in the kit.]
>
> PROCEDURE: [What the teacher is to say is in boldface type.]
>
> 1. INTRODUCTION **I'm going to show you a puppet play about these two puppets, Ginny and Jerry. Put on puppets. Be very quiet until the story is over and the puppets bow like this.** [*Make puppets bow.*]
> 2. STORY AND ENACTMENT **Now Ginny was Jerry's friend. In fact, she liked him so much, she wanted to be exactly like him.**
>   **When Jerry wore a beanie, Ginny took off the pretty scarf she was wearing, got a beanie, and wore it.** [*Unwind scarf and put a beanie on Ginny.*]
>   **When Jerry climbed a tree, Ginny tried and tried to climb the tree.** [*Have Jerry climb the tree easily; have Ginny keep sliding down.*] **This made Ginny angry with herself because she didn't do it very well. When Jerry would swing a bat, he could really swing, but Ginny could hardly swing it at all.** [*Show*

vigorous swing for Jerry, weak swing for Ginny.] **Ginny felt she was not as good as Jerry when she couldn't swing the bat very hard.**

When Jerry got a newspaper route, Ginny helped him. She could only carry one paper, while he carried three. [*Show puppets carrying and throwing newspapers.*] **Sometimes Ginny got very tired along the way and wished she were home making doll clothes and doing other things.**

Then one summer Jerry went to visit his grandmother. Ginny couldn't go. She just sat around sadly and did nothing.

Then one day something happened. Ginny found out that trying to be like Jerry and doing only the things Jerry liked wasn't making her happy. She decided to do the things she liked to do. She wore pretty scarves, she jumped rope, she played with dolls. This made her feel much happier. When Jerry returned, sometimes she did the things he liked to do, but not all the time. Ginny found she could be Jerry's friend, but she should be herself.

3. DISCUSSION **What happened to let Ginny know she should be herself, not Jerry?** [*Help the children see that when Ginny stopped feeling sorry for herself and stopped trying to be like Jerry, she was not only able but happier.*]

4. EXTENSION **What is there about you that is special?** [*Elicit responses. Encourage children to use the puppets to show something about themselves that makes them unique as a person. . . .*] (Dinkmeyer, 1970:69-70)

What might students learn from this puppet play? Throughout it the stereotypes that girls are weaker than boys and what constitutes "girlish" things are obvious. It seems more than possible that this lesson implicitly reinforces the stereotypes that girls are weak and enjoy wearing pretty scarves and playing with dolls and that boys are active and strong.

The Null Curriculum

A third kind of curriculum, the *null* curriculum, consists of what students do not have opportunities to learn. It may seem odd to call it a "curriculum" unless one considers that its absence creates ways of thinking by negating opportunities to learn alternate skills and knowledge. Thus it is crucial to consider what we do *not* teach in schools as well as what we do.[3]

Conceived in this way, curriculum is at the very heart of schooling, for decisions about what opportunities students should have to learn are the most important ones we make about schools. The curriculum "drives" all else in school; ideally, all other decisions should support these fundamental decisions and be ancillary to them. Because the process of making curriculum decisions is so central, we need to understand how educators—working alone and in groups—make such decisions and to consider how the process can be facilitated and enhanced.

OVERVIEW OF THIS BOOK

In this book I portray both what I found in the literature and in classrooms and meeting rooms in my quest for understanding how people make curriculum decisions, the contexts in which they make their decisions, and the assumptions they make. I've found no certain answers but have found great elaboration on and use of processes to address curriculum problems. Quite simply, this involves deliberation to resolve practical problems. When *individuals* deliberate, the process rests heavily on the individual construction of reality: the creation of their personal theories, images, or practical theories of action. When *groups* deliberate, this is also the case, but the process is made more complex because it relies on a *social* construction of reality. This means it is accompanied by conflict among and varied interests of people in their effort to reach group agreement.

Solo deliberation constitutes mental planning when individual teachers make curriculum decisions. Group deliberation includes the discussion and weighing of alternatives people employ when making curriculum decisions such as the development of a graded course of study or curriculum guide or the adoption of educational materials. It rests heavily on the development of the group, which occurs simultaneously with the development of the curriculum.

In chapter 1 I discuss the nature of deliberation as a process central to decision making about curriculum. I include a part about solo deliberation. In chapter 2 I detail how individuals engage in curriculum decision making and examine the nature of teacher thinking, teachers' practical theories of action, and teacher planning. Taken together, teacher thinking and planning and teachers' practical theories comprise solo deliberation. I follow these two literature-based chapters with two chapters describing solo deliberations of teachers at the elementary school level (chapter 3) and secondary school level (chapter 4). I relate the nature of the curriculum these teachers make available to their students to their practical theories of action and solo deliberations as depicted in these chapters.

While I included case studies of elementary and high school classrooms and teachers' deliberations about them, I did not include portraits of classrooms in middle schools, colleges, or in-service courses offered in business, health-care professions, the military, and other places. I limited my research for this book so it would not rival an encyclopedia in length. The organization of such settings may differ somewhat from cases I presented in this book, but I believe many of the issues and processes are fairly similar. However, I encourage people to do research in these settings as well.

The problems of making curriculum decisions are similar enough among settings that I believe other similarities probably also exist. Details undoubtedly vary because of differing personalities, policies, organizational constraints, and possibilities, as well as other factors that make each situation idiosyncratic. However, I believe that because the task itself is a human enterprise, many matters are similar in various settings.

For example, some high schools and middle schools, unlike those I visited in chapter 4, are organized into interdisciplinary teams rather than by departments. Based on my experiences working in such settings, I believe an interesting interplay occurs between solo and group deliberation during their planning sessions. While planning in a group, they develop a sense of general goals and outcomes and perhaps a general strategy about how students learn as well as their appropriate roles in facilitating this, and through solo deliberation they decide how specifically to enact and achieve these goals.

The next part of the book concerns group deliberation. In chapter 5, I examine group deliberation, the social construction of reality, conflict, competing interests, and the roles teachers' practical theories of action play in the endeavor. Interest fuels conflict, and conflict drives the deliberative process as people strive to develop agreement to resolve the curriculum problem they face. In chapter 6 I portray group deliberation about a reading textbook adoption in a school system. Here I focus primarily on the roles of conflict and teachers' practical theories of action in group deliberations. In chapter 7 I portray a group developing a graded course of study for social studies, the way it developed agreement, and the roles of conflict, stress, interests, and teachers' practical theories of action in group deliberation. I close the book with chapter 8, where I analyze, compare, and contrast the cases to the literature, exploring issues about differences among cases of deliberation and then outlining implications for various people. The case studies I present in chapters 3, 4, 6, and 7 illustrate the nature of deliberation in a variety of settings to facilitate understanding its nature and processes. My other purpose is to compare and contrast deliberation in practice with its portrayal in the curriculum literature so I can raise and discuss relevant issues and questions.

In the research appendix I describe my beliefs about research, the philosophy underlying my research approach, and detail the strategies I used to collect, analyze, and interpret data.

ACKNOWLEDGMENTS

No book is merely a solitary venture; many people supported, helped, and challenged me in writing this, and I am indebted to all of them. Foremost among them is my secretary, Linda Jones, who patiently typed various drafts of this on the computer. Moreover, she helped me maintain some semblance of organization during the years I developed and wrote this.

My husband, George Disch, and my son, Ian Chávez, also deserve my deep appreciation for their support and patience while I undoubtedly selfishly neglected their needs, yet talked incessantly about teaching, planning, and the goals of education. I'm sure I was so preoccupied by it and at many times seemed distracted from their interests and concerns. I love them both and hope they'll forgive me. I'll try not to slight them when I start another project.

Other people assisted by agreeing to help me with my research. These people appear in this book under altered names, and they know who they are. I am extremely grateful to them for their efforts at helping me understand how they made curriculum decisions and for discussing earlier drafts of the case studies, teaching me patiently how they saw things. Of course, I'm also indebted to John Dewey, Joseph Schwab, Peter Pereira, Bill Reid, Decker Walker, and Ian Westbury for their earlier work about deliberation.

Finally, many people supported this venture merely by asking how it was going and encouraging me when it went more slowly than I'd hoped or I reached a particularly troublesome spot. Chief among these people was Elliot Eisner. Naomi Silverman was instrumental in encouraging me to develop my prospectus, and Laura McKenna was very helpful in talking about the project and seeing it through. Several colleagues and former students were also helpful simply by letting me discuss my work with them and by asking me how it was going. These people include Elsie Alberty, Bob Backoff, Gary Best, Jeff Cornett, Beverly Cross, Keith Hall, Gisele Hinkle, Ken Howey, Dan DeMatteis, Burga Jung, Brad Mitchell, Bill Pasters, Richard Pratte, and Nancy Zimpher. Many students read earlier drafts of various chapters; discussions with them, their questions, and comments enriched my work greatly. Elsie Alberty, Beverly Gordon, and Robert Lawson helped me obtain two ten-week research leaves to observe in elementary and high schools, and without those leaves I could not have developed and written this. Several people reviewed this for me, and their criticisms helped me rethink a few parts. Bill Pasters proofread this and helped me develop the index for this book, and I appreciate his thoughtful help on it. Most of these people are truly a pleasure to know, and I feel very fortunate to have that opportunity.

I would like also to thank the following reviewers, commissioned by Longman Publishers:

Daisy Arredondo, University of Missouri

Gerald Bailey, Kansas State University

Carol Barnes, California State University, Fullerton

Kathee Christensen, San Diego State University

Ellen Clark, University of Texas, San Antonio

William Doll, Louisiana State University

Elliot Eisner, Stanford University

Thomas Erb, University of Kansas

Joann Ericson, Towson State University

Sandra Gray, Southwest Missouri State University
Lillian Hart, Clemson University
Edmund Short, Pennsylvania State University

Their comments were very helpful.

NOTES

1. I first developed and wrote about this definition in 1982. Cleo Cherryholmes borrowed and employed this definition in his recent (1988) book.
2. From *Developing Understanding of Self and Others, Level 1* (DUSO D-1) by Don Dinkmeyer. © 1970 American Guidance Service, Inc. 4201 Woodland Road, Circle Pines, MN 55014-1796. All rights reserved.
3. For elaboration on these definitions see Eisner (1985:87–107).

part

Deliberation in General

This part of the book contains one chapter, which discusses theoretical literature and research about the concept of deliberation.

chapter 1

The Nature and Role of Deliberation in Curriculum Decision Making

Whether people engage in it individually or in groups, deliberation is the central process of curriculum decision making. It is exciting to watch people tackle curriculum problems and develop plans to resolve those problems. It is even more compelling to be involved in curriculum decision making. During deliberation, people reveal, exchange, and weigh many ideas and values. Deliberators examine and discuss ideas about the content of education and its function and organization. They discuss how students learn, how teachers teach, the social context of classroom life, and broader social needs and purposes of education. Through deliberation, people also speculate about the future and envision ideas in action. The discussions and thinking underlying these ideas are frequently spirited. Ideally, when people deliberate they identify problems, generate alternatives, and examine each fully. In a sense, deliberation is the process of weighing the many possible resolutions to problems and the many matters that vie for attention, affect the curriculum, and otherwise shape teachers' decisions about what to teach in order to act in their students' best interests.

Group deliberation is frequently an opportunity to develop policies and plans for coordinated action—an important matter worthy of close attention. Solo deliberation involves many of the same processes, and it too is a complicated and intriguing process. Alone, teachers plan what opportunities to make accessible to their students. Although teachers deliberate alone, they envision actions and the effects of actions on a group of students, so it is a social enterprise as well. These deliberations are crucial to the profession of teaching. Indeed, deliberation may be the most professional part of teaching, for through it teachers conceptualize, envision, and plan by applying their knowledge of students and the context where they work as well as many diverse theories that they and others have developed about their situation.

Solo deliberation (where teachers plan alone) and group deliberation (where teachers plan in groups) are interrelated methods of curriculum decision making. Because deliberation is a process, it may be more difficult to understand than if it were an object, easily labeled, framed, and placed on the wall. This chapter concerns the nature of the process in general.

I begin by examining the nature of deliberation. Then I turn to several categories of knowledge ("commonplaces") that are helpful to apply in deliberation. In a third section, I discuss phases of deliberation, then explore such impediments to deliberation as the influence of stress and particular habits of thinking on decision making. I close the chapter by applying concepts from the chapter to excerpts from three cases of curriculum decision making, and I challenge readers to do this as well. Finally, I summarize the chapter.

DELIBERATION: A DEFINITION

Deliberation is a process of reasoning about practical problems. It is solution oriented, that is, toward deciding on a course of action. A deliberative approach is a decision-making process in which people, individually or in groups, conceive a problem, create and weigh likely alternative solutions to it, envision the probable results of each alternative, and select or develop the best course of action. It is not a linear process, although specific activities are necessary. It is important to recognize that not *all* thinking and discourse about the curriculum constitute deliberation. Some of these activities might be termed "reflection" or "discussion" because they do not have all or most characteristics of deliberation.

Further, some thinking might comprise what Simon (1976) refers to as "satisficing," where people search for a course of action that is good enough to meet a minimum set of requirements, for instance, the objectives of a state or local school system. Satisficing is characterized by settling for less than the optimum course of action because it is acceptable (e.g., to a board of education, state or local policymakers, parents, or administrators) rather than meeting the ethical and moral needs of society and students. When people satisfice, they can plan how to "get by," and this does *not* constitute deliberation.

Adopting an approach of satisficing rather than deliberation may result partly from the bureaucratic organization of schools, where people other than teachers themselves make many curriculum decisions and where policies hold teachers accountable for teaching students to meet a set of minimum standards—in effect, controlling the teachers. Teachers may thus develop a civil service mentality toward teaching, a natural outgrowth of which would be satisficing rather than deliberation. Ultimately, this approach lowers the quality of education because decisions favor playing it safe to keep one's job. Indeed, Duckworth (1984) decries such a civil service conceptualization of teaching because it causes teachers to curtail using their own rich and illuminating knowledge and thus deprives students of the benefit of this enormous potential.

Nine Characteristics of Deliberation

Deliberation has at least nine important characteristics. Deliberators (1) consider and weigh *alternative* possible solutions and actions, (2) envision potential actions and outcomes of each, and (3) consider equally means and ends, facts and values, and must (4) act within time constraints. That is, a decision has to be made within a particular time span because an action *must* be taken. For instance, materials must be ordered; lessons must be conceived of, developed, and taught; or topics must be revised, added to, or deleted from the curriculum by a particular time because school is due to start, the board of education has scheduled a meeting, or other events are going to occur. The need to act in this way can have a deleterious effect on deliberation, as I explain later in the chapter.

Deliberation also (5) has a moral dimension. Deliberation is not an objective, value neutral, totally rational enterprise, nor should it be. While deliberators make purposeful, rational decisions, their decisions are inescapably informed by values and ethical commitments, a sense of social responsibility, and a vision of a better society rather than by a system of accountability to an *external* authority or following an objective technical set of steps.

By extension, deliberation is (6) a social enterprise with at least five elements. One element is the social responsibility educators have for making decisions that affect children and society as a whole. A second social element of deliberation is that in group deliberations, people employ social interaction skills exchanging ideas, disagreeing at times, and learning how to work together to make decisions. Together, people create the process of deliberation as they engage in it by formulating their own social rules, such as whether interruptions are permitted, conversations are possible, or raised hands are needed to be called upon. Third, in solo deliberation, teachers must consider what other teachers are teaching as they attempt to provide coherence, continuity, integration, and sequence in the learning opportunities in their own classrooms. Fourth, deliberation is also a social enterprise the teacher must anticipate and consider students' reactions. Finally, deliberation calls for educators to anticipate the future of society. That is, as they educate students today, teachers are really preparing them to contend with their future lives. In this way, the curriculum both reflects and changes society, and deliberation yields responsible rather than accountable action.

Another important quality of deliberation is (7) *simultaneity.*[1] That is, when people deliberate many things simultaneously vie for their attention as they think and speak. The decisions to be made are complicated and affected by a number of matters, and so individuals and groups may be attracted to various ideas. Missing from much of the deliberation literature is this idea of simultaneity. Instead, deliberation is mistakenly thought of as a linear, totally rational process, but because of simultaneity it is not.

Finally, two other important characteristics of deliberation are the presence of (8) interest and (9) conflict, which interact to fuel deliberation and drive the process. As a result, whether engaging in solo or group deliberation, it is important to be aware of the nature of the interests and the resulting conflict, to weigh them, to voice one's own interests, and to be highly involved in participating in and understanding the resolution of the conflict. It is important to be tolerant of the conflict, to weigh differences of opinion inherent in deliberations, and thereby to judge the alternatives.

According to Pratte (1977) interest is a disposition to act held by an individual because *only* an individual can be interested in something or be motivated by an interest to act. Interest is a useful if confusing idea to apply to deliberation. In daily life, the word *interest* has a preferential use and a normative use (Chambers, 1983). The former means merely a liking, or preference, for something. In the preferential sense, a person might have an interest in Chinese cooking, the game of bridge, or sports cars. The normative use concerns our own or someone else's welfare. In this sense, people talk about self-interest and vested interests. For instance, an elementary school teacher might like teaching science more than teaching reading (a preferential interest), but if the administration said that raises would be determined by students' scores on reading tests, it would be in the teacher's interest (in a normative sense) to focus on reading. If the reading-test scores formed the basis for students' grade-level promotions, it would also be in the students' interests (in a normative sense) to perform well on the test whether they were interested (in a preferential sense) in the test or not.

Mansbridge (1980:24–25) defines the term *interest* as enlightened preference, although she acknowledges that no information is perfect. Further, she believes her definition is better than one differentiating between preferential and normative interests because, in her own (1980:26) words:

> It does not seem a distortion of meaning to speak of my having an interest in someone else's welfare or in ending famine in Biafra if I have no material stake in the outcome but have so identified myself with the achievement of these goals that they have become part of myself in the same way as my need for clean air or a higher income.

This applies in particular to individual teachers engaging in solo deliberation (see chapter 2) because their practical theories of action become their interests in Mansbridge's sense. That is, teachers so identify themselves with their beliefs, concepts, and images about their work that they have a stake in applying their own practical theories of action to their private deliberations or to a group's deliberations.

However, the distinction Chambers makes between preferential and normative interest is also a useful one. I take interest to mean enlightened preference, but interests can be of two types, following Chambers's distinction. Jung's (1991) analysis, after closely examining the interests of a group deliberating about the mathematics curriculum for an affluent suburban school system, revealed that three "interests" predominated: interest in the group process itself, in professional development, and in accountability. For deliberation, the normative application of interest is highly relevant. Teachers might decide to be involved in group deliberations due to several normative interests; for instance, having their ideas taken into account to protect themselves from inordinate or disagreeable change;

learning more about the curriculum; gaining the attention of an administrator in charge of promotions; or resolving a problem directly affecting them. Normative interests are the basis for much of what individuals say in group deliberations and plan in solo deliberations, and for this reason interests can be thought of as the fuel of deliberation. If interest is the fuel, then conflict is the engine.

Conflict concerns disharmony and disagreement. It can run the gamut from dispassionate debate through heated debate to all-out war. When people disagree but continue to think and talk, they examine ideas more carefully than they would if unanimity existed. Some social groups try to smooth over or avoid conflict, but it has several positive roles to play in deliberations. Simmel (1955) distinguishes between conflict motivated by personal goals and conflict in which individuals represent a group's goals. This latter type can be complex because when people see themselves as representing a cause they are frequently imbued with a sense of respectability and self-righteousness because they are not acting solely out of their own self-interests. (See chapter 6 for an example of this.) In social processes such as curriculum deliberation, individuals are prompted by interests that may partially or wholly conflict with the interests of colleagues. As they deliberate in the group, they construct knowledge as a group—socially— that is, through discourse they create ideas. Through the conflict, people come to understand one another's positions more clearly than if there were no conflict. As a result, they can more clearly evaluate the alternatives that arise.

According to Park (1941), conflict helps groups integrate and rate ideas and group members. In Park's (1941:578) view, conflict is important because "only where there is a conflict is behavior conscious and self-conscious; only here are the conditions for rational conduct." As with politics and world events, much curriculum change can occur through differences of opinion, discussions of alternatives, weighing and making self-conscious decisions about these alternatives, and the resulting social construction of knowledge.

Finally, Simmel (1955) believes conflict unifies people because it brings about interaction between antagonists who must create both the norms and conditions under which the conflict takes place. That is, when conflict brings the antagonists together, they discuss not only the conflict itself but also the ground rules for that discussion. In the course of the conflict, the antagonists develop the norms under which the discussion can occur (e.g., whether interruptions are permitted, the extent of formality or informality desired, and the sort of language to be used). In the end, because they have established these social norms and attended closely to each other's positions, a resolution can be reached. Deliberators can commit themselves to their resolution because they have undergone the process to reach it. Conflict virtually *forces* people to examine alternatives, which is a characteristic of deliberation. The group also becomes unified as a result of developing a common interest. However, this conflict among competing interests is one reason that deliberation consumes so much time and seems so disorganized. Deliberators simultaneously develop the rules for discourse and the curriculum, and this takes time and does not flow easily in one direction. (I shall have more to say about conflict in group deliberations in chapter 4.)

Conflict might appear not to exist within individuals, but it does and is commonly described as "having mixed feelings," "on the one hand . . . and then the other hand," or "being of two minds." Such conflict occurs when we are simultaneously attracted to and repelled by things, when we find two things equally attractive, when we are supposed to do one thing but prefer to do something else, or when we believe we *should* do something else. In such cases, each person examines closely the merits of both sides to understand the matter and resolves it; afterward the person is committed to a decision because of this process.

For example, a number of years ago I facilitated a middle school faculty's deliberations about how to organize the curriculum. One social studies teacher voiced an interest in organizing all the disciplines around the concept of change. The art teacher disagreed because in her view many significant elements of art would not fit tidily. The mathematics teacher concurred, arguing that only by stretching the idea of change to the point of absurdity could he incorporate some of the more crucial features of his curriculum. The science teacher, keen on continuing to teach the periodic table of the elements and worried about the availability of suitable materials, added his voice to this side. Because of their interests, these teachers wanted to maintain the status quo, in which the key concepts of their separate disciplines were primary.

The language arts teacher, however, took up the change idea, arguing that although it would take some massive reorganization on everyone's part, in the end everyone (including the teachers) would be excited about learning. The school psychologist supported the language arts and social studies teachers by pointing out the changes adolescents confront daily, so the concept would certainly be relevant to them. Deliberators examined both sides of the issue and in the end opted to organize the curriculum around change. Their unity was evident when two representatives from the state department of education visited and demanded to see their behavioral objectives. However, the faculty had been working for ten days on curriculum reform and replied that they were not ready to begin writing their objectives. They were adamant about the matter. They also related their commitment to change as a concept to unify the curriculum. As their work progressed, they traded and suggested ideas, pulled each other along, examined each other's syllabi and objectives, ordered and developed new materials. Two years later they implemented the new curriculum. They continued to meet every other week to discuss troublesome details that had eluded them. At the beginning of their deliberations the teachers were divided by competing interests. Conflict actually brought the group together to such an extent that they developed a common interest in change. As this example demonstrates, when educators take conflict seriously and pay close attention to opposing interests, they can make informed decisions.

Deliberation consists of a search for an *optimum* course of action, given the dynamic balance between constraints and resources. People make their choices purposefully, having examined alternatives and likely consequences. At times it is an uncomfortable process because of the lack of certainty about how to proceed, as will be illustrated in the cases in the subsequent chapters. It is important to recognize that uncertainty and lack of comfort are common and universal problems in the process of deliberation, but that through patiently examining various courses of action and their nature and consequences, people have been successful in deliberating and selecting a course of action appropriate for the time and setting. They frequently have to reconsider the same problem on subsequent occasions because today's "answer" may become problematic as conditions, students, and teachers themselves change. Further, the original decision may have been flawed due to impediments to deliberation, as I discuss later in this chapter.

I turn now to several other scholars' views on deliberation.

Deliberation According to Other Theorists

Several theorists have developed ideas about deliberation. In Dewey's (1922) philosophical work about the nature of thinking he termed one kind of thinking "deliberation." Schwab (1978) applied that idea to curriculum development and elaborated on Dewey's work. Reid (1978) continued to apply Dewey's and Schwab's work to education and to elaborate on those ideas further through his own philosophical and empirical work. Walker (1971) also employed philosophical and empirical methods to explain deliberation and clarified and systematized the process somewhat.

Dewey (1922) portrays deliberation as a form of practical reasoning useful in solving problems. In his view, merely utilitarian approaches "degrade morals" (1922:189). They are ultimately false to facts because they ignore moral knowledge and have the potential to separate means from ends and moral knowledge from empirical knowledge. Dewey regards deliberation as "a dramatic rehearsal (in imagination) of various possible lines of action." This dramatic rehearsal consists of envisioning an action in order to see what it would entail. One positive feature of this is that "thought runs ahead and foresees outcomes." Hence the deliberator avoids having to undergo the action itself, for, as Dewey says: "An act overtly tried is irrevocable, its consequences cannot be blotted out. An act tried out in imagination is not final or fatal. It is retrievable." The act of rehearsal can be simultaneously a solitary as well as a social act because deliberators rehearse the social consequences of their planned action.

Schwab (1978), who was heavily influenced by Dewey's work, argues that a method for treating practical problems should neither be deductive nor inductive; rather, it must be deliberative. Elaborating on the nature of deliberation, he describes it as complex and arduous. Through deliberation, people treat both ends and means as mutually determining; identify facts relevant to both ends and means and to the case in general. Further, through deliberation, people generate alternative solutions and trace various likely consequences of each alternative on the case and on what is desired in general. Deliberators compare each alternative and its likely consequences with other alternatives to "choose not the *right* alternative, for there is no such thing, but the *best* one" (Schwab, 1978:318, emphasis in original). Although this may sound like a linear view, Schwab does not view deliberation as a linear process.

Reid (1978:43) continued to develop the idea that deliberation is a form of practical reasoning and characterized deliberation as "the method by which most everyday practical problems get solved." For Reid, it comprises "an intricate and skilled intellectual and social process whereby, individually or collectively, we identify the questions to which we must respond, establish grounds for deciding on answers, and then choose among the available solutions." Again while Reid's view of deliberation makes it sound like a linear process, he does not intend that.

Reid (1978:42) discusses the nature of practical problems themselves and delineates seven features common to practical problems that I find helpful:

1. They are questions that have to be answered—even if the answer is to decide to do nothing. In this they differ from academic, or theoretic, questions which do not demand an answer at any particular time, or indeed any answer at all.
2. The grounds on which decisions should be made are uncertain. Nothing can tell us infallibly whose interests should be consulted, what evidence should be taken into account, or what kinds of arguments should be given precedence.
3. In answering practical questions, we always have to take some existing state of affairs into account. We are never in a position to make a completely fresh start, free from the legacy of past history and present arrangements.
4. Following from three, each question is in some ways unique, belonging to a specific time and context, the particulars of which we can never exhaustively describe.
5. The question will certainly compel us to adjudicate between competing goals and values. We may choose a solution that maximizes our satisfaction across a range of possible goals, but some will suffer at the expense of others.
6. We can never predict the outcome of the particular solution we choose, still less know what the outcome would have been had we made a different choice.
7. The grounds on which we decide to answer a practical question in a particular way are not grounds that point to the desirability of the action chosen as an act in itself, but grounds that lead us to suppose that the action will result in some desirable state of affairs.

Walker (1990:162-163, emphasis in original) also echoes the theme of deliberation as practical reasoning when he says:

Practical problems arise when someone identifies conditions that they want to ease or eliminate. A practical problem can only be settled by an action or a decision to undertake a course of action designed to eliminate the problematic conditions. If we believe that thoughtful, considered actions are more likely to be effective, then decision-makers should consider in light of the best available knowledge what action, if any, is best for this situation, all things considered. This consideration of possible actions is called *deliberation.*

THE NATURE OF CURRICULUM PROBLEMS

When decisions have a clear, single solution, deliberation is not necessary. However, there are probably few of these in curriculum decision making. Complicated practical problems with multiple solutions may be best treated through the process of deliberation. Curriculum problems are typically of this sort.

The following problems exemplify ones recently treated through deliberation:

How can we get economics inserted into the curriculum in elementary and secondary school?

How should we sequence the curriculum in this elementary school?

What should be taught to gifted students in this school system?

What set of curriculum materials about reading should our school system purchase?

What should this hospital teach in our course about parenting?

How can we go about energizing the science curriculum at this elementary school?

How should I structure mathematics for my students for the entire year?

Should our school system require an additional course in American history for graduation? If so, what should we delete?

For male students in our school system, we offer both basketball and football. What sports should we offer the female students? Which sports can we teach coeducationally?

How can I incorporate these adolescents' fears, interests, problems, and concerns into the drama curriculum I teach?

How can we, at these high schools, integrate the curriculum so our students can more easily see connections among the subjects we teach?

This middle school cannot afford to publish both a school newspaper and a literary magazine. Which one should we do? Is there any way to raise money to do both?

How can this (Eastern European) country start to teach English as an important foreign language? What can we do to sustain that effort? At what grade level should we begin this?

How can we get law into the curriculum at the elementary and secondary school levels?

What should we change in our curriculum so that Native-American students don't drop out?

What should this college of education consider to be foundations courses?

How can I determine the nature of my implicit curriculum so I can change it if it's deleterious?

What should this state require second-graders to know?

These problems call for deliberators to apply different strategies, such as developing new curriculum materials, developing policies, resequencing or otherwise reorganizing lessons, reorganizing materials, and developing altogether new courses. Further, the problems range from huge, molar ones that cut across disciplines or grade levels to more molecular problems about subject matter at a particular grade level, and from plans for an entire nation or state to those for a particular classroom or school. They concern extracurricular as well as curricular problems, and the implicit as well as the overt curriculum. To resolve each problem, it is necessary to gather different facts and to apply different values. The problems to be dealt with range across all levels of schooling and include problems at sites other than traditional schools. Some involve group deliberations and others solo deliberations. Despite the many variations, deliberation, alone or in groups, is the process of resolving such practical, everyday curriculum problems. In all the cases cited above, the policies and plans were developed for a particular curriculum problem for a particular group of students in a particular setting. That is, each curriculum problem is unique to its setting. Furthermore, because education has conflicting aims, the grounds for making decisions vary and are unclear. People who make curriculum decisions hold differing ideas about the goals of education, and different interests are served by the solutions. While the *process* of deliberation can be transferred to different contexts and problems, the content of the deliberations and resulting decisions cannot be because each problem is rooted in a unique set of factors.

THE COMMONPLACES

Another matter fundamental to understanding the nature of deliberation concerns what Schwab (1978) calls the "commonplaces," several focuses that help to organize the uncertainty and variability of curriculum problems.[2] They can be thought of as types of knowledge to apply to curriculum decisions.

Schwab suggests applying four bodies of knowledge ("commonplaces") to each curriculum problem in addition to applying knowledge of curriculum development, which is necessary to organize and facilitate deliberation. Each of these bodies of knowledge should be considered in group deliberations. They also have implications for solo deliberation, so teachers planning alone are well advised to consider them. They comprise the content for reflection during deliberation. Schwab calls the four commonplaces *subject matter, learners, milieus,* and *teachers*.

By *subject matter* Schwab means the scholarly materials under treatment and the discipline from which they come. While Schwab himself concentrates here on "disciplines," several other sets of beliefs about what should be included in the curriculum have been advanced and could be considered through this commonplace. For example, Eisner's and Vallance's (1974) categories of orientations include curriculum as the development of cognitive processes, as self-actualization, as academic rationalism, as social reconstructionism, and as social adaptation. Ideas about the subject matter to be included in the curriculum encompass more than merely subject matter represented in academic disciplines.

A second commonplace, according to Schwab, is of *learners,* the students who are to be beneficiaries of the curriculum. Knowing learners includes knowing characteristics of the age group, what it already knows, can be expected to learn easily, or is likely to find more difficult. It also includes their aspirations and anxieties likely to affect learning.

Schwab's third category is *milieus,* the contexts in which a student's learning will take place. A milieu encompasses the school and the classroom as well as relationships among students, relationships between the community and the school, the status of educators in the community, relationships between the school and the individual families, and values of the community—its climate or ethos. I believe it should also include knowledge of students' cultures (such as Hispanic, African American, Asian American, and Native American).

Schwab's fourth commonplace, *teachers*, includes what teachers are likely to know, their flexibility and readiness to learn new materials and instructional strategies; their personalities, characters, and prevailing moods; relationships between teachers and students, each other, and school directors. Here Schwab is most clearly discussing factors that play a significant role in group deliberation about the overt curriculum rather than solo deliberation about the curriculum as presented in a classroom.

Finally, in addition to the four commonplaces is what Schwab terms the *curriculum specialist,* who holds a crucial role combining several functions, task master, agenda setter, attention director, clarifier, and summarizer. This category is different from the other commonplaces. For one thing, like the commonplace of teachers, the commonplace of curriculum specialist, as Schwab discusses it, concerns group deliberation. Moreover, the other commonplaces comprise categories of the content of deliberation, but this one concerns the process of facilitating deliberation. Here Schwab (1978:368) discusses the general function of this role:

> It is he [sic], as chairman, who monitors the proceedings, pointing out
> to the group what has happened in the course of their deliberations,
> what is currently taking place, what has not yet been considered.

One role of the curriculum specialist is to remind deliberators frequently of the importance of considering the commonplaces. Indeed, from the very beginning of the process, it might be a good idea for one person to assume primary responsibility for this. The curriculum specialist helps the group reflect on whether each commonplace is being applied as fully as is warranted. In solo deliberation, the curriculum specialist can be thought of as a voice reminding the individual educator of the commonplaces and calling for clarification about goals, organization, instructional and evaluation strategies, and the interrelationships among them all.

Another function of the curriculum specialist concerns the curriculum bit. The curriculum specialist facilitates the examination of the curriculum bit—a syllabus, set of materials, or lesson plans—to enable deliberators to study whether the meanings and ideas about which they deliberated are embodied in it. So, for Schwab (1978:369), "the second function of the curriculum specialist is to instigate, administer, and chair this process of realization of the curriculum."

Yet another function, according to Schwab, is to instigate, encourage, and monitor the examination of the curriculum bit in terms of the values it embodies in comparison to the values of the deliberators. Like the second function, this is a reflexive process in that scrutinizing the bit may change the deliberators as well as the bit itself. The process permits questioning whether students should be exposed to a given value in the curriculum as well as whether the curriculum bit should carry the value in it.

Schwab argues for reflectively considering these four commonplaces and the curriculum specialist's knowledge by applying the commonplaces to the curriculum problem during deliberation. For this reason, each commonplace is to be represented in groups and solo deliberation. Several other scholars' research about deliberation focuses on aspects of deliberation in an effort to understand the process. I turn to this work now.

ASPECTS OF DELIBERATION

Walker (1971) develops a model of deliberation and refers to it as a "naturalistic model," as shown in Figure 1.1. This model consists of three elements, the *platform,* the *design,* and their associated *deliberation.* By platform Walker means each deliberator's values and beliefs. This idea is similar to my idea about teachers' practical theories of action. (See chapter 2.) The curriculum design consists of relationships among features of the curriculum being developed. According to Walker, the deliberators enter with their individual platforms and deliberate about a curriculum problem, calling for facts ("data" in his model) about key issues on occasion. Eventually through deliberation they agree about some matters, which become policies (for instance, a policy to internationalize the undergraduate business curriculum by developing five supplementary textbooks; to hold a schoolwide science fair based on science, mathematics, and language arts; to integrate the middle school curriculum; or to individualize the mathematics curriculum). Then the group links the separate policies and decisions into a coherent design.

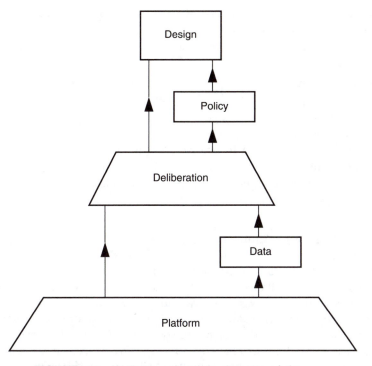

FIGURE 1.1 Walker's schematic diagram of the main components of the naturalistic model

SOURCE: D. Walker (1971). "A Naturalistic Model of Curriculum Development," *School Review* 80, pp. 51–65.

Each feature of the model is helpful in providing language to use to refer to processes of deliberation, but the unidirectionality of the arrows in the model is misleading. For example, as people deliberate, examine a curriculum bit, or consider data they requested, they might amend and alter their original individual platforms. Further, while the model appears to portray the curriculum design as the end, these alterations in people's platforms might also be a significant outcome. Another outcome might be understanding the nature and processes of curriculum decision making through deliberation. Moreover, while deliberation is an approach for considering and formulating *various* alternatives, this model appears to design only one alternative.

Another curriculum scholar who concentrates on phases of deliberation is Pereira (1984), who analyzes Schwab's practical arts necessary to curriculum development into four kinds: arts of perception, problemation, prescription, and commitment. In schematic form, Pereira's (1984: 347–351) analysis of tasks within the four arts is:

Perception
List the symptoms which indicate something is wrong.
Describe the details which are relevant.

Problemation
Make a diagnosis of what is going wrong and why.
Formulate the problem which will require attention.

Prescription
Inventory the resources and constraints.
Generate a plan of action to resolve the problem.

Commitment
Rehearse the consequences of the proposed action.
Terminate deliberation and take action.

Pereira (1984:349) acknowledges that deliberation is not linear and does not aim to produce only one action. Rather, he suggests that it allows for entertaining alternatives. Again, the schematic is helpful if deliberators note and follow cautions, but as with Walker's model the schematic is somewhat misleading, for deliberation does not necessarily follow these stages and is more dynamic than the stages convey. This dynamism is due partly to the roles of interest and conflict and partly to the nature of the social construction of reality. However, the list of stages can serve as a kind of checklist to see if any process has been omitted.

Walker and Pereira are right; particular deliberative tasks, such as conceiving of the problem, do reasonably precede others because decisions build upon one another strategically. In deliberation, a decision aims at resolving a problem. However, in practice, conversations or thoughts may initially be somewhat undirected, as people strive to understand the problem they are considering. So deliberation may sound linear, but in practice it is not. Be wary of believing that deliberation is linear and also be cautioned against adopting Pereira's schematic or Walker's model as a prescriptive set of steps that will lead to curriculum decisions. Their work represents post facto analyses of curriculum development projects, describes the sense they made of those projects, and does not constitute a prescription.

It is difficult to portray the nuances and interrelationships among features of the process of deliberation, and this leads to problems with drawing a model or developing a scheme on paper. A false impression of linearity of design might result. Instead of portraying a deliberative process that is constantly reforming itself, in these schemes the process appears static. In action it is anything but that; deliberation is in fact dynamic. In her study of three groups of deliberators, Battison (1990) finds deliberation not to be linear when deliberators on several occasions discussed themes they had previously discussed. Even late in the enterprise, they were still involved in understanding the nature of the problem and redefining it. Walker's and Pereira's work do provide concepts and termi-nology useful in understanding and discussing how deliberation proceeds, and each could be used as a sort of checklist to be sure everything had been done.

In the next section I explore several potential impediments to deliberation and reasonable measures for countering them.

IMPEDIMENTS TO DELIBERATION

Stress

Earlier in the chapter I noted that deliberation involves conflict. Indeed, conflict occurs throughout the process of deliberation and can produce stress because many people find disagreements to be uncomfortable. Stress seems to be a major factor that can inhibit decision making. The literature about stress and its influences on decision making appears to have many implications for curriculum deliberations. This research started in psychology and currently has expanded to industrial management and industrial psychology,[3] although curriculum scholars do not seem to have recognized its importance.

How does stress influence decision making? The primary motivation of people under stress, not surprisingly, is to alleviate that stress and return to normal conditions. In order to do this and to cope with the distraction of the stress, people under stress tend to rely heavily on experiences that worked well in the past. Additionally, people under stress tend to narrow their vision and the range of matters they consider. This helps them cope by preventing information overload (Keinan, 1987; Smart and Verlinsky, 1977), but this coping strategy can create cognitive oversimplification, as people attend only to information they judge to have the most potential for resolving the stress. Further, people under stress try to respond quickly to alleviate the stress and return to normal conditions rapidly (Anderson, 1976; Festinger, 1957). Finally, people under stress tend to be distracted as they attend primarily to the perceived source of stress. This brings about forgetfulness, disorganization, impatience, and a tendency to block out what they perceive to be secondary information. The person under stress desires to act as quickly as possible. However, curriculum problems are generally complex ones, which require time and attention to myriad details for resolution in an optimum manner. Table 1.1 summarizes the potential dilemma that stress brings to deliberation by contrasting characteristics of deliberation and the effects of stress. As can be seen in the table, the conditions that stress produces directly oppose the sort of thinking and work required during deliberation.

What sources of stress appear germane to curriculum decision making? Two sources cited in the psychological literature are fear (Baddeley, 1972) and time pressure (Janis and Mann, 1977). I think that educators are typically under stress because while they do not believe that problems cannot be resolved, they *do* worry about whether they will be able to develop a workable plan in the time they have.

Fear of failure seems relevant as educators worry whether their decisions are good ones and likely to create optimum conditions for students to learn the content. Fears here include that lessons will not work, discipline will become a

TABLE 1.1 Characteristics of deliberation and the effects on stress on decision making

Characteristics of Deliberation	Effects of Stress
Considering alternatives	Cognitive oversimplification:
Envisioning potential actions	• narrowing perspective
Considering means and ends, facts and values	• disregard of alternatives
	• disorganization
Deciding in a timely manner	• impatience
Conflict about how to proceed based on interests	• forgetfulness
Spiral (not linear)	
Moral dimension	
Social dimension	

problem, and students will not demonstrate that they learned from the lessons. Teachers who are committed to do an excellent job of educating their students and administrators who desire to develop policies to create optimum conditions under which teachers can do this may be particularly susceptible to such self-induced stress. This is exacerbated because curriculum problems cannot be resolved in a "correct" way since the grounds for judging curriculum decisions are sometimes unclear or controversial and since consensus does not exist about the aims of education. This source of stress is likely to influence decisions people make, whether they deliberate alone or in groups.

Another source of stress is a deadline mentality. The stress of time pressure is significant in curriculum decisions since they require elaborate attention to the nature of the problem and its potential alternative resolutions, thus necessitating that a great deal of time be devoted to them. As a deadline nears and time begins to run out, deliberations can take on a frantic quality. Time pressure can short-circuit full consideration of a matter as people become impatient and see the deadline nearing. The coping mechanisms of narrowing the range of matters under consideration and relying greatly on previous experiences may come into play and cloud the deliberations.

Some individuals actually thrive on such stress and find that competing with it is challenging, even exhilarating. In such cases, the negative influences of stress may not apply. Hence, while the literature depicts stress negatively, some individuals may actually find it to be positive. However, for many people it influences decision making negatively by interfering with the normal thinking processes that would permit careful and thorough consideration of a matter. One must be vigilant in observing the effects of stress on oneself and try to resist them by maintaining patience, attending to details carefully, and considering a range of alternatives.

Other Habits Impeding Deliberation

Roby (1985) delineates several habits besides stress that impede deliberation based on his research and experiences with curriculum development. Some of the habits he discusses may entail manifestations of stress. He organizes these habits into impediments at the beginning and end of deliberation and those that influence the general process.

Two habits impede deliberation as deliberators are conceptualizing the current problem. One concerns externalizing elements of the problem. In this case, people are not inclined to see themselves as part of the problem. Rather than questioning their own habits, biases, beliefs, or other internal factors that might be part of the problem, these deliberators blame elements external to themselves. A second habit that occurs at the onset of deliberation is excluding the commonplaces or shortchanging their importance. The commonplaces are important as organizers that help to shape and clarify the problem and its potential resolution.

Roby also cites two faulty assumptions that inhibit deliberation severely throughout the process: the expectation of a linear process and the intolerance of uncertainty. These values seem embedded in modern Western culture and may be difficult to resist, but expecting deliberation to be a linear process creates difficulties because people might be reluctant to reconsider matters for further deliberation when discussions reveal flaws in previous decisions. This is important because failure to attend sufficiently to decisions could lead deliberators to make flawed decisions that would jeopardize the entire project, thereby forcing them to later revise the curriculum.

Intolerance of uncertainty also yields difficulties because people believe that decisions have to be made so actions can be taken whether one is certain or not. This is particularly troublesome when educators desire to make excellent decisions that will create optimum conditions for students to learn. As the literature about stress reveals, this could create stress, and people could become impatient and make flawed decisions because they failed to examine alternatives sufficiently.

Roby also cites several impediments to deliberation at the end of the deliberative process. A serious one is a rush to *the* solution. Perhaps this also relates to stress, for people desire to reach a decision to alleviate their stress as quickly as possible. One way of rushing to the solution is to move to what Roby terms a "pet solution" based on deliberators' unquestioned vested interests. A second way is to engage in "global mentality," that is, to assume that universal methods (e.g., outcome-based education or mastery learning) are a panacea.

Roby cites two habits that can inhibit both problem formulation and reaching resolutions: "either/or thinking" and a "lone ranger approach." Either/or thinking inhibits deliberators from considering alternatives between the two extremes. For example, in seeking an optimum approach for an elementary school reading curriculum, deliberators might consider only a whole-language or a phonics approach and not attempt to fashion a curriculum merging the two approaches.

A lone ranger approach consists of not exchanging ideas but making up one's own mind. It may prevail among educators accustomed to planning alone in situations where cooperation and collegial planning are lacking or unsupported. Further, in some situations, the teacher's role is merely to implement the administrator's readymade decisions and state or local mandates. Lacking both practice in deliberating in peer groups and deliberative habits, these people may develop idiosyncratic pet solutions. A lone ranger approach may result from deliberators' working in isolation and developing territoriality about particular content.

In addition to the rush to *the* solution, Roby sees "crisis consciousness" as interfering with solutions. In this case, people are uncomfortable initiating curriculum development or deliberating unless they perceive a crisis because they conceive of their role as one of fixing crises. Again, if a crisis induces stress and a deadline mentality, people under stress will strive to alleviate it. They will become virtually consumed with the desire to remove the stressor—in this case, the crisis. This may then serve to bring on the apparently counterproductive effects of stress, such as narrowing the range of alternatives considered and becoming impatient.

In Roby's view, a third habit interfering with solutions is "utopian antici-pation," where deliberators see a possible, but idealistic, solution as realistic and feasible, even if it is novel. In this case, a sort of magical, wishful thinking takes over where people see only the positive features of a potential solution. Again, this habit may relate to stress and the propensity for people under stress to remove the stressor expeditiously so they can return to a more normal condition. In this case, oversimplifying the problem and disregarding alternatives seem to be the effects of stress at work.

New Habits for Deliberation

What does this literature about stress and habits impeding deliberation imply about facilitating deliberation? In this section, I address that question.

As Table 1.1 showed, several important effects of stress are in sharp contra-diction to deliberation. This seems to imply that if a person desires deliberation to occur about a problem, time should be set aside when deliberators are not likely to be suffering from stress. For instance, meetings should not be scheduled immediately following the school day, when many teachers have experienced the frustrations of a hectic day of teaching. It is better to schedule necessary meetings during the summer and to pay the teachers for their time, or to release teachers from teaching duties by hiring substitute teachers.

Time can be a stressor too in that as an individual or group starts to exhaust the available time for deliberation, they press for more organization and clarity about decisions in order to bring closure on the process. Needing more time occurs frequently in deliberation. Again, stress can short-circuit the process; due to impatience, the deliberators might not be careful to examine alternatives and the fit between the proposed solutions and the problem as they conceptualized it. Being aware of this as time grows short and reminding oneself to be patient might help; scheduling what seems to be too much time might be even more helpful to avert a frenzied finish to the project.

Another general way to improve the quality of deliberation might be to develop and present a short in-service course about the nature of deliberation and its potential impediments so deliberators can reflect on and monitor their work. An alternative is that during the process of deliberation, the curriculum specialist who facilitates the deliberations could discuss the impediments and also comment occasionally on the deliberations in light of the research on it. The point is that deliberations might be facilitated by educating deliberators about the process before and during their work. It is also important to create a school climate where teachers deliberate publicly about lessons and approaches, discussing why they were unsuccessful or successful. Such a climate of sharing might help teachers to consider alternatives and to avoid the lone ranger approach.

Cross (1992) researched the deliberations of three secondary school teachers as they cooperatively planned the core curriculum for 90 students. She attributes their success to several factors. First, the administration had built an extra hour of planning time into the school day and reduced class size. Second, the teachers were given flexibility about how to use class time for the core subjects. Third, the teachers and administrators had accepted several of Sizer's tenets of school reform, which became their platform, thus minimizing conflict. Major tenets selected from Sizer's (1984) Common Principals for Essential Schools included "backward" curriculum building, students as workers and teacher as coach, performance-based assessment and student exhibits, and personalized teaching and learning.

Here is a set of questions about some of the habits that Roby cites. It might be a helpful checklist for deliberators to see if they are using a deliberative process efficaciously.

Habits	*Questions*
Utopianism	What features of this proposed solution are feasible and likely to succeed? Why? Which features might be problematic? Why?
Lone ranger approach	What are other deliberators' views of this solution? Why do they hold those views? What are alternative solutions? How does each fit the problem?
Crisis consciousness	What are some alternative solutions? Do they fit the nature of the problem?
Global mentality	What are specific details of this problem? How can they be grouped together?
Either/or thinking	What specific solutions and problems could rest between these extremes? In what ways does and doesn't each fit the problem?

APPLYING THESE IDEAS TO EXAMPLES
OF CURRICULUM DECISION MAKING

In this section, I present three brief excerpts of curriculum decision making. No one excerpt fully exemplifies deliberation. I have chosen to present counter-examples so as to permit specific analysis of how they do not exemplify full-blown deliberation. I invite readers to analyze the three excerpts by applying concepts from this chapter. One way of organizing this analysis is to reexamine Table 1.1.

Internationalizing the Undergraduate
Business Curriculum

In this excerpt, a group of business professors meets to begin planning how to internationalize the undergraduate business curriculum because business has increasingly international dimensions. As a group, their professional association had recently mandated internationalizing this curriculum throughout the United States, so their problem concerns how to effect a change on a national basis.

DR. ABRAMS: The easiest way to do this would be to write a textbook.

DR. CARRUTHERS: Well, maybe the *easiest*, but would it get used?

DR. BROWN: There's no sense writing it if it isn't used.

DR. ABRAMS: Well, if we write it to accompany the basic text as a supplement it might. And plenty of us nationally are concerned about the international dimensions of business in our various areas.

DR. CARRUTHERS: If we secured the top-selling texts in each area, we could use them as a sort of outline for each book.

DR. ABRAMS: Oh, now you're talking about a supplementary book for each area.

DR. CARRUTHERS: That's the only choice I see. Then maybe someone might use them to offer a senior seminar that cuts across the areas. Or each one could be used to supplement the text in the basic course in each area. Each college could decide.

DR. BROWN: Then our task isn't simple, but the route to take is clear if we're agreed. Well-known writers with track records should write each supplement, and if they're published in paperback it'll keep the price down so instructors might be more willing to adopt them. It's gonna take some time, and that has to be understood from the beginning. But I can see us doing this well and the books being used.

Dr. Abrams begins by talking about the "easiest" way. This opening may focus the group's attention on the solution to the problem rather than its nature. In an interview, he confides that he had reflected greatly on the problem ever since his association voted for the mandate.

DR. ABRAMS: This bothered me a lot. *I'm* interested in internationalism, so I think my personal plans have reflected that interest for several years. But just because that happens in *my* university doesn't mean it happens in Pennsylvania, Ohio, Colorado, and Florida. It might, but not necessarily. So the problem is how to make it easy to comply with our mandate for professors whose expertise *doesn't* run to internationalism. Well, *you* know (since you teach in a university) that textbooks are a fairly easy way to do this, and the topic could easily be handled in paperback supplementary texts. They'd have to be well written, so people in these five major fields of business who've written successful texts might carry this out well, especially if we critiqued each other's work.

Even though he doesn't articulate it during deliberations, Dr. Abrams has considered the commonplace of milieu (the university). This also arises in the deliberations when Dr. Carruthers says the texts could be used either to supplement the textbooks in the five core courses or to teach in an integrated senior seminar focusing on international business. A second aspect of the milieu to which the group attended was the wider society. In this case they were considering how to attend to their association's mandate, undertaken because they believed that business could serve society better if its international dimensions were treated in coursework. Another commonplace to which Dr. Abrams refers is teachers, when he acknowledges their possible lack of expertise in the topic. The deliberations did not apply the subject matter commonplace and treated no commonplace overtly; they implied some commonplaces. No curriculum specialist led the discussions.

While alternatives might have been generated, such as offering workshops about each topic for professors attending the association convention, they were not. In the rush to a solution, they formulated *one* solution, a solution that seems workable in Dr. Carruthers's view because, "Textbooks are virtually an inextricable part of undergraduate education, aren't they?" Aiming for the solution early in this particular decision-making process may have resulted from the tendency to reach for quick solutions, and this influenced their thinking.

In comparing Dr. Abrams's reflections to the group deliberations, the amount of interplay between solo and group deliberation becomes apparent. His platform, although not fully articulated to the group, ultimately became policy, although the group elaborated upon it.

This excerpt does *not* exemplify deliberation in that alternatives were not generated, equal attention was not paid to means and ends, and neither conflict nor interest was apparent. More than anything, they considered only one solution. Later, they formed five committees (one for each subject) to write outlines to parallel the major texts for each subject, to write the books, to critique each other's work, and to field test the books.

What are possible effects on the curriculum of not considering alternatives and rushing to the solution? One possible result is that the decision makers may have oversimplified the problem. It was not only the unavailability of readable, affordable textbooks that accounted for undergraduate business professors not previously internationalizing the curriculum. For example, some professors may not be knowledgeable about international dimensions of their core subjects. Their lack of knowledge could have formed an implicit message to students: This is not an important topic. Perhaps international business would move out of the null curriculum but have a negative attitude accompanying its teachings by way of the implicit curriculum. Further, if professors are not knowledgeable, what discussion questions can they raise? Will they be sufficiently challenging? It is unlikely that they can add examples to the discussion to clarify and illuminate unclear points. Perhaps a series of workshops need to be offered to professors who believe they need to update their knowledge. Other alternatives are also possible, but the problem may not have been as simple as it seemed.

In Table 1.2 I summarize the first excerpt by comparing it to Table 1.1.

Revising the Geography Curriculum

This second excerpt (Marsh et al., 1990:107–108) concerns parts of the fourth meeting of a geography revision committee.

MARK: Do you ever do role playing in geography or anywhere?

ARCHIE: I have maybe once.

MARK: I never have. I've sort of toyed with the idea. . . . How do you do it?

LYNNE: [*provides several examples*]

MARK: I'd like to see that [examples] because I don't really know that much about role playing. I mean I know the general drift of it but I stop and think to myself "mmhm, I can't." Maybe I don't give enough thought to it.

ARCHIE: I think role playing and most of those types of strategies demand a heck of a pile of preparation because the better they're prepared, the more successful they will be in the classroom. I find I just don't have that kind of time most times. I've never seen an example in my teaching career. You know, say in teachers' college or something like that . . . I think that is why I tend to stay away from it.

MARK: I always wondered how do you motivate them [students]? How do you get them to care that much [about role playing]? I mean you do it, I do it for the fun but some of the kids they don't want to spend the effort.

ARCHIE: I think it's one of my greatest reasons for not doing this kind of stuff in the past was I never felt comfortable when it came to an evaluation. How do you evaluate?

ARCHIE: I'll give it a great deal of thought because I really do think that in my teaching right now I'm looking for variety because I can see where I get into a rut.

TABLE 1.2 Comparing Table 1.1 to the internationalized business curriculum excerpt

Characteristics of Deliberation	Possible Effects of Stress
No envisioning of potential alternatives to textbook solution	Narrowness of perspective
	Disregard of alternatives
Expedience considered rather than values	
Linear decision making was possibly the most dominant factor	
No moral considerations	
No social dimensions discussed	

This discussion represents an instance of teachers' reflecting aloud on their practice and exploring alternatives that have grown out of their emphasis in the previous deliberations on process learning. They are wondering about the nature of role playing as a possible teaching strategy to help students understand some geography concepts. The basic question underlying these deliberations concerns feasibility: Can teachers implement this curriculum? This is interesting, for in doing this these teachers apply the commonplace of teachers. Moreover, they avoid two potential impediments to deliberation. By asking each other about role playing, they avoid the "lone ranger" impediment. When Mark confesses, "I really don't know that much about role playing," he acknowledges that part of the problem might be his own lack of knowledge about one of the processes on which this curriculum could rest. Clearly, for Mark at least, the deliberation context and process are comfortable enough that he could be very open in confessing ignorance. The social setting they have developed is supportive by being non-threatening. This discussion might also help the group avoid applying "utopian consciousness" to the problem, which might result in unrealistic plans.

Interestingly, the geography group does not consider (at this time, anyway) alternative possibilities, such as making and using project maps or globes. Nor do they discuss other commonplaces. The curriculum specialist (Lynne) has little role here.

In Table 1.3 I summarize the second excerpt by comparing it to Table 1.1.

Revising the Graded Course of Study for Gifted and Talented Students

A final excerpt (Marsh et al., 1990:127–128) included here concerns developing a graded course of study for gifted and talented students in an affluent community near a large city. Early discussions are characterized by attempts to clarify some of the problems being faced.

LEONARD: Michelle's concern is a concern I share. She's saying if we are man-dated (Mary, we're talking about the grammar issue. Here's a copy of the minutes.). The issues here are that we have received a mandate from the

TABLE 1.3 Comparing Table 1.2 to the geography curriculum revision excerpt

Characteristics of Deliberation	Possible Effects of Stress
Alternatives to role playing not discussed	Narrow perspective
Envisioning potential actions outcomes discussed	
Time, student motivation, threat of evaluation discussed	
Disorganization	
No decision mentioned but there seemed to be change for a spiral type of decision making beginning, not a linear one	Impatience and forgetfulness could result from time restraints on this discussion
Moral considerations not directly discussed	
Social considerations not extended outside classroom	

Board of Education to give students a comprehensive grammar proficiency test at the middle school level. Because of this order, it's relatively counter-productive and contradictory to what we're trying to do in language arts education districtwide and that is writing process. Although the Language Arts Graded Course of Study does prescribe the teaching of grammar, it does so as a tool for editing.

MICHELLE: Right! It's not isolated.

LEONARD: This mandate is to be that kind of thing. . . . It came out of a Board member's request for a Board Curriculum Committee meeting.

MICHELLE: You mean at the last Board meeting or something?

LEONARD: No. Not exactly. All year long representatives for the Board attending these curriculum meetings have been expressing concerns about the secondary gifted program. So finally we asked, "What are these concerns?" And the two Board of Education representatives on the sub-committee, who speak on behalf of the community, and then fellow Board members. . . .

MARY: It's interesting. One thing that came out that they wished. I would pre-test grammar. It's in our plans.

LEONARD: Right! And you said that at the last meeting too—you said the same thing. . . . I think the Board wants to make teachers more aware of the concern that students need more formal instruction in grammar. So, you at the middle school need to articulate better to your students and parents that we are giving them grammar proficiency tests to determine where they are in grammar and that I, as a teacher, will provide independent work or group activities if need be in areas that are deficient.

WILMA: Right, in the case of group work, it's the gifted kind of syndrome coming out. The kids told me we don't want grammar; we don't need it. Being new to the district, I read the graded course of study as grammar being in there and that I need to teach it—whether it was misinterpreted or not. I thought this was part of my job. So, I went ahead with it and I may have 6 students out of 100 who did not do well in the proficiency tests. I didn't think that was not something I wanted to send home—such a weakness—and I would take care of it—get them up to par—and continue onward. . . .

MICHELLE: This is part of a much larger philosophical problem and I think it needs to be put on hold and let language arts graded course of study people handle it. I think it's a part of the problem. . . . And I know of those two members. I know how each one feels about grammar. But there lies the challenge through the year. We have to. . . .

LEONARD: Yes. It's a matter, too, of educating people about what the writing process is all about.

As can be seen, the grammar issue has become of paramount importance, at least partly because the local board of education recently mandated a language arts proficiency test, affecting not only the language arts curriculum but this one as well. Although this group's task is to develop a graded course of study for gifted students, Michelle argues for holding the issue of the test in abeyance so the language arts people can handle it. An enormous difficulty here is that in Chester, the language arts curriculum is composed of a writing process that is based on reflecting upon and editing the work as well as writing it. Hence, a proficiency test in grammar is at odds with the curriculum.

Two other difficulties that had prompted the curriculum revision were not discussed in this meeting but arose during subsequent ones. Both concerned communication. A lack of communication with principals had caused a number of practical problems about scheduling and room assignments. A lack of communication with the community had caused problems because parents did not know what to expect of the program. While the group is trying to make sense of the nature of the problem, they do not raise some important aspects of it during this first meeting. Understanding these dilemmas is important if identical problems are to be avoided with the new curriculum. The deliberation in this early phase of curriculum development may seem to be freewheeling and inefficient, but it is essential for the success of the venture. This illustrates how deliberation is not unidirectional even though it has an aim.

In this excerpt, developers apply some information about the milieu commonplace (the new board policy) but none from subject matter. Mary (who favors teaching grammar), Wilma (a new teacher who wants to know what is expected of her), and the other teachers represent the commonplace of teachers, but they do not raise the matters Schwab associated with it. The focus here is partly due to a problem of curriculum organization—the nature of the language arts curriculum, the role of grammar in it, and its influence on other parts of the curriculum. Lacking an overall design, the pieces run the risk of being disjointed, piecemeal, and unharmonious, a curriculum crazy quilt. Again, the curriculum specialist (Leonard) does not assume the roles Schwab suggests.

In Table 1.4 I summarize this final excerpt by comparing it to Table 1.1.

TABLE 1.4 Comparing Table 1.1 to the gifted and talented curriculum development excerpt

Characteristics of Deliberation	Possible Effects of Stress
Alternatives to consider how to treat the grammar issue discussed	Cognitive oversimplication (such as narrowing perspectives)
Potential actions and outcomes discussed	Time constraint probably not a factor (no evidence of disorganization, impatience, or forgetfulness)
Means and ends considered as well as facts and values related to how the issue might be resolved	
Some conflict about how the issue might be resolved	
Spiral, not linear decision making seemed dominant	
Larger or perhaps moral issues deferred to another group of people	
Social dimensions such as educating parents about the education process discussed	

SUMMARY

Deliberation is a dynamic process of making curriculum decisions alone or in groups. It is social because educators deliberate on behalf of society. While deliberating, Leonard, Lynne, Dr. Carruthers, and other people consider alternatives, envision potential actions and outcomes of each, make decisions in a timely manner, bring to light their interests, entertain conflict, thereby making decisions in a spiral—not linear—manner. They also consider moral and social dimensions, means and ends, and facts and values. In short, deliberation is a complicated yet organized approach to making curriculum decisions, not merely a discussion or debate about curriculum. In group deliberation, deliberators mutually create the process during the enterprise. This occurs in part through the two dynamic processes of conflict and interest, which unify the group and cause people to be vigilant in examining what occurs as they socially construct knowledge.

In making curriculum decisions it is important to consider four bodies of knowledge accompanied by specialized knowledge of curriculum development. These four bodies of knowledge are about the "commonplaces" called students, subject matter, the milieu, and teachers. The curriculum specialist facilitates the process of curriculum development by calling attention to these commonplaces and by guiding the group to examine in detail their decisions and curriculum bits such as a curriculum guide, syllabus, graded course of study, or curriculum materials.

Several factors can intrude on deliberations to such an extent that they impede the deliberations. A major impediment is stress, which can create psychological reactions and patterns of thinking directly opposed to deliberative thinking. Some other thinking habits can also impede deliberations such as a lone ranger approach, a rush to one solution, and either/or thinking. The policy-driven, bureaucratic nature of many school systems can also impede deliberation by stifling creative possibilities. If everything has to be standardized, creative solutions do not emerge. Ignorance as to the nature of deliberation can also impede it.

Finally, I related three excerpts of curriculum decision making and analyzed them according to the characteristics of deliberation and the influences of stress on decision making. None fully exemplified deliberation. This implies a need for understanding deliberation and how to nurture it so educators can make optimum decisions about what opportunities students should have to learn in schools. People are already doing bits and pieces of deliberation, but more is possible. The rest of this book elaborates on the nature of deliberation and illustrates instances of curriculum decision making.

STUDY QUESTIONS

1. Explain in your own words how conflict supports deliberation. How can it improve deliberations? How does this apply to your own practice?
2. Explain Schwab's commonplaces and their roles in deliberation in your own words. How are these ideas helpful in reflecting on your own planning?
3. Compare the discussion of satisficing to characteristics of deliberation. What are some reasons why satisficing is not a form of deliberation? What state and local policies where you work might support an attitude and practice of satisficing instead of deliberation? How could this be harmful and actually counteract what policymakers were trying to achieve? What are issues here for policymakers to confront? Why is it harmful for teachers and administrators to adopt the attitude of satisficing in their work? How can you counteract it in your own practice? Do you think this changes as teachers get more practice? What makes you think that? What other characteristics of educators (in addition to being novices) might explain why they engage in satisficing instead of deliberation?
4. Give an example of deliberation from your everyday life. Explain the roles each characteristic of deliberation played in your example.
5. Further analyze Roby's habits impeding deliberation in light of the literature presented about stress. Which of his habits might be induced by stress? How? Why do you think this?
6. What about the culture where you live might relate to some of the habits impeding deliberation that Roby cites?
7. Based on the three examples at the end of chapter 1, what would you say are some ways to improve deliberation in groups? How might you effect such changes where you work?

NOTES

1. I am grateful to LeAnne Puglielli for this term.
2. This section draws heavily on Schwab's work, so it is helpful to understand the origin of his views about curriculum development. Schwab developed his views on the basis

of his experiences in course development at the University of Chicago, where groups of highly respected scholars met to deliberate the curriculum of each undergraduate course. These groups would deliberate about, say, the biology course. A person who was going to teach it would develop a syllabus and provide it to the group, which would examine it and redeliberate. The syllabus was an example of what Schwab refers to as a "curriculum bit." In this instance, group and solo deliberation are clearly interrelated, for the group's decisions informed the individual, who designed the syllabus, and the individual planned the syllabus for the group to examine and critique. The redeliberation might bring about changes in the values and ideas of the deliberators, in the curriculum bit, or in both. Indeed, such a process of examining and deliberating might occur several times before the best solution possible is arrived at, given the circumstances. Examining the curriculum bit seems to be a useful way of checking whether deliberators understand the implications of their deliberations.

3. I have two misgivings about this literature. One is that the research reports are unclear about their samples, making me conjecture whether only white men (perhaps possessing particular traits) were included. If so, the research may apply less to education, where women and minorities have a higher rate of employment than they do as managers in industry. My other misgiving is that the nature of decision making and stress in curriculum may differ substantially from the nature of decision making in industry. However, the literature is compelling and raises interesting points that appear relevant to difficulties in curriculum deliberation. Thus, while I discuss it briefly, I encourage people to do more research about it in the context of curriculum deliberations.

part II

Solo Deliberation

In this part of the book I examine how individual teachers think about their work and make decisions about it. In chapter 2 I review literature about individual teachers' thought processes and decision making. In chapter 3, I present three case studies about elementary school teachers' solo deliberations. In chapter 4, I include three case studies about secondary school teachers' solo deliberations. In chapters 3 and 4, I also describe the school and community contexts where the teachers work in order to place the deliberations in their settings.

chapter 2

Solo Deliberation:
How Individuals Conceptualize and Make Decisions about the Curriculum

One occasion for curriculum deliberation is when individual teachers conceive and plan what and how students are to learn in their classes. Chapter 2 examines how teachers conceive of their role and how this bears on their planning and deliberations. In this chapter, I discuss how teachers' own practical theories of action are influenced by experiences and expectations from both within and outside their teaching practice. By combining my own field observations with other scholars' research and literature, I demonstrate how teachers' practical theories dominate their attempts at solo deliberation and, as a result, their teaching and the curriculum they provide to students.

In the first half of this chapter, I discuss teachers' practical theories of action, starting with three basic themes. The first deals with the nature of these theories, while the second and third cover how teachers develop and use them in their work.

In the balance of the chapter I focus upon the relationship between teachers' practical theories and solo deliberation. I first present a brief section concerning teachers' planning and follow this with an extract from a fifth-grade teacher's research into her own practice, where she reveals the thoughts behind her planning. I also include an example of a college instructor's work. These examples are used to demonstrate how people develop practical theories and to show how teachers' theories of action affect their curriculum and lesson planning. After analyzing the link between theories of action and planning, I demonstrate how these thought processes do and don't constitute deliberation. I close the chapter with a brief summary.

TEACHERS' PRACTICAL THEORIES OF ACTION:
WHAT THEY ARE

Practical theories of action are interrelated concepts, beliefs, and images teachers hold about their work. They guide the decision-making process before and during teaching and form the interpretive lens teachers apply to their post-teaching reflections. These reflections inform teachers' future decision making as well. In sum, they affect teachers' preactive and interactive planning and postactive reflections.

Teachers express their practical theories in a range of individual ways. Some teachers state them as a logical, orderly set of concepts, others as a collection of beliefs, others as a cluster of loosely interwoven images, and still others as a combination of the three. Regardless of the teacher's phrasing, my research indicates that a teacher's practical theory of action contains a combination of concepts, beliefs, and images. This theory is, of course, more clearly expressed in a teacher's actions themselves. These theories result from a teacher's life experiences, current endeavors, and expectations for the future, not from an arbitrary selection.

By its nature, teaching, at any grade level, in any community, or in any specific discipline or area (e.g., teaching behaviorally handicapped or learning disabled students), is a complex task. Not only must the teacher adhere to a curriculum policy, but he or she also must adapt such policy to fit comfortably with his or her own practical theory. Moreover, teachers are provided with particular curriculum materials. Administrative curriculum policies may be somewhat consistent from one educational system to another, but teachers' practical theories vary. Curriculum policies treat school systems as a whole, but teachers work alone in classrooms with particular students in specific situations and apply their theories to their work.

The school is literally backed by the force of law; the implied will of the people dictates, "Teach this." Teachers receive such dictates but completion is not assured. Theoretically the individual teacher must simply determine what learning is primary, what teaching methods should be utilized to reach the greatest number of students, how to motivate students, and then implement those decisions. In reality, though, each teacher develops an idiosyncratic set of concepts, beliefs, and images about what to teach, how students learn, how to treat the curriculum guidelines, how to treat other adults, how to motivate students, and how to evaluate them. As a result, teachers transform curriculum policies and materials to such a degree that it is more appropriate to think of them as curriculum developers than as mere implementors (see Ross, Cornett, and McCutcheon [1992] for more on this topic).

When discussing their practice, some teachers refer to their practical theories as their reasons, theories, or philosophies; others phrase them more metaphorically (see chapters 3 and 4). Connelly and Clandinin (1988:70) cite Lakoff and Johnson's (1980) notion of the role of metaphor in people's conceptual systems and view teachers' actions and practices "as embodied expressions of their metaphors of teaching and living" (1988:71). They exemplify this by pointing out that it makes a great difference whether we think of children as clay to be molded, as players on a team, or as travelers on a journey. Clearly, teachers' practical theories are partly metaphorical in nature.

The idiosyncratic nature of teachers' practical theories of action is due to the individual experiences teachers have had before teaching. These theories are shared to some extent when people grew up in a similar culture because the character of that culture was shared by those teachers and shaped some of their thinking, such as a belief in the importance of family, equality, and the work ethic. Teachers' practical theories drive the action in a classroom and underlie a teacher's plans and decision making. In a sense, they represent how an individual (in this case, a teacher) has constructed reality in terms of schools.

HOW TEACHERS DEVELOP PRACTICAL THEORIES

The Roles Preteaching Experiences Play

Teachers develop these practical theories largely on the basis of their personal experiences. Through personal experiences, people individually and socially construct meanings about the world. Experiences while growing up, going to school, traveling, working, and interacting with people and the world shape people's knowledge and attitudes. In writing about ideological realities and knowledge construction, Watzlawick (1984) describes humans' seeming psychological inability to exist in a universe lacking meaning and order. Hence, he reasons people fill this vacuum by interpreting the world around them. My research demonstrates that teachers create meanings through their various experiences about what is important to learn, about how students learn and are motivated, and about what to teach and evaluate. The result is each teacher's practical theory of action.

For example, Iris Robole[1] (see chapter 3) teaches elementary school in a small, upscale community. I observed her giving more and longer turns to answer questions and participate in demonstrations to boys than to girls. Why? Her preteaching background applies here. She grew up with brothers. Later, she and her husband had a son of their own as well as raising foster sons. In an interview, when I asked her what sort of student she believed she taught best, she confided that she probably taught boys better than girls. She stated that she understands how boys think, "but I just don't understand what makes girls tick." In conversation she became aware of and began attending to this tacit (unconscious) aspect of her practical theory. She was clearly disappointed with herself and troubled by her realization because she said she believed in equity and hoped she was a role model for her female students with an interest in science. Following the interview, Iris began to treat girls and boys more equally than she had, probably because she recognized the problem, brought her once tacit belief into consciousness, and could now change it and act on the change.

In another example, Mark Schaefer's (see chapter 3) work background before becoming a teacher consisted of managing apartments for low-income people and working at a family-owned small manufacturing company. He believes managing those apartments and having grown up in a working-class neighborhood helped him understand and communicate well with low-income people such as the parents and students where he teaches. Another element in his thinking is precision, which to him is reminiscent of what was needed in cutting gaskets and maintaining records in the family manufacturing business. He also enjoys the variety of tasks involved in teaching, as he had enjoyed the variety in his job at the M. J. Schaefer Company.

Differences exist in the nature of these experiences. They further vary because individuals construe identical occurrences differently and because teachers place differing degrees of importance on even the same issue. As a result, many aspects of teachers' practical theories differ widely, although having grown up in a similar culture, some aspects may be common to teachers.

Teachers do not frequently ascribe their practical theories to preservice teacher education, in part because much of it seems so far removed from the work they do. Much preservice education is generalized, but teachers have to make specific decisions within a particular context. In my view, some serious rethinking of preservice teacher education is necessary if our aim is to develop reflective professional teachers.

The Role the Context Plays

In addition to being idiosyncratic because teachers' backgrounds differ, these practical theories are also unique because contexts of teaching differ. The context affords opportunities for constructing meanings and for placing importance on different issues. Contextual differences include: the nature of administrative practices and policies, the discipline or field and grade level taught, the nature of available materials, the classroom in which teachers work, colleagues' practical theories, opportunities for professional discourse, sociocultural, racial, and other differences within the student body. Teachers' practical theories will vary because teachers take such matters into account when they make decisions. Such differences appear in teachers' practical theories as well as their practice, for their practice is continually informing their theories, and vice versa. Such matters shape the arena within which teachers make decisions. As a result, these features of the context also affect teachers' practical theories because of the importance that teaching itself plays in teachers' thinking about their practice. While considering the context concerns the surroundings of a teacher's practice, the next consideration may be more idiosyncratic and critical in teachers' developing their practical theories.

The Role Teaching Plays

A teacher's practice itself is a crucial source for developing practical theories. It permits the teacher to focus on particular aspects of work. While teaching, teachers work to refine their proficiency; they try to increase the professional expertise necessary to educating students and to increase the likelihood that most students will have access to and be successful in an excellent curriculum.

A professional teacher's pragmatic aim is to produce desired consequences since this is what the teacher was hired to do and was presumed to be professionally skilled in accomplishing. However, while professional aims in education are pragmatic, they are neither dispassionate nor value-free. To the contrary, curriculum decisions include normative aspects, and professional teachers care deeply about their work and students' progress. Indeed, because of this and because education makes efforts on behalf of society, teachers work to improve their efforts. This is one reason why facts and values cannot and should not be separated. The reason professional teachers try to improve their actions and understandings is their sense of responsibility to their students, families, and society rather than a mandate or law.

These practical theories are vital to success in teaching because, as Reid (1978) notes, curriculum problems are practical problems. That is, they cannot be solved merely by discovering new knowledge or inventing solutions. To be effective, teachers must develop and put solutions into action in ways that are appropriate to the circumstances. Carr and Kemmis (1983:110) argue that all practical activities are guided by some theory because teachers need some knowledge of their particular situation and some idea of what needs to be done before they even begin. "Anyone engaged in the practice of educating must already possess some theory of education that structures activities and guides decisions." These sorts of theories are at the heart of teachers' practical theories. Whether they are aware of it or not, teachers develop generalizations based on their previous experiences and current teaching that underlie and guide their work. In a sense, this simplifies their task because their practical theories imply and guide particular actions. Remember, these theories are developed by the teachers themselves and are somewhat unique to each. There are also two other important characteristics of these theories.

Tacit and Rational Characteristics of These Practical Theories

Teachers do not operate on the basis of a single practical theory, but rather on the basis of a set of interrelated ones. Some aspects of teachers' practical theories are *tacit*—that is, teachers are unaware of them. Perhaps when teachers refer to their "intuition," they are really acting on their tacit knowledge. Through reflection on their practice and professional conversations, teachers uncover some of this tacit knowledge, which they can examine, weigh, and articulate. This is evident in the example about Iris Robole and her teaching of girls and boys. Teachers might enhance such reflection by maintaining professional diaries or journals about their work. The process of putting their actions and reflections into words might help them focus on those ideas and gain a deeper understanding. Through this process of reflection and discussion, teachers refine their practical theories and come to understand them more fully. Then teachers are in a position to reject some, as Iris did, or to continue acting with conviction.

These practical theories are also *rational* because they are intentional, whether or not teachers are conscious of these reasons, according to Argyris (1982). Teachers may not be fully aware of all their reasoning, but the fact that teachers are always trying to accomplish something when they act professionally is inherent in teaching. As Argyris's (1982:41) research shows,

> People have intentions about what it is that they are trying to accomplish. The degree to which they are aware of their intentions varies, but so far we have found that their actions are intentionally rational. Their actions are explicitly or tacitly designed to achieve some intended consequences.

Teachers select and enact every teaching practice because they are engaged in intentional, purposive action to create optimum conditions for learning to occur. Some actions merely support the general aim (e.g., distributing materials, having students get in a line, rearranging the room, washing tables after an art or science project), but others support educational aims (e.g., teaching multiplication facts, how flight occurs, or how people in other countries live).

For example, Michael Davis is a high school social studies teacher in an affluent suburban school system. Here he articulates such intentionality to students on the third day in his East Asian studies course. Material in brackets gives background information; material in parentheses tells his actions:

> I want to call attention to the three sorts of things I have on the black board. One thing you can see here is the day's date—a practical thing. So you don't have to look far to find out the date in here! Then I have three items that change each day. In the first one you can see that U.S. history has some interesting events. Some of them start creeping in and they affect each other and other countries. [Today's is about developing a way to fasten boots, then developing the zipper from that preliminary patented item.] In the middle is something else I believe in. Social studies is interdisciplinary. (*He writes the word on the board in the front of the room.*) You take a variety of subjects in school, and they all fit together, interrelate. When you live your life you don't really draw on just one discipline—the arts, economics, mathematics and so forth. You draw on a lot of them at the same time. That's particularly true in social studies. To pretend that's not true would be wrong. So I'll do it deliberately, right up front. In a week or two you'll be thinking, "This guy thinks he's an English teacher." For instance, in a few weeks you'll be studying vocabulary, and I'll expect you to spell the words right, too, not just know the meanings. And I'll look at what you write for its structure, grammar, word usage and other things, not just its content. So that's appropriate to this course. I'll reinforce some things from English class. (*He writes "Literature" on the board, then "Literature both reflects and affects history."*) You know, our textbooks are sort of literature. Poems, pamphlets and novels, too. Some are nonfiction and some are fiction. Some of Michener's work is

a good example. Harriet Beecher Stowe's *Uncle Tom's Cabin* stirred up passion in the United States before the Civil War. Rachel Carson's *Silent Spring* contributed to the banning of DDT. And Ralph Nader's *Unsafe at Any Speed* helped get seatbelts and padded dashboards in cars. Now, you might not think that's necessarily good, but Nader's book helped with automobile safety. (*On the back board a section about Today in Literature describes Robert Frost's beginning a good-will tour of the USSR when he was 88.*) A third broad thing I believe in is multiculturalism, and the third board concerns today's holiday. You know, many cultures celebrate different things and in different ways. [The board labeled "Today's Holiday" describes how the Gele de Nigeria is celebrated by the Yoruba.]

In this example Mr. Davis explains his routines to his students and shares his intention with them to connect social studies with the discipline, other disciplines, and other cultures. He does this throughout various lessons and clearly considers that providing reasons to students is part of his practical theory. Further, the interconnected, multicultural, and interdisciplinary view of his discipline pervades his lessons, and it figures in his practical theory because it is part of how he has constructed reality in terms of his discipline.

Teachers base some aspects of their practical theories on experiences prior to teaching and on recreational experiences outside of school while they are teachers. More importantly, teachers develop them as they observe their own small experiments aimed at improving their work and ascertain what works well. Undergraduate education probably has less influence on these conceptualizations than teachers' experiences because the latter involve more responsibility. Faced with the responsibility to educate a group of students and feeling motivated to do so, teachers find they have to solve myriad practical problems. They soon realize that no one else—not another teacher, a supervisor, or former professor—can resolve them or is responsible for doing so, and that they ultimately bear the responsibility for educating their students well. By closely observing students and lessons, students' written work and projects, their responses and discussions, teachers accumulate and develop ideas about how students learn, what they should learn, how to maintain discipline and motivation, and how to organize their planning and teaching. They do so by acting, observing, reflecting on, and interpreting their teaching experiences and students' actions.

Kolb's (1981) work in cognitive theory provides a general way to understand how teachers develop their conceptualizations of practice. His theory, remarkably like Dewey's theory of experience (1938), emphasizes the dialectical nature of human transactions in experience. Kolb portrays such learning in a four-stage cyclical model beginning with a concrete experience on which a person observes and reflects, forms generalizations, goes on to test implications in new situations, and then repeats the cycle. By way of explaining this model, Kolb (1981:233) says,

Immediate concrete experience is the basis for observation and reflection. An individual uses these observations to build upon an idea, generalization or "theory" from which new implications serve as guides in acting to create new experiences.

An illustration of Kolb's model is appropriate here. Starting at the observations and reflections point of this model, Mark Schaefer, third-grade teacher (see chapter 3), recently observed that his students did not understand the definition of even numbers in his school system's mathematics curriculum, and that he was to implement the concept that "even numbers are numbers that can be divided by two." Compared to previous classes he'd taught in Mapleton, he viewed these students as somewhat less capable, but he was momentarily perplexed because not even his brightest students in class understood or could apply the concept. He quickly realized that they could not understand this definition until they had learned about division (which was not to occur until fourth grade, according to the graded course of study). He saw it as a sequencing problem in the graded course of study. He used this reflection in his decision to remind students of the chant, "Two, four, six, eight, who [sic] do we appreciate" and to return to the definition later in the year after he introduced division (he was permitted to exceed the grade objectives). Following the teaching of the chant, students were able to sort numbers into odd and even on worksheets he made for pages in the mathematics textbook. In April, he taught students division facts because he believed third-graders might as well learn them in conjunction with all the other facts. In May, he returned to the original definition of even numbers in the graded course of study. The incident arose out of concrete experience and puzzled Mr. Schaefer, leading to the observations and reflections, a generalization (a sequence problem), and a plan (two, four, six, eight . . .) he could test. A schematic of this anecdote organized through Kolb's model is shown in Figure 2.1.

HOW TEACHERS USE PRACTICAL THEORIES

Teachers employ their practical theories in several interrelated ways. When they plan, teachers use these ideas to help them decide what to teach and how to motivate students, present ideas, and otherwise orchestrate lessons. They examine an idea they've encountered (e.g., in a teacher's guide, at an in-service meeting, or from another teacher) and consider whether to use it. They compare it to parts of their practical theory. Does the idea embody the ideals they hold dear? Is it consonant with how they believe students learn and what they should learn? Is it likely to work with their particular students? If they adopt the idea, they further reflect upon it to consider how to adapt it based on their practical theory. This is one reason why many curriculum innovations bear little resemblance to their developers' intentions: Teachers change the ideas by deleting some features and grafting others onto them. Indeed, at times teachers alter the written curriculum to such an extent that it bears virtually no relationship to the developers' original intentions. As Jenkins and Shipman (1976:63) note, teachers extract bits from

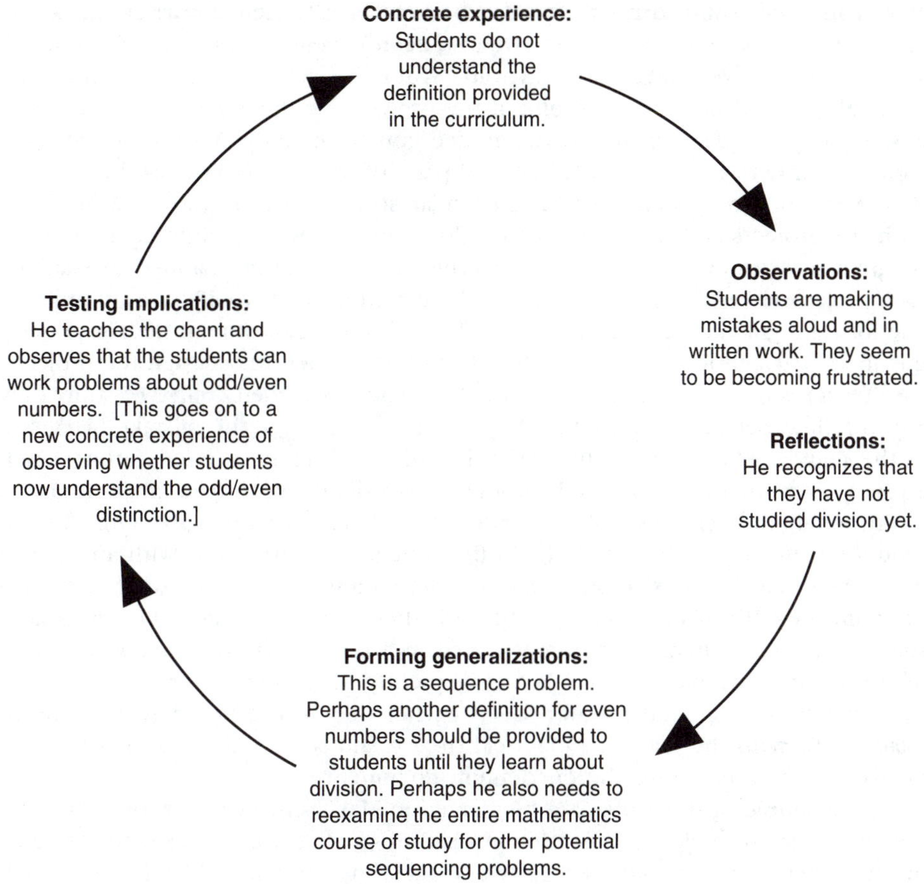

Concrete experience:
Students do not
understand the
definition provided
in the curriculum.

Observations:
Students are making
mistakes aloud and in
written work. They seem
to be becoming frustrated.

Testing implications:
He teaches the chant and
observes that the students can
work problems about odd/even
numbers. [This goes on to a
new concrete experience of
observing whether students
now understand the odd/even
distinction.]

Reflections:
He recognizes that
they have not
studied division yet.

Forming generalizations:
This is a sequence problem.
Perhaps another definition for even
numbers should be provided to
students until they learn about
division. Perhaps he also needs to
reexamine the entire mathematics
course of study for other potential
sequencing problems.

FIGURE 2.1   Applying Kolb's model to an example

documents they believe fit their situation when they believe the program is not consonant with how they conceive of practice. These revisions are to be expected. Also, teachers shop around for clever teaching strategies, accumulating strategies from many sources and altering them because of their practical theories. This further accounts for why teachers can be thought of as developing the curriculum rather than merely implementing it.

For example, Mark Schaefer was concerned about his science curriculum. He recently attended an in-service workshop that brought together teachers, businesspeople, and people from a scientific institute. The last two groups agreed to assist with science lessons in nearby elementary school classrooms, and Mark was keen on obtaining such a volunteer because it would afford his students opportunities to meet a potential role model working in an academic discipline. At the workshop, a physics program was discussed and some lessons demonstrated.

Mark had been troubled by a lack of substance in his science curriculum, so he sent away for the science program. He also aggressively and humorously solicited and obtained a volunteer, Mr. Reynolds from the science institute. After the materials arrived, Mark selected one of the projects Mr. Reynolds liked that would develop physics ideas related to the graded course of study and that he believed would work with his students. He deleted parts of the project because he believed they were too complicated for his particular students. In his view, the first year with the projects and the volunteer would be experimental, while he altered the program to see how well it worked. During the summer he planned to examine each project described in the materials and redesign it so he would have six projects, one for each grading period. When he suffered a retina detachment he had to delay this for a year and found that troubling, but he continued to redesign the projects.

Teachers often rearrange the curriculum guide or graded course of study they are to follow because of mistakes they perceive in it (e.g., the mistake Mark saw in the mandate for teaching the definition of even numbers, cited earlier). Such a policy is frequently developed through group deliberation (see chapters 5 and 7). Although the school's policy is intended to organize the curriculum of the school system, it may frequently be in fundamental disagreement with a teacher's practical theory. This is another factor compelling the teacher to transform a program they are given to implement with their students. It also illustrates how solo and group deliberation are interrelated. As we see, curriculum guides, courses of study, and curriculum materials are frequently developed by groups, and then significantly redeveloped by individual teachers. Some redevelopment is due to a lack of fit with the teacher's practical theory, and sometimes it occurs because of oversights or errors in the curriculum document.

An example of this can again be located in Mark Schaefer's practice. The only objective related to clocks appearing in his third-grade mathematics graded course of study reads: "Given pictures of two clocks, the student will tell how much time has elapsed between the two." Mark recognizes that his students must be able to tell time on *one* clock before they can hope to make such a comparison. As a result, he has constructed a series of lessons using manipulative clocks and worksheets to teach this first. He will then construct the ones for the comparison objective. This is a clear case of a teacher developing the curriculum by planning lessons to provide skills preliminary to achieving the districtwide goal. It arose out of Mark's perceiving the problem that students need prior knowledge to achieve the end objective—the comparison.

Teachers also employ their practical theories as they react to students' questions, actions, and written work. The teacher's beliefs about motivation, appropriate expectations, and the nature of the subject matter being made accessible to students frame the nature of his or her conversations with students.

For example, Beverly Koenig teaches mathematics at a secondary school. A student recently asked her, "Mrs. Koenig, do parallel lines ever intersect?" Beverly quickly considered two options. One was simply to reply "No," based on the definition of parallel lines. Her alternative was, "It depends on what you believe about the nature of the edge of the universe." She chose the latter course of action because, in her view, "In high school—maybe before—students start to wonder about things, and I shouldn't put a damper on that. We need to show them that some questions simply don't have neat and tidy answers. Not having definite answers to everything is okay." Further, she argues that recent astronomical theories raise questions about the nature of the edge of the universe and that this student would follow those news stories.

This response based on Beverly's practical theory is in direct contrast to an elementary school example in science where the teacher asked, "What is infinity?" She called on Billy, who replied, "Infinity is like a bowl of cream of wheat." The teacher replied, "Billy, don't be silly." To a child, cream of wheat may seem to stretch into infinity as it forms gluey wads if not promptly eaten, and the contents of the box make look infinite (tiny pearls that will expand to fill bowl after bowl . . .). To him, this description may actually reflect Billy's concept of infinity. Suggesting that the box for a popular brand contains a picture of a chef holding a box of it (which contains a picture of a chef holding a box with a picture of a chef holding a box . . .) reinforces the concept of infinity that Billy may have understood. He responded with a metaphor that the teacher, perhaps anticipating a literal response, did not understand. Perhaps an aspect of her practical theory defines school knowledge as objective.

Teachers also select materials and arrange their classrooms on the basis of their practical theories. For instance, in a classroom where the teacher believes that knowledge is objective, produced by experts, and delivered unchanged to students, the teacher would probably select books and other materials written by those experts. A lecture method or one where students read those texts then answered factual questions might predominate. By contrast, if a teacher believed that students have to construct their own understandings, the teacher might have a variety of resource materials and manipulative materials for them to use. A great deal of time might be devoted to student projects and individual discussions of readings and other work. Cooperative learning might be used, with small clusters of desks or tables for such work in evidence.

Finally, teachers employ their practical theories when they discuss their practice with parents, administrators, and other teachers. Teachers who are knowledgeable about their theories are self-confident and competent when talking with parents and administrators, which may assist in gaining their support. Through such discussions teachers can uncover tacit dimensions of their practical theories. Such conversations are even more helpful then. This occurs in group deliberations, when curriculum decisions are being made for a grade level, department, or school system. During these deliberations, teachers' practical theories comprise one aspect of their interests. This is another way in which solo and group deliberations are interrelated. Teachers' practical theories, then, are sets of concepts, images, and beliefs constructed from preteaching experiences and current practices in order to make sense of their knowledge and work. They have three important characteristics: They are idiosyncratic, frequently have tacit dimensions, and are rational. Teachers use them while they plan, while they teach, and as lenses through which they look at their practice.

Different Terminology about Practical Theories

Theorists have developed and use different terms for unique practical theories in their discussions of teacher thinking. Kelly (1955) argues that people construct the world through sets of opposing polarities. Several researchers (e.g., Elbaz, 1983; Oberg, 1987; Taylor, 1970) have used this construct theory as a starting point to understand teachers' "constructs." Referring to teachers' practical theories as "personal knowledge," Connelly and Clandinin (1988:13) argue:

> We have . . . said that the teacher is the most important agent, after the students of course, in a curriculum situation from the point of view of its planning and development. It is the teacher's personal knowledge that makes all the difference.

On pages 14 to 17 of their book, there is an excellent chart displaying research on teacher thinking, and I recommend it highly. Hammersly (1977) writes of teachers' "perspectives" as ordered sets of beliefs from which teachers make sense of their situations. Clandinin (1986) and Elbaz (1983) refer to these interrelated beliefs as "images." Schön (1983) examines "theories" professionals develop from their practice, and Sanders and I (1986) discuss "practical theories of teaching." Ross, Cornett, and I (1992) refer to "teachers' personal theories." In the field of psychology, Sternberg and Wagner (1980) use the term "practical intelligence" to explain the wisdom that workers attain through their on-the-job experiences. They find that such information is never explicitly taught to workers but is necessary for their success. The terms differ, but the idea that teachers and other professionals construct knowledge based upon their autobiographies and their practice is common to these theorists' work.

Theorists also employ different terms for processes people use to develop meaning. Gadamer (1977) refers to "hermeneutic consciousness," Dewey (1922) to "deliberation," and Lewis (1955) to "introspection."

For example, Gadamer (1977) points out that reflection is a powerful process in bringing to consciousness tacit (and therefore unquestioned) assumptions and beliefs. For Gadamer, developing such understanding is largely an interpretive enterprise. He argues that the real power of this process rests in a person's ability to see what is questionable, what occurs behind one's back, and what one takes for granted. When people are able to see what they take for granted and to examine it, they bring such matters to consciousness and question their assumptions and beliefs. This makes it possible for people to understand and transform their actions. The product of such interpretation and reflection is hermeneutic consciousness.

Lewis (1955) terms this kind of thinking "introspection," an attempt to look inside oneself to see what has been occurring. Lewis cautions that one potential difficulty is that at the moment of pausing to look inside oneself, the occurrence itself is frozen in order for the mind to examine it. The danger is the potential for neglecting the occurrence's fluidity, thereby misrendering and not truly seeing it. In everyday life, many people reflect almost continuously in an effort to improve their understandings and actions.

I believe it is critical for teachers to uncover and understand as much of their own practical theory of action as they can since understanding it permits them to critique and change it if they believe certain aspects are untenable, unfair, or improper. Through such a process, teachers come to possess their theories rather than holding them blindly. Such a process also enables teachers to articulate their theories to administrators, parents, and colleagues.

Teachers can uncover and understand their theories by keeping a reflective journal (see Holly, 1989). Also, audiotaping and videotaping one's practice and then reviewing and analyzing the tape is another tactic. Talking with colleagues trying to understand their practices is helpful to teachers. Describing their practice and conjecturing about why they took a particular action, why a practice worked well, and what beliefs underlie those actions are fruitful sorts of contemplations. Another way to think about this is through metaphors and images. Here too a reflective journal and discussions with colleagues can be used to uncover and examine metaphors and images about what to teach, how children learn, appropriate roles for teachers, and the like.

In this next section I examine research about teachers' planning. How do teachers plan? What do they take into account? What is the nature of those plans?

TEACHERS' PLANNING

Virtually every teacher education program devotes a considerable amount of time teaching undergraduates how to write detailed linear lesson plans that begin by specifying instructional objectives (Clark and Peterson, 1986; Kauchak and Eggen, 1989). This seems rather odd in that research has consistently revealed that experienced teachers do not develop or use written lesson plans when making decisions about what to teach and that their planning is not linear.

When teachers plan, their plans do not resemble the linear models taught in university courses (Clark and Peterson, 1986; Clark and Yinger, 1979; McCutcheon, 1982). Apparently teachers—even those with only a few years of classroom experience—find that writing detailed lesson plans does not help them conceive lessons except when they are planning a lesson for the first time.

Most lessons are planned mentally and not committed to paper. At most, a teacher may jot down an outline or list topics to be covered during the lesson. This outline does not approximate the complexity of a teacher's plan, which typically exists as a notion of a particular flow of activity (McCutcheon, 1982; Morine-Dersheimer, 1979). For the most part, teachers' mental planning seems more significant to them than the act of committing ideas to paper. Such a mental rehearsal of the lesson seems to be an integral part of their planning. Teachers have in mind a general approach and sequence for the lesson. They envision it in action and rehearse what they will say, what questions to ask, when to distribute which materials, what to assign for practice or evaluation purposes, what difficulties are likely to occur, and how long the lesson is likely to take. This rehearsal in imagination demonstrates one way in which this mental work resembles deliberation as I described it in chapter 1.

Moreover, the brief written outlines of lessons are typically nonlinear and rarely entail explicit instructional objectives (Clark and Peterson, 1986; Clark and Yinger, 1987; Zahorik, 1975). Indeed, several surveys indicate teachers spend a relatively small proportion of their total planning time thinking about instructional objectives (Morine-Dersheimer and Vallance, 1976; Peterson, Marx, and Clark, 1978). This does not mean teachers never consider objectives, but they may do so more when teaching (interactive) than planning (preactive). Teachers point out that since their courses of study, curriculum guides, and textbooks include objectives, listing them would be superfluous. They also say that objectives are inherent in what they do, so writing them in plan books is wasted effort. Despite the negligible use of objective-driven plans, most teachers are able to state their lessons' goals (Clark and Yinger, 1979, 1987; Kauchak and Eggen, 1989), perhaps because of the rational nature of their work.

It is less clear whether teachers are aware of or reflect upon the implicit curriculum, since it is not typically planned in advance, but rather emerges out of what occurs in the school and classroom. However, when asked about their overall goals, teachers frequently list some that could be classified as implicit, such as developing a healthy self-concept. At times the implicit curriculum is intended. For example, Karen Smith (see chapter 3) wants her students to learn to enjoy good literature. More examples of this can be found in chapters 3 and 4.

Teachers who do not begin with instructional objectives commence their planning by considering the learning situations most likely to interest their pupils (Taylor, 1970). This supports the idea that teachers translate intentions and beliefs into the curriculum through instructional activities, which may or may not be physically active (Bromme and Juhl, 1988; Sardo-Brown, 1988; Hollingsworth, 1989; Leinhardt, 1982; Zahorik, 1975). It is important to recognize the influence of simultaneity here. Teachers think simultaneously about their students, the content of lessons, and instructional strategies while they engage in solo deliberation as well as outcomes and the teaching/learning processes.

Clark and Yinger's research suggests that lesson planning is cyclic and recursive. That is, each planning event is heavily dependent upon prior classroom experiences (Clark and Yinger, 1987; Yinger, 1980). Some teachers begin with a vague conception of an activity, and then elaborate upon it progressively until it becomes a set of routines that may be nested within weekly or even yearly plans (Yinger, 1980; Sardo-Brown, 1988). For example, Mark Schaefer developed a system to assess and teach his third-graders number facts. He displayed a huge chart, "Power Math Facts," in the hall outside his room and taught students how to study their number facts by focusing on one set a week (e.g., addition with fives) so they would not be overwhelmed by the task. He administered timed tests to students, and those who passed had that box checked off on the chart. Students seemed to be highly motivated to compete with themselves and they eagerly checked the row beside their name each day to see whether they had mastered that set of facts. From addition, he proceeded to subtraction, multiplication, and division, transferring the system he developed for addition to the other operations. Teachers do not always write such plans, but more often keep them in mind, critiquing and refining them, envisioning what they will say and do. In Mark's case, the system worked so well that he used it the following year and was able to oversee his students' mastering arithmetic facts in all four functions, which he believes is essential to learning mathematics. Other teachers in his school have also started doing this. Now Mark keeps the chart inside the classroom so students can see it more often, and he has developed other systems related to homework.

Some teachers keep lists of things to be sure to do ("see Chris—studying spelling words," "Remind Anne: homework frequency"). These frequently concern particular problems that need attention so as to preserve the general flow in the classroom.

The nature of planning appears to vary with the subject matter and grade level to be taught, the instructional materials available, and the school context (Clark and Yinger, 1979), as chapters 3 and 4 illustrate. Even when one particular model of lesson planning is advocated in a school district, teachers tend to individualize it to be consistent with their own styles and classroom contexts (Sardo-Brown, 1990). An emphasis on detailed written lesson plans may even be somewhat detrimental since they may interfere with improvisation and unforeseen events. Too much planning can make a teacher less sensitive and responsive to pupils (Zahorik, 1970).

Planning does not occur only before teaching. Jackson (1990) reminds us that teachers do not merely plan before teaching, but also while teaching, and they relive and critique those plans and actions after the lesson is completed. He refers to these as preactive, interactive, and postactive planning.

One important phase of planning some teachers employ is interactive. Yinger (1987) conceives of one form of interactive planning as "improvisation." He characterizes it as holistic and patterned, and as he points out, it is particularly well suited to situations that do not permit extensive prior deliberation. In his view, improvisational planning is a compositional process in which teachers apply contextually grounded patterns for thinking and action. (See examples in chapters 3 and 4.) I think teachers create these patterns because they are based upon their practical theories of action—known or tacit. This is why teachers need to know their theories of action.

Many experienced teachers appear to improvise. They begin with a mental outline of activities, and then fill in details to elaborate the plan as they perform it (Borko et al., 1988; Leinhardt, 1982; Yinger, 1987). Moreover, a single prescriptive format for lesson plans may make it difficult for teachers to use nontraditional instructional models such as cooperative learning (Sardo-Brown, 1990). Perhaps this is the case because planning involves a great deal of thinking and learning. As a result, teachers' mental planning is much more significant than what they actually write in their lesson plans. Because a model oversimplifies it cannot capture the complicated interrelationships and multidimensionality of the decision making involved in planning.

Teachers themselves regard written lesson plans as useful only for student teachers or substitute teachers or on occasions when they plan completely new lessons or units. On such occasions, teachers write the plans because the activity of writing helps them to think and gives them a document to examine. However, they do not refer to such plans while actually teaching.

Quite often teachers write very detailed sets of plans for substitute teachers to follow that are different from what they actually do. They also rethink and reorder what is to be done in their absence since they are reluctant to leave the introduction of an important concept or the implementation of a complicated lesson to a substitute teacher.

In short, do teachers plan? If "planning" is considered as writing down in detail what is to be accomplished, the answer is no. If it is considered as developing a course of action, the answer is yes. The plan is a sketchy outline of events upon which teachers elaborate while teaching. Teachers consider previous lessons while planning current and future ones. They think about both the content and their students while conceiving of a plan. Although these plans do not focus upon instructional objectives as much as upon ideas about what to do, inherent in the lessons are aims.

This next section of the chapter contains an extract from an action research project by Angela Valtman, who discloses her planning a new unit. It demonstrates interrelationships between her conceptualization of practice and her planning.

VALTMAN'S ACTION RESEARCH
ABOUT HER PLANNING

Angela Valtman teaches fifth grade in a large metropolitan school system. She reflects on her planning processes in designing a series of lessons that relate the study of Native Americans, science, and language arts:

> To begin with, I must state that I have not looked at my planning or my teaching in the sense of deliberation prior to this. I now believe that the greatest part of what I do is deliberation. I deliberate all day long. By deliberation I mean a process by which I make decisions. *Webster's New World Dictionary* defines deliberation as considering carefully; and as consideration and discussion of alternatives before making a decision. In planning a lesson or a unit for my students, I weigh alternatives for many variables. In carrying out the lesson, I am still weighing alternatives, based on how the lesson is progressing. Also, throughout a typical school day, I may be involved in discussions with other teachers deliberating about procedures, or I may deliberate within a committee meeting.
>
> It takes deliberation to search for alternatives to my beliefs or values about teaching. In planning many of my social studies or science units,

it would be very easy to follow the adopted texts. Yet, they do not always fully meet the objectives and definitely do not match my belief about students constructing their own meaning in learning about a topic. Also, I feel a strong commitment to teaching the children how to gather information on their own. In planning a unit on Native Americans, I had to decide how much I would pull from the book (if anything) and what other sources I would use among many other decisions. If I had chosen satisficing as my course of action, I would have carried on with very little deliberation.

Realizing that my beliefs and values about the teaching/learning process cause me to deliberate during planning, I would like to compare my planning a unit on Native Americans in relation to chapter 1 [of this book]. In my study I examined characteristics of deliberation and how each one was evident in my planning process. However, I found that they were all interrelated and I had difficulty in isolating them. Also, I planned to do the same with Schwab's commonplaces. Again, I had the same problem. Therefore, I will proceed with the planning of the unit and attempt to point out what elements and commonplaces were evident at the time. I must point out, though, the first element, which involves the deliberator weighing and considering alternatives, runs through every stage.

My first step in my planning was deciding with what unit I would start the year. Among my possibilities were starting with our heritage or roots. In past years, I have had the students begin with their beginnings. They were to trace where their ancestry began. This allowed me the justification and motivation to study history. I could give the children a reason to study history, by making it relevant to them and showing them how their families have a history. In another alternative I considered starting with the present and working backwards in history. Part of my reasoning was that I always seem to get to the end of the year before I get that far. It would also give the children something to relate to up front, since they have some idea of what is happening in the present. At any rate, the resources of the TV, radio, and newspaper are more familiar. Up to this point, my deliberations centered mainly around subject matter. There were some peripheral considerations going on at the same time. Do I start with the students' world and work out, or do I start with the world and work back to the student, or start with the familiar and work toward the unfamiliar? At this point, I brought into the deliberation the student and possible learning styles. The deciding factor to this question in my planning came from a class I attended this past summer in which I was introduced with an alternative of a "big picture." With the approach, I had a more holistic view in the respect that I would relate social studies to other areas of the curriculum in a natural way. This helped me with my struggle to integrate across curriculum without being superficial. I was not focusing on my values and beliefs about learning and teaching. If the students were going to be able to make meaning out of what they are learning, then they need to see how the pieces fit together. The curriculum cannot be taught in fragmented segments. I now decided that my "big picture" would be based on a time line. I would go back in history and relate it to developments in science. By starting with the Native Americans, which is about as far back in history that the fourth graders are expected to go, I would be able to bring out nature (animals, plants, ecology) and the attitudes toward them. To tie it together, I would bring in *Sign of the Beaver*, by Elizabeth George Speare. I have now made the first decision.

As I look back, I see that conflict entered into the deliberation. Since I did not feel some of the alternatives would be compatible with my beliefs and values, I could not feel comfortable with them. To use Walker's explanation of deliberation, I was establishing my platform.

Already it had become quite evident to me that deliberation is not linear. If it were, I would have been able to relate the process I went through in this one decision to a series of steps I followed. Yet, I went back and forth among the elements and across the commonplaces until I had a decision with which I could feel comfortable. That is not to say I did not continue to deliberate as to whether this was the route I would take. I still would reflect during future decisions to see if I still wanted to maintain this position. Apparently, I did not come up against any conflict that was great enough to make me totally redeliberate this point. To use Pereira's (1984) terminology, I was ready to make a commitment. I did start the year with a unit on Native Americans.

My next deliberation was how to present the topic. I needed to answer questions like: What materials will I provide? Will the students work in groups, individually, or in pairs? What do I want them to learn as a result of this unit? How will I evaluate them? Are there items that I perceived had been in the null curriculum that should be brought out into the open? Where do I begin the unit?

I probably deliberated the least on the last question. Since the book, *Sign of the Beaver*, tied in both elements (science and social studies) it seemed natural to start with the story. First of all, the book would give me the opportunity to introduce Native Americans through one of the main characters in the story. Second, it took place in the period that I wanted to introduce. Third, one of the driving elements of the story was the different attitudes toward nature between the Native American, Attean, and the white boy, Matt.

I was probably simultaneously deciding what specific objectives, or goals I wished to accomplish with this unit. I was not able to isolate all the components. Everything was related and influenced other elements. The elements at this point were for the most part Schwab's commonplaces: subject matter, learners, milieux, and teachers. There was also a strong consideration as to how each of these fit into my beliefs and values.

Since I was deliberating about this unit prior to the start of the school year, I was not aware of the zone of time as I normally might be. However, as the end of the summer grew closer, I was becoming more aware of time. My deliberations were not as long. I probably cut down on the number of alternatives that I would actually consider. I could probably say that stress was starting to enter as an inhibitor.

I feel fortunate that I have had enough confidence in my teaching to not feel the stress of planning a lesson a "correct" way. This is probably a result of feeling safe in my undergraduate training. As I look back, I find I was in situations in which deliberation with a supervising teacher was a norm, even though it was not expressed in those terms. Therefore, I probably have enough confidence in knowing I can, either by myself or with other educators, deliberate sufficiently about a lesson to a point in which it is the best for the given moment and conditions. This is not to say I feel I do the best on every lesson I teach. It is just that I do not see this as an inhibitor to my deliberation process.

I have tried very hard in the last few years to match my teaching to my beliefs and values. In solo deliberation, I feel that it is now second nature and is not an inhibitor. If anything, it frustrates me greatly when, because of something like a time constraint, I cannot come up with enough alternatives to consider what would accommodate my values and beliefs.

Most of the time, I have been able to tolerate the uncertainty that seems to go along with deliberation. However, I find it interesting that there have been times in which I have been deliberating over what direction to take without seeming to arrive at a comfortable alternative. Then suddenly, when it comes down to the wire, I just happen upon the best solution. Occasionally, this occurs moments before I am presenting the lesson. I am not sure what might be a plausible explanation. Is it a positive effect of stress? Or, could it be that when I have made a content satisficing decision to take a course of action, I remove the stress because the decision is made and now I feel a freedom to explore alternatives? A third explanation might be that subconsciously, I know it will work out. Fortunately, this is not a norm. Yet, if I were to find my greatest deliberation flaw, it probably would be not giving myself enough time to come to a close in deliberation. At times, I probably deliberate too long, which puts me into this type of situation.

My deliberation did not stop once I had planned my Native-American and nature unit. Throughout the lesson, I would deliberate upon the feedback I was receiving from the students. While I read a section in the story that dealt with gender differences (in relation to chores) between the two cultures, I had to deliberate on the spot as to whether or not to approach the issue at that time. It was not originally one of my goals. However, I did see it as an opportunity to deal with an issue that is many times part of the hidden curriculum—attitudes toward gender—and here the two cultures had opposing views on what was considered "woman's" work. There are such times in which I will make the students aware of my deliberations and let them deliberate with me. I will come right out and tell them I am trying to decide if we should proceed in this manner or that manner. I will even give my reasons for each consideration. They have freely expressed their opinions in the matter. (Valtman, 1991)

As is evident in this extract, two of Valtman's fundamental beliefs shaped what she ultimately planned. For one, she believed that students construct meanings. Therefore she planned to make many resources available to them so they could do so. Secondly, she believed that the curriculum should not be fragmented with firm boundaries separating disciplines. Therefore she planned to integrate science, social studies, and language arts in her teaching.

The second example of solo deliberation, from Annink-Lehman's (1992) research, is useful in revealing some dimensions of a teacher's development of her practical theory. In this case, Marchia taught in high school for seven years before returning to college to seek a Ph.D. in multicultural education. At that college she is a teaching associate for a preservice professional introduction to education (PIE) course. The course has a required textbook, and its objectives are about educational psychology, although Marchia infuses multicultural education into it as well.

MARCHIA'S SOLO DELIBERATIONS

Marchia characterizes her teaching as "action, participation, research and presentation." She emphasizes student learning, student involvement, and student control in the classroom. As she sees it, her role as an instructor is to promote research and to function as a resource person.

In Marchia's view, the act of teaching should be made as real as possible to these future teachers. Teaching should not only connect with the students' lives but also expand them to permit students to see how their ideas fit into the total realm of possible ideas about teaching.

Marchia indicates that her practical theory is not specifically related to a particular subject, in her case, professional introduction. Although Marchia doesn't mention them as such it seems that she holds several other beliefs that are part of her practical theory. Marchia is a strong believer in the value of multicultural education, which seems to emanate from a strong commitment to equity. For Marchia, the emphasis seems to be on educating *all* students, regardless of race, and she reiterates this point throughout the interview.

Later Marchia says she believes reflection on teaching is important. She mentions it several times while talking about her own teaching and the teaching of her preservice teachers. Next to reflection, she emphasizes the value of cooperation between (preservice) teachers quite a lot. Marchia indicates she is conscious of the fact that reflections refine practical theories by giving teachers a fuller understanding of their theory of action.

When asked what preteaching experience she considers to be of influence on her theory of action, Marchia recalls the political environment of the 1960s, when she was in high school and became convinced that the phrase, "Ask not what your country can do for you; ask what you can do for your country," was correct. Kennedy was president, and everybody seemed to be joining the Peace Corps. Because of personal circumstances, she could not join the Peace Corps, and she decided to work toward change in the domestic situation by becoming a teacher.

The men around her also influenced her decision to become a teacher. Her father and her boyfriend steered her away from the less traditional occupations she was considering. Later in her life she realized that as a woman she let other people limit her possibilities. Even further down the road she started pursuing the goals she set aside at the beginning of her career.

As Marchia indicates, her theory of action has developed with growing teaching experience. As a novice teacher, she stuck close to the content as described in the curriculum for political science. After one and a half years, she began adjusting it. She began by emphasizing bringing the community into the classroom.

An early breakthrough in her teaching occurred when she developed what she considered to be a great lesson. She says, "The lesson bombed and when I reflected I realized that in developing the lesson I'd done all the fun work, the research." On reflection, she realized that the research should have been done by the students themselves.

The practical theories inform what the teacher should teach and how to teach it, before, during, and after teaching by influencing planning content, method, material, and classroom organization. Factors outside the teacher also influence planning.

Another important starting point for planning is the curriculum guide, which is very much related to conceptualizations of practice. As said before, each individual teacher's practical theory of action influences the way he or she actually translates the curriculum guide into teaching practice. The curriculum guide also influences teachers' practical theories, illustrating how solo deliberation and group deliberation are interrelated, as Marchia's planning illustrates.

Marchia indicates that some instructors in the professional introduction course merely teach from the book. In contrast, she assumes that students read the book, so she focuses more on important current topics related to teaching and on application of ideas. Increasingly, Marchia emphasizes teaching students how to reflect on their field experience. To achieve individual reflection and small-group reflection she uses interactive small-group sessions. In her view, this teaching strategy further achieves collegiality and the ability to receive criticism, and it increases information about content.

The course Marchia is teaching for PIE has a theoretical emphasis that should cover understanding the learner. Marchia feels comfortable teaching this because she has a good psychology background and because of her teaching experience. Thus, although she accepts the curriculum guide up to a certain level, she feels uncomfortable that PIE does not yet have a multicultural aspect and has been inviting speakers to talk abut multicultural education.

She thinks people slowly are coming to recognize the importance of multicultural education. Marchia played a large role in initiating a recent seminar for all PIE teaching assistants about multicultural education. According to Marchia, not giving attention to multicultural education in preservice sets up future teachers for failure. She stresses the predictions that in the near future about 95 percent of the teachers will be white suburban and rural women one-fifth to one-third of whose students will be from different racial and ethnic groups.

Marchia reports that the way she plans what she teaches has changed over the years because of her growing knowledge of the content she is teaching and her growing familiarity with teaching aids and resource persons. When planning, she uses her former experiences and does more research on the topic and the appropriate teaching materials (films, television, journal articles, her own graduate courses in education).

She characterizes the above described part of planning as not very structured. The result of her planning and research will be written on one page with about four major topics she wants to cover, at the bottom of which she will write down special things she wants to discuss or show to individual students.

So if you're wondering if I have a picture perfect paper to do it, I don't, absolutely don't. As far as lesson plans, if I would turn in what I have, I'll get an F, I know it. Because I just don't function that way. . . . I can function and get the test graded at a certain time, I can get all the bureaucratic situations done. But in the classroom I need to be able to make or not make a formal lesson plan according to what I need to do in the classroom. It would take me an enormous amount of time to do it the way they would want me to do it. And then I don't have time to do what I need to do.

At the beginning of class, Marchia gives the students an overview of what they will be doing that day and that week. She also directs them in scheduling time for major projects they need to work on. In this way, the students have a time reference and know where they are going.

The start for planning a lesson, or a unit, is usually a blend of topics she wants to cover, activities, and objectives. "I truly think it all interrelates. You know that schemata where you build a web; I truly think that's the way I think. I web everything, everything interrelates."

Marchia indicates that at times she does improvise, but "when I flow there is always a purpose. There is an understanding that this is a key topic that needs to be discussed."

Marchia's story reveals that her planning does not resemble linear models; instead, it is like webbing, she says, based on previous experiences and changing continuously. Like many teachers, she is improvisational in that she does not make detailed lesson plans. Instead, she jots down ideas on paper that resemble notes to herself rather than any formal lesson plans. She says her planning starts with thinking about objectives, topics, and activities, but it seems her topics are the genesis of her plans. Marchia seems to feel somewhat guilty about not writing "picture-perfect lesson plans" and that her planning is not structured in a linear fashion. She was taught the "proper" way to plan, but experiencing that in practice yields mixed feelings for her (Annink-Lehman, 1992).

COMPARING INDIVIDUALS' PLANNING TO CHARACTERISTICS OF DELIBERATION

In chapter 1 I argued that deliberation is a form of practical reasoning embodying several characteristics, including developing alternatives; envisioning potential actions and outcomes; considering means and ends, facts, and values; operating within a zone of time; having conflict and interest and a moral and social dimension. Solo deliberation is a form of practical reasoning because it comprises a process of identifying problems to resolve and grounds for making such decisions, generating solutions, and selecting among them to resolve the problem. It is a thoughtful consideration of possible actions that employs one's practical theory of action, as exemplified by Valtman's action research.

Valtman saw these characteristics of deliberation as inextricably interrelated but acknowledged that generating alternatives was true of all phases of her planning. Research on teacher planning demonstrates that teachers also envision their actions while planning as they virtually "see" what they and their students will say and do. Because teaching is rational and intentional, teachers also envision outcomes. Indeed, professional teachers are concerned with creating optimum conditions (helping the most students learn the most possible), so their work has this element to it and focuses on ends as well as means. It is also time-bound because teachers must take action. They have to cease preactive deliberations at some point and act. They elaborate upon the decision while actually acting.

As is true of deliberation in general, conflict occurs within individual teachers about what to do because, although they generate several alternatives, realistically they can only pursue a few without chaos ensuing. Conflict is also inherent in the process because the grounds for making selections are ambiguous. Society has not agreed upon the purposes of schooling and revises or adds items to the agenda as current events and society change. Also, the best course of action for most students may not be suitable for all students, as is evident in Mark Schaefer's recent reflections:

I've developed this great creative idea for teaching an important geographic concept. But implementing it means the kids have to control themselves. The idea is somewhat unusual because it's not like our usual routine. But I think all the kids can except possibly Joshua. He is so volatile that he could create massive problems and the whole class could fail. On the one hand, it's an excellent idea and teaches important content. Also, I can't see that Josh will ever learn self-control unless he's virtually thrown into situations where he has to exercise it. I don't want to sacrifice the whole class just because Josh might flip out. But on the other hand, he could ruin a week's worth of social studies lessons. I think I'll go for it anyway and see how it goes. I can always give him a regular assignment to do while the other kids are doing this.

Teachers' interests also come into play in solo deliberation. Following Mansbridge's (1980) work, these sorts of interests are based largely in teachers' practical theories and appear in what they plan to do. When a teacher believes it is crucial to teach something and has developed a series of lessons about it, this interest is very evident. Thinking back to Michael Davis's lesson, his interests in social studies and its interdisciplinary, interconnected, and multicultural nature comprise some of his interests, as they do Marchia's. Also true of Marchia is that she identifies problems in need of solutions (such as a lack of multiculturalism in PIE), identifies solutions and potential actions, weighs alternatives in terms of results, and selects the best course of action. An analysis of such work makes it appear to be linear, but in the process of planning it is not, as both Valtman and Marchia indicate.

Because solo deliberation bears the general characteristics of deliberation, I believe it is appropriate to say that teachers deliberate as they conceive of and plan their lessons.

SUMMARY

Solo deliberation is a form of practical reasoning with its roots in teachers' practical theories. These are the philosophies, theories, and guiding images teachers develop based upon their personal experiences before and while they teach. People develop such generalizations to make sense of the world. Teachers employ these to decide before and while they teach what are the optimum actions to take. Because teachers' practical theories differ, their interests and actions are highly idiosyncratic. This results in teachers' developing and redeveloping the curriculum policies and materials they are given to such an extent that it is more appropriate to say that teachers develop the curriculum through their solo deliberations than it is to say they implement it.

Merely because teachers develop and redevelop the curriculum does not mean they do so based on whim. As I have shown in this chapter, they do so based on their practical theories of action. Further, this does not mean that because teachers have idiosyncratic practical theories that the curriculum necessarily has to be chaotic and disorganized. I will have more to say about this theory and curriculum organization in chapter 8.

STUDY QUESTIONS

1. Give an example of a change you made in the curriculum you were supposed to teach or in the curriculum materials you were to use. Why did you make that change? In what ways did it work and not work in the way you anticipated? In what ways did it go along and not go along with the goals of that policy or materials?

2. When I was beginning to conceive of and write this book, a friend of mine said, "Teachers *plan*. They don't deliberate. *Groups* of people deliberate." Having read this chapter, how would you respond to this?

3. In your own words, explain what practical theories of action are. Give an example of one of your practical theories of action. What is its source? What makes you believe it? What would it take to make you doubt it?

4. Why are teachers' practical theories of action idiosyncratic? What does this imply about curriculum policies and materials?

5. One important part of enhancing one's professionalism as a teacher is to uncover tacit dimensions of one's practical theory of action. Why is this the case? How can teachers do this? Who might be able to help you?

6. Clarify one part of your practical theory of action. Reflect upon what you believe your students should learn. Defend your views. Then collect students' work for several lessons you teach and audiotape those lessons. Analyze the work audiotapes to discern what actions you took that were in keeping with your beliefs and what actions might have contradicted them. Also analyze these for the implicit curriculum, its sources, merits, and negative aspects.

7. Why does preservice education account for so little of teachers' theories of action? What does this imply for teachers who are supervising preservice teachers, such as student teachers?

8. Reflect upon the kinds of planning you do. To what extent do you preplan? How do you do this? What characteristics of deliberations apply and do not apply to the process? When you're planning interactively, what do you take into account?

9. Immediately after you teach a lesson, reconstruct in a journal entry your interactive planning. Then reflect upon ways it does and does not resemble deliberation.

10. Why might Angie Valtman see the characteristics of deliberation as so interrelated that they are difficult to disentangle? If this is true, of what value *are* the characteristics?

11. Many teachers are like Marchia, who jots general ideas down on paper; some claim they do not plan. Is this true? In what ways do they do themselves a disservice by saying or thinking that?

12. Keep a journal about your planning processes for three days of lessons. Analyze them by comparing what *you* do to what I presented in this chapter. What can you say about how you plan? In what ways is and is it not deliberative in nature?

13. Plan a lesson you could use with a student teacher about theories of action and planning.

NOTE

1. Teachers and school names have been changed in an effort to disguise their identities. This is true throughout the book.

chapter 3

Solo Deliberation in Elementary Schools:

Three Cases

Chapter 3 consists of case studies of three elementary school teachers' deliberations and teaching. The focus here is on what the theory presented in chapters 1 and 2 looks like in practice in elementary schools. These three cases are located in two different communities, two cases in Potomac and one in Mapleton. I begin each case by describing the community and school, then the teacher and classroom, the teaching, the practical theory of action, and the deliberations of each teacher.[1] Following these cases I discuss and summarize them.

I developed these portraits and those in other chapters by doing case studies that focused on the questions associated with the theory presented in chapters 1 and 2. I discuss my research methodology in an appendix. I did research in the two classrooms daily in Potomac for ten weeks during a winter 1990 research leave.[2] I did not have a research leave for the Mapleton study, so it took longer; I observed and interviewed the teacher and his class there more sporadically in 1990–1991 during my nonteaching days. In all, I observed for about 300 hours and interviewed teachers, students, principals, parents, and community residents. After reanalyzing over 500 pages of field notes, I can locate no evidence to negate the theory that teachers develop and hold idiosyncratic practical theories of action on which they base decisions while deliberating and teaching. These three cases reveal nuances of how these teachers develop their practical theories and deliberate to decide what to teach.

Potomac

Potomac is from 30 to 100 miles from various cities in Ohio, thus escaping from urban sprawl and serving as a bedroom community for these cities. The people of Potomac cherish the smallness of their town. Its proximity to metropolitan centers permits citizens to travel there to shop and to attend cultural or sports events. It also permits city dwellers to visit Potomac to attend the popular annual Potomac County Fair and to relax for a getaway weekend of antique shopping and a slower pace.

Potomac is the largest town in Potomac County, with a population of almost 21,000. Manufacturing predominates, followed by sales, services, government, construction, and agriculture. Potomac consistently has a lower unemployment rate than the rest of Ohio and the United States. In a local coffee shop, some citizens say they believe this is because Potomac is a small town, which makes it easier to know about job openings and to make contacts than in bigger communities. Others contend it is because Potomac has a well-educated work force. Yet others maintain it is due to the presence of many family-owned enterprises and to Potomac's fairly stable population. Probably a combination of these factors leads to most adults being employed in Potomac.

According to a report by the chamber of commerce, 97 percent of Potomac's population is white, and the median number of school years completed by its citizens is 12.3. More minority families have been moving to Potomac. In the past ten years several African-American and Asian-American families have relocated to Potomac. They say they like the employment opportunities, the relaxed pace of the community, and the welcome they have received.

Brick buildings dominate the ten-block downtown, and the architecture reflects the styles of various decades of its 100-year history. The campus of Potomac-Powell College, a four-year liberal arts college, consumes several blocks of the downtown area. Its large trees and architectural style blend into the rest of the area, and town citizens are usually patient with students' pranks, acknowledging that these are an inevitable part of growing up. They are less tolerant of serious pranks, such as when two students slowly cruised by Hughes Elementary School in a white station wagon with out-of-state plates one recent wintry day, instilling fears of kidnapping. On that day, the nearby police station buzzed with concern for several hours. The police investigated and later arrested two college students in the case.

HUGHES ELEMENTARY SCHOOL

One residential area in northern Potomac has spacious lots, huge trees, and large, ranch-style homes intermingled with occasional two-story Victorian mansions. In 1990, the average house price in this neighborhood was $102,000. Nestled among these homes is Hughes Elementary School, contained in an L-shaped building of one floor with a basement under a portion of it that adds height to the gymnasium and contains a few other rooms. Built in 1950, Hughes was added to in 1958 and 1982. The 1982 addition included an airy, well-lit media center where 100 students typically work during the day in various areas at tables, on large couches, in chairs, or on the floor.

Artwork and other students' projects festoon the neat, quiet halls. Teachers, children, and others smile as they pass one another in the halls. Classroom doors are open, and a quiet hum of activity spills out into the hall from most rooms.

Most parents of Hughes children are professionals. A few children of working-class families ride buses from a nearby tidy and well-landscaped mobile home park. Eighteen teachers work with 424 students at Hughes. The student body consists of 407 white, 14 African-American, two Hispanic-American, and one Asian-American students. Typically, 11 percent of the school population transfers into or out of Hughes annually.

Each year the faculty identifies a theme around which they plan activities, including assemblies and special events. Recent special events have included an artist-in-residence, who taught about customs of western Africa. Another recent theme combined physical education and health. In 1989–1990, the theme was space and space exploration.

In October 1988, several faculty and administrative personnel were on hand in Washington, D.C., to receive an award for educational excellence from then-Secretary of Education William Bennett. The principal, Ted Berry, is committed to administering the school in partnership with teachers, so shared decision making about policy matters is common here.

KAREN SMITH TEACHES SECOND/THIRD GRADE

Karen and Her Background

Karen Smith is in her thirties and has light brown, curly hair; she is slim and taller than average. She usually dresses somewhat casually in slacks or a full skirt and blouse so she can hunker down or sit on the floor with her students. She always seems ready with a gentle smile of encouragement. She has taught for 13 years, 11 in first grade and two in second. She grew up in Kansas City and moved to Ohio from Chicago for her senior year of high school. She had originally planned to go to Iowa State University to study home economics, but she attended Powell-Potomac College instead, majored in elementary school education, and is completing her master's degree in language arts education at a nearby university. Being a teacher seemed natural to her probably because her mother and father, aunts, and uncles had been teachers. She says it would never have occurred to her not to go to college because college seemed to be a natural extension of high school. Her earliest memories are those of her mother reading to her extensively and correcting her speech. Her sister is 12 years younger than she is and her brother, six. She reflects that she has always liked children, perhaps because of her younger siblings. She taught for one year before getting married. Her husband and she have two children, a seven-year-old son and a two-year-old daughter. Before having their own children she and her husband cared for a foster child. She further remembers having liked books as a child, perhaps due to her mother's having read to her so much. This year Karen teaches a combined class of 22 second- and third-graders.

The Classroom

Books abound in her classroom. On the floor sit two large boxes full of books, one with books by Dr. Seuss and the other with books about snow. Some books are shelved and others are stacked, perching atop the piano, teacher's desk, and window ledge. Most are trade books, although some are textbooks, dictionaries, and other reference books.

Tall windows stretch along one wall between a bookcase, a ledge, and the ceiling. On another wall are hooks and shelves where children hang coats and stow their lunches and equipment to use on the playground. Twenty-two students' desks are pushed together to form two islands in the room. Around the room's periphery are other work areas—a wooden frame shaped like a tepee or pine tree, small chairs, a piano, a computer on a desk, and the teacher's desk. Children sit in the chairs, stretch out on the carpet under the tepeelike frame, curl up in the kneehole under the teacher's desk or underneath the piano bench, and work alone or in quiet groups. A busy hum of quiet chatter permeates the room even though it is usually busy with movement and activity.

Teaching and Learning in Karen's Room

Karen typically devotes most of the morning to language arts. As children enter, they record their presence, hang up coats, retrieve their journals from their desks, and begin to write their daily entries. Topics include making pizza last night, worries about a sick pet, what their family did over the weekend, or wishes for snow with reminiscences of snowy adventures. Most entries consist of two or three sentences with a few misspelled words, but they do contain a sense of the sentence and do convey ideas. For instance, one morning, Angelo writes, "Last night we made pizza with sauce, cheese and sausage. We watched TV and ate. I hleped [sic]." Karen helps him spell "sauce," "cheese," and "sausage." Teri writes, "This weekend I *really* wanted to play in the snow. But it didn't snow, so I helped Mom wash curtains and then I read a library book. Maybe it will snow soon. I have a new sled." They interrupt their work with the Pledge of Allegiance, led by a rotating Star of the Day, who also selects a patriotic song for the class to sing. Finishing their journals, children obtain books to read. Today they scurry to the carton of Dr. Seuss books, examine their bibliographies to see what they have not read, then shuffle through the box to select one so they can write another book report. Other children are completing journal entries. Any time during the day after they complete work they get Dr. Seuss books and find places in the room to read or write their book reports. Thirty minutes after beginning their school day, the children return to their seats, following Karen's direction. Some are slower than others; they may be engrossed in diary entries or a book or may be more serious procrastinators than others. Karen reminds them, "Please finish up and move here, people. It's time to move on." Later, she calls individual names to prod them. Once all assemble she directs third-graders to obtain a snow book from the box and to read it to a second-grader and then have the second-grader read it back to them. Third-graders go to the box, get a book, and select a second-grader. Then the pair locates a spot to work. One pair is lying down head to head under the tepeelike frame. Others are under the teacher's desk or piano bench. Still others are sprawled on the rug or sitting in small chairs. A few work at desks, clearly the least favorite spot, but acceptable. They quietly read snow books to one another, taking turns and chatting amiably about their story and pictures. After reading the book twice—first with the third-grader and then with the second-grader taking the lead—they get Dr. Seuss books. Karen monitors this month-long Dr. Seuss activity in which students are to read ten books a week and write short book reports summarizing the plot and telling what they did and did not like about it. Students have copies of a Dr. Seuss bibliography and check off books they read. Karen reminds them through each week of how many they should have read to complete their ten-a-week diet.

On another day, Karen says, "Okay, third-graders get out your literature journal book—the paperback. Second-graders, back in your seats and get out your literature journals, too. Angelo, Robert, it's time to move on. Let's start by looking at page 53. There are ants at the bottom of page 53." Tim, Angelo, and Robert scurry to sit down and find their books and the page. On it appears a chart, "Things I'm Choosy About," for students to complete. Karen asks, "If you're choosy about your food, are you the same or different? What are you choosy about?" A chorus of answers comes forth, but students wait for each other to finish, and they talk quietly. It is not a boisterous chorus:

ANNE: Where I play.

ROBERT: Games!

AARON: If I should make my bed or not.

NATHAN: What I wear. My corduroys.

TAD: Certain friends.

AMY: Where to do shopping.

Karen continues, "If you go to Kroger's or Big Bear, what kind of store are you in?" Aaron says, "A grocery store." Karen smiles and continues, "If you're in the grocery store in a section where there are rolls of plastic bags and scales hanging, what section are you in?" Amy says, "Vegetable and fruit." Again, this has the tone of a conversation rather than a sing-song, rote-response question-and-answer session. Karen asks if people are choosy about produce, as she tries to extend students' understanding of the word *choosy*. She directs them to observe the next time they're in the produce section at the store. Continuing to develop the meaning of the word *choosy*, she asks, "How many of you are choosy about pizza?" Many hands go up, very enthusiastically. Then she asks how many would eat it even with anchovies, green pepper, or onions on it. Several groans and scowls are evident. "Okay, let's go on," she says. "At the bottom of the page, Arthur's mother wants him to eat red ants. What words does she use to describe them? If you don't remember an adjective she uses, look in the book on page 31." Many consult the book, *An Anteater Named Arthur,* by Bernard Water. They find it quickly and quietly, but this time they excitedly call out words, pointing them out to one another enthusiastically: "scrumptious" (p. 34), "beautiful!" (p. 31). Karen calmly says, "Okay, find three answers." She walks around, looking at the answers they write and occasionally prompting, "You need one more answer here, don't you?" After a pause, she says, "Okay, let's go on to page 54. Anyone need help there at the top?" They read the directions silently. Mark says he needs help in answering the first question, which asks how one knows from the story that Arthur does not like red ants. Robert says he (Arthur) wants brown, not red, ants, and Karen asks Robert to remember a verb that tells what Arthur *did.* "What's something little kids do when they don't like something," she prompts. Robert responds, "Shake his head, stuck out his tongue, said 'Ik.'" Laurel needs help finding another, so Karen has Maggie read hers, which is the same as what Robert said. At the bottom of the page another chart appears, and Karen directs third-graders to help second-graders complete it:

What Arthur Forgot   Why He Came Back for It

Then third-graders read their Dr. Seuss books while second-graders complete their work. Karen reminds Maggie to finish her journal entry. When students are working or responding to questions in discussions, Karen is constantly looking around, monitoring what all are doing.

One day Karen reads *Wacky Wednesday,* by Audrey S. Geisel, to them. Students are to follow along and count wacky things, page by page. Because Chad also has a copy of the book, students gather around the two books and excitedly point out the odd things to one another, giggling and squirming as they do.

On yet another day third-graders silently read part of *Matilda,* by Ronald Dahl, then respond conversationally to Karen's questions about that part. Many of her questions tend to be lower-order what, when, who, or where ones, although a few call for interpretations. She directs them to continue to read to page 100 for tomorrow's discussion while she works with second-graders.

Now it's almost time for recess. Twenty minutes before that break, Karen reads Mary Ann Hoberman's poem, "Pockets." Then she says, "If you have a pocket, put your hand in it and see if anything is there." They do and contribute suggestions of what they found in their pockets:

RANDY: crud

AMY: lunch money

LANCE: lint, air, and a seam

She continues the conversation by pulling her pocket inside out and showing other students what a seam is. Abraham enters the conversation by doing the same. Then she directs the students to count how many pockets they have and to hold up fingers to indicate the number. She adds out loud as she goes around the room to find out how many pockets the class has: "Four and four are? And four more?" Soon the problems get a bit more difficult: 22 plus 4? 26 plus 0? 26 plus 1? 27 plus 4? 31 plus 5? At last, it turns out they have 67 pockets! She asks if they have any other kinds of pockets. After pausing for responses, which are not forthcoming, she suggests that they could think of their lungs as pockets for air. Lance says the library books all have pockets. She beams and agrees, then asks what animals have pockets. Randy mentions kangaroos. Following that, they line up by grade level for recess with their coats on, and Karen asks them to count how many pockets are in their coats. She quickly adds these aloud. Third-graders have 28, and second-graders, 32. "Who had more pockets, second-graders or third-graders?" she asks. Perhaps by now they are bored by pocket hunting or see the question as too easy for their attention, or perhaps it is the weather, for no one has an answer to this easy question. Excitedly, she says, "Look out the window!" (It has just begun to snow in an almost snowless winter.) As they go out to play they talk quietly about pockets, despite their obvious excitement about the rare snow.

The students say they love to read books. Second-grader Angelo says, "I really like Dr. Seuss. He's very funny and I laugh at his rhymes." Christina, a third-grader, adds superciliously, "He's really very silly, you know." Whether reading is assigned or not, children read a great deal during the day. Teri suggests, "It's obvious what Mrs. Smith likes best. She loves books. You can just tell."

Following recess they tumble into the room more noisily than at the day's start, excitedly remembering snowier days, unwinding scarves, shaking out, removing and depositing coats, hats, and mittens, and stowing playground equipment they'd taken outside. Unprompted they move to their seats, and a few children take out unfinished morning work. Others obtain a Dr. Seuss book or a snow book and start to read. Karen distributes a packet of arithmetic problems consisting of two-place addition without renaming for second-graders. Third-graders continue to read *Matilda* silently with Karen while she simultaneously monitors the arithmetic work. Neil softly complains about the number of problems (32) on one ditto. Karen says, "I want to see if you really know how to do these." Neil responds with a quiet and gentle "Humbug." "You do the first two rows and I'll check them," she replies. After checking them, Karen finds all are correct. She circulates quickly, seeing the others have also done the problems correctly, so she directs each to go on to the following worksheet.

Another day all second-graders have completed their mathematics except Abraham, who is laboring over his paper using his pencil to count out answers to himself. Neil takes his paper to Karen to check. She examines it, puts a dot above each of three problems, and tells him to fix them. He has missed three problems. He says this is due to errors in number facts ($9 + 5, 5 + 9, 6 + 9$). He quietly and quickly returns to his seat and changes the answers; then he turns the paper in and joins others working on social studies projects. Meanwhile, third-graders continue to read and discuss *Matilda*.

This week Karen has a week-long project about famous people. Second-graders select famous people to study, write about, and paint. This will be part of an assembly for students and parents later in the month. They select Jane Adams, Teddy Roosevelt, Francis Drake, Abigail Adams, Franco Harris, Neil Armstrong, Frank Robinson, and Miles Standish, largely on the basis of leafing through biographies of many famous people. A detail catches their eye or imagination, and so they select that person for their report. Jason likes how Neil Armstrong dressed for the mission to the moon and likes science. Allison likes the way Abigail Adams dressed. Robert is impressed with Francis Drake's sword in one picture. They read about their famous person, and then they work in the hall to trace around each other's own bodies on large sheets of paper to make pictures of the characters. Then they use magic markers and paint to dress their famous people appropriately, at times referring to books for details. Karen and I help students cut out the tracings, using the big scissors. They read more about their person all week, soliciting help from third-graders. Each writes a report and select parts to give in the speech for the assembly. Bits are copied on a large notecard if needed for practice on Friday morning, but they must be memorized for the actual assembly. Meanwhile, third-graders paint scenery to surround and stand behind the famous people. Much of this work is done during students' spare time when they have completed other work. One rainy day contributes an indoor recess to the project. After the assembly, Karen and I hang the paper versions of the famous people and the accompanying notecards on the brick wall in the hall adjacent to her room for all to see.

On another day, Karen reads *The True Story of the Three Little Pigs,* by Jon Scieszka, aloud. This book calls into question whether a wolf was really as nasty a character as depicted in Mother Goose. After that, they hold a trial of the wolf to determine whether he was guilty of huffing, puffing, destroying property, and killing pigs. While the trial bears none of the formalized characteristics of the legal system, through their play children begin to consider issues of why society has laws and the rights of the accused and accuser.

The snow has abated significantly since earlier this morning as they get ready for lunch and leave the room, causing many disappointed comments. The afternoon begins with students continuing their social studies projects, reading Dr. Seuss books, or completing morning work. Then they assemble and line up to go to science or social studies. Karen and other teachers exchange children for part of the afternoon, so Karen teaches health while Miss Glass teaches social studies and Mrs. Peterson science. Karen augments other teachers' lessons through her own social studies projects, a science lesson that she co-teaches with Iris Robole, and reminders about things to study for tests, such as patriotic songs and symbols for second-graders, who are helped by third-graders.

Like many other subjects she teaches, Karen frequently uses literature as a vehicle to teach some of her health lessons. Third-graders enter from other rooms until ultimately 76 jam her room. As all 76 are seated on the floor or at desks, Karen reminds them, "Everyone should be facing south—toward the Ohio River." She pauses momentarily while they wriggle around to face south and get settled, and then she continues, "I want to read a book with you today very quickly." Holding up the book for all to see, she goes on, "This one takes you inside the human body. Raise your hand if you've read it." No one does, so after a pause, she says, "I'll read parts of it." This book, *The Magic School Bus Inside the Human Body*, by Joanna Cole, is a story of a school bus that miniaturizes and goes inside a second-grader who wasn't listening. The pictures illustrate the inside of the body as the bus benignly ventures through it. Karen retells the story, reading only occasionally, holding up each picture for all to see, and circulating among students. She pauses sometimes to point out something in an illustration and to inquire about it: "See how dull these red blood cells are? Why is that?" Jan replies, "When they're *bright* red they have more oxygen in them." Karen asks, "How do you get more oxygen in your brain?" She inhales deeply and reminds them that a deep breath carries oxygen into one's lungs and then asks, "What goes out when you exhale?" Allison replies, "Carbon dioxide comes out because your body can't use it." Again, the questions and answers take the form of a conversation, not a drill. This lesson follows last week's lesson about respiration, where Karen used an overhead transparency to show the path of oxygen into the body, the use of oxygen, and the exhalation of carbon dioxide. Meanwhile, students traced the path on photocopied drawings of the respiratory and circulatory systems. As Karen reaches the book's end, she notices aloud that it contains a test. Many students clamor to take it. This seems to surprise Karen, who says, "We'll do three questions," which she reads aloud, and students respond conversationally.

The remainder of the afternoon is consumed by Karen's lessons in social studies or science to augment what occurs in other classrooms. Today her friend Iris Robole (see next section of this chapter) enters carrying a metal briefcase accompanied by her fourth- and fifth-graders. One of her students carries an off-white sphere. Iris enters in a white laboratory coat adorned with NASA patches. She says, "You saw me come last week with a special little briefcase." Karen obtains the case and reads the label, simultaneously pulling down a wall map of the United States. The label says, "United States Government Property. If found, return to NASA, Johnson Space Center, Houston TX 77058." She asks, "TX. What does that stand for? Where is it? Is it in the north? The south? Then where?" Nathan confesses, "I can't really remember whether it's east or west, but it's Texas." Karen smiles and then remarks that "Mrs. Robole has brought a globe, too, although her globe is somewhat different from the one we're used to because it's a globe of the moon."

In a storytelling tone, Iris begins, "Many years ago before you were even born, a special spaceship landed on the moon. The first one that landed on the moon was Apollo 11. I have some rocks with me that came from the moon. Not from Apollo 11. From Apollo 16." Opening the briefcase to show them, accompanied by soft oohs and ahs, she asks, "Why are they so small?" She pauses and then continues, "There's no water at all on the moon. So if we take these little rocks, unprotected, they'd start to rust. When things start to rust, they start to disintegrate. Now, the *lunar* samples are in lucite, and that's why they're so small. If we had them bigger, it would take three or four of us to carry in the lucite."

The children are extraordinarily attentive to Iris, her story, and her moon rocks and murmur, "Oh, wow!" "Golly!" "Wow!" and "Geez!" She smiles beamingly and then goes on, "*This* is what most of the rocks on the moon are made of: lava. Now, *this* lava is from Hawaii, and it isn't in lucite so you can see it clearly."

Karen directs the fourth- and fifth-graders to help the second- and third-graders. They are to print "LUNAR" down the left side of their paper after looking at the lunar samples. They are to write a word beside each letter about their observations of the lunar samples and what they learned from what Iris has said. Karen interjects, "Let's try not to use 'neat' or 'awesome.'" Knowing that Iris's students have been working with the lunar samples for several days, she encourages, "Fourth- and fifth-graders, tell the second- and third-graders some scientific terms you've heard or read." They consult dictionaries and discuss the lunar samples as they begin to work. They write:

L: light, lift-off, lucite, lunar

U: unique, unusual

N: NASA, nitrogen

A: Apollo

R: rock, rocket

Following that, Karen directs them to write eight adjectives to describe the samples. She reminds all that "adjectives are describing words." Then they are to list eight things the samples consist of, such as volcanic ash and iron. While doing this the partners talk quietly as they collaborate on answers. They also refer to dictionaries for correct spellings, read definitions, and discuss words animatedly for 20 minutes. Then Iris, her class, moon rocks, and lunar globe return to their classroom down the hall.

Before closing the day, Karen asks students to check around their desks for litter, passes back papers she'd checked during lunchtime, and reminds students that library books are due tomorrow. They retrieve coats and personal items and talk animatedly about daily events and their anticipation of afterschool play as they line up to go home. Most of the snow has melted as they leave.

Karen's Practical Theory and Deliberations

One obvious part of Karen's practical theory of action is a belief in learning language as the most important ingredient of education for young children: "You can't do anything unless you're at home in your language. Everything else follows *from* that because you learn everything else *through* it. The best way to learn it is through outstanding children's books that are out because they use the best language and are exciting to kids, beautifully illustrated and creative." Excellent examples of children's literature are a necessary condition for quality education for young children in Karen's view.

She further demonstrates her desire to help children become independent learners as she oversees their many independent projects. Children work in different spots, direct their own work, make choices within boundaries she establishes, and complete the work as due, from their brief journal entries to the month-long ten-a-week Dr. Seuss book reports and the week-long work about famous people. They also work during free time on unassigned activities, most typically reading alone or with a friend. A few children occasionally also work on arithmetic games on the computer. Along the same theme of independent learning, Karen also demonstrates that learning is a social enterprise as she has children collaborate and seek help from one another. They discuss snow books, famous people, moon rocks, and justice for three pigs and a wolf.

The curriculum here centers around language arts, focusing primarily on reading, talking, playing, and writing about children's literature. It should surprise no one that Karen's students score very well on language arts examinations and that their arithmetic scores are a bit lower. Through the implicit curriculum children know Karen appreciates literature. Perhaps this is one reason why they read so extensively, although they also say they love books. Mathematics and other disciplines are less emphasized here, so people favoring more balance in the elementary school curriculum might find this troublesome. However, Karen sees her curriculum as "efficient because I'm teaching many things at once." A lesson where she reads children's literature aloud is also a lesson about health, arithmetic, historical figures, law-related education, or other subjects. Children practice thinking, listening, and speaking. They read and write. She also makes available occasional other lessons, as when Iris, her globe, class, and the moon rocks visited. On this occasion, both science and language arts predominated, although not through children's literature.

Karen was also concerned about the mathematics scores. It may stem partly from the fact that her previous experience had been in first grade; through teaching first grade she may have developed first-grade outlook on mathematics because she is used to the first-grade curriculum. Two years after this research was done, Karen took workshops in mathematics education, and the school system purchased many manipulatives for use in the mathematics curriculum. Now she begins her mornings with math lessons but continues organizing the rest of the curriculum around children's literature.

Karen's penchant for reading and children's literature stretches back to her childhood, when her mother read to her and she read to younger siblings and other children.

Her belief in language arts and children's literature causes some difficulties for her deliberations. "There are just so many great examples of children's literature! I spend hours (and a lot of money each year) collecting and poring over them trying to decide which ones are best for my kids and how to weave them into the day, the month, and the year." Her deliberations begin with the examples of children's literature; her alternatives consist of which ones to use. A second important consideration in her deliberations is her knowledge of *her* students. Criteria she employs in her choices include the quality of the book, its suitability for this particular class, and how she can envision using it in terms of both its content and her instructional strategies. Karen sees goals inherent in the books and their use, and so means and ends intertwine in her thinking. She envisions her actions with the books and enters upon lessons "with a general game plan in mind," not a plan in which every detail has been firmly fixed in her mind.

As is true of many teachers, Karen establishes some routines such as journal writing to use throughout the year. She also accumulates ideas about which projects, routines, and individual lessons worked well in the past, such as the Dr. Seuss and famous people projects and the pockets and snow books lessons. This aids her deliberations because she can predict their likely success with her current group based on this past success. The adoption and use of routines assists her in planning because through them she establishes parts of the day that are relatively less problematic.

While teaching she changes plans as warranted, such as when she tried to extend students' understanding of *choosy,* and then curtailed the discussion when she saw that they liked pizza but did not understand the distinction between liking something and being selective about it. She further alters her plans while teaching when children negotiate her plan, such as when Neil argued *against* too many arithmetic problems and the class argued *for* taking a health test included in a book she read during health class.

IRIS ROBOLE TEACHES FOURTH/FIFTH GRADE

Iris and Her Background

Down the long hall from Karen is her friend Iris Robole, who teaches a combined class of fourth- and fifth-graders. Iris has taught for 18 years in Potomac, primarily in fifth grade. Friends encourage Iris to become an administrator, but she rejects the idea, saying, "I'd miss the kids too much—the action is in the classroom, teaching and watching the kids learn." Her bachelor's and master's degrees are from Ohio State University. She also holds a certificate in gifted education and has accumulated many graduate credits. She and her husband have four sons.

Iris continues to take courses because she says she enjoys learning and is curious about the world and the nature of learning. This year she drives to Cleveland occasionally to participate in day-long seminars sponsored by NASA. At one time Iris was a finalist for NEWEST (NASA Educational Workshop for Elementary School Teachers), a two-week experience. When she was originally accepted she imagined it would be held in Cape Canaveral or Houston and seemed somewhat disappointed to learn its location was Cleveland. Nonetheless, she attends and is very excited about the projects, content, and activities she can plan about science in general and space in particular as a result of the workshop. This year Iris was nominated as elementary school science teacher of the year, a national award. Speaking ardently, she says, "My love of science has grown over the years. I don't know where it came from or when it started; it seems like it's always been there. Science is a part of everything, and it's really important for America's future! Science and technology are what made America *great*, and that'll continue. Where do you get a love of science unless it starts in elementary school? It's the most important thing we teach for our kids' sakes and for the whole country."

Iris is of medium height and weight with shiny, medium-length chestnut hair. Trim and in her early forties, she generally wears a skirt and blouse with a jacket, although one very wintry day she wore a pantsuit. Hair glistening, she seems businesslike, enthusiastic, energetic, and happy, but she claims, "It's an act," when asked how she maintains her energy and enthusiasm all day, every day. Whether it is an act or she gets absorbed in what occurs is difficult to say. I suspect she begins each day acting but is fueled by her genuine joy at being with children, watching them learn, and thinking about her tasks while teaching. At any rate, at no time during the ten weeks I observed there did Iris seem grumpy, tired, or short-tempered. If it's merely an act, Iris pulls off the act convincingly and consistently.

The Classroom

Huge, colorful NASA posters hanging on the walls depict various space missions, vehicles, planets, the moon, and other bodies in the galaxy and solar system. Near them on one wall above her desk are charts Iris has made listing 120 terms, names, and words she and students use in their studies of space.

Encyclopedias, dictionaries, and trade books are neatly shelved in bookcases beneath the windows on one long wall. Above the bookcases are suspended three impatiens plants brought in from Iris's yard for the winter. Students hang their coats and stow gear along a shorter wall. Desks congregate to form four islands comprised of four or five desks each. In the center of the room, two tables are pushed together; they hold a tiny frog and assorted reference books. A computer sits on a desk along the room's periphery near the door. Space on another shorter wall, near the teacher's desk and blackboard, is at various times full of seated students assembled for small-group lessons.

This year Iris teaches a combined class of 18 fourth- and fifth-graders. Last year she had 31 students. Of the difference she says, "We can do more group work, more activities and projects. And I get to know each kid much better so I can pick out what's a favorite for them or a strength or weakness and plan around those things somewhat."

Teaching and Learning in Iris's Room

Iris starts today by calling attention to several new items she's just placed in the room: a book of pig riddles, an activity book about solar eclipses, a filmstrip and cassette about the space shuttle, and booklets about astronomy and constellations. Then she quickly gives an overview of the day, pointing out she is unsure exactly when some lessons will occur because she cannot predict how long others will take. A second concern she shares is that she did not retrieve the moon rocks from the bank vault where they must be stored each weekend; unless she can get them during lunchtime, the lesson will have to be postponed a day. Students seem disappointed, emitting quiet groans, ahs, gees, and shoots. She assures them they'll have science anyway.

Each day a different island of desks is responsible for brief reports of current events. Today Scott reports, "This isn't exactly a current event, but the dinosaurs are back at the Center of Science and Industry [in Columbus]. I know 'cause we went there this weekend." Iris conversationally asks what he learned. "They weren't all enormous, and they lived in different environments," replies Scott. Stephanie gives a vague report that "a man who burned his son badly is out on parole." Iris asks what that means, but Stephanie shrugs. Iris suggests, "It means he has to learn to live by some rules." In his turn, Shawn reports that "the newspaper asked citizens to start looking for a white station wagon with blue plates because two men asked a child to get into the car with them." A few children gasp and Iris urges all to remember the license plate numbers if seen. Joel reports that in February Mike Tyson will have a fight in Tokyo, prompting brief and hushed speculations about whether it would be a good fight. John continues, "The space shuttle was spinning." Iris asks, "Do you know why? Several things all happened simultaneously. The fire alarm went off. Then several engines fired and it kept flipping. When is it supposed to land?" John says, "Tomorrow." "Right," says Iris, "When you get up in the morning turn on the television and you'll probably see it or a replay." Finally, Wayne says he heard "something about oat bran not being as good for you as they thought." "They can't decide what's good for you and what isn't!" is his frustrated editorial comment. On other days children mention possible trials of drug lords in Colombia, a lawsuit about being infected with AIDS, liftoffs and landings, arrests for drugs in Columbus and for murders in Cleveland. Not all the news is bad. All tidbits about space are reported. A huge snowfall in Colorado is wistfully reported. Following current events, attendance and lunch count are quickly taken. This completed, they say the Pledge of Allegiance. To assist them in staying (or getting) organized, Iris distributes forms like the one in Figure 3.1 where students can list assignments and check whether all have been submitted. Many students put their names on the forms and this week's dates along the top.

After a pause Iris explains, "Today we're going to start reading Elizabeth Speare's *Sign of the Beaver*. I'll want you to do a long-term project like you've done for other books we've already read." Then she asks whether students thought making a game about the book read previously had been worthwhile. Walter claims, "It was incredibly worthwhile 'cause I had to look up all these little details to make the game exactly follow the book." Scott, Shawn, and Miranda concur, with Miranda adding that she had to use her imagination, too. Iris says, "Let's vote. Who thinks this was worthwhile to do?" All hands go up, and she smiles, saying, "Well, asking the opposite's really pointless, isn't it?" Then she asks what other worthwhile projects they'd like to do that they haven't done yet. Walter

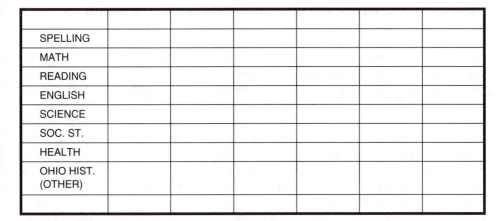

SPELLING						
MATH						
READING						
ENGLISH						
SCIENCE						
SOC. ST.						
HEALTH						
OHIO HIST. (OTHER)						

FIGURE 3.1 Iris's student assignment form

and Wayne want to make dioramas; Miranda, write an additional chapter for the book; and Sandra, draw settings and characters. Shawn says he doesn't want to commit himself until after he sees what the book is about. Iris agrees but cautions him to decide this week so he'll have plenty of time to finish. He assures her he will. After calling attention to the fact that she has only 12 copies of the book, she solicits suggestions of how to deal with the problem fairly, since the class has 18 students. Walter says, "Well, four or five of us sit together, and we have four groups. Why don't you just give each group three books and let us decide? When we aren't using one we can put it in the middle for everyone else." All agree this is a fair solution. Iris does this, then passes out photocopies of material to accompany the book, and students assemble the pages in order because today the photocopying machine did no collating. When all students have all the pages in order, Iris directs them to turn to page 1 of the book. With some students sharing, they read page 1, with four students taking turns reading aloud. At one point Iris interrupts, asking "What's an heirloom?" Jessica, who had been reading that section, says, "Something that might get passed on?" Then Iris remarks that there is no vocabulary sheet in the photocopied packet, "Which means what?" Walter says they need to make their own. Iris agrees and suggests, "Look up and put down whatever interesting words you see that you don't know or aren't sure of." Then she directs all to read the entire first chapter, which is only five pages long, so it should not be a problem. Sharing books appears to cause no problems during the time they read it because students have many other things to do as well.

On another day she has brief conferences about projects students have completed after finishing a different book. As she confers, she asks how the project is related to the book and asks specific questions about each project, entering a mark in a grade book as she proceeds to the next student. In this case, most have made games, and some are very elaborate. Walter's game board is a three-dimensional model of the sewers that are the setting of the story. He points this out to Iris, who asks his neighbor Bill how the game worked out when he played it earlier this week during indoor recess. Bill says, "Just fine. The object is to collect three rats and five scum pieces [the currency used in the sewers]. If you land on a rat hole space you get a rat token, and if you land on a money space you collect the number of scums indicated. I lost though." Iris says to Walter, "Wow, you really thought that out!" Walter smiles and is proudly enthusiastic about his game. He says he learned in making the game "what the sewers were really like and the dangers encountered." Iris agrees, "Yes, you have to pay attention to what you're reading so you can stay with the facts so they match up. This is true of other projects, too, like dioramas." Miranda says, "Yes, although I made a game too. The plot for my game comes from the plot of the book. The dangers are the same." Similar conversations occur about each project, with students briefly showing the project to Iris and Iris commenting on how well or poorly they match the book's plot or on difficulties associated with the game itself. Eddie, for example, has included neither a set of rules nor a mechanism for game pieces to move ahead such as a spinner or pair of dice.

Following reading with the whole group, Iris calls upon fifth-graders to get out their spelling books, leaving them closed, along with a clean sheet of paper. Fourth-graders are to go ahead in *The Sign of the Beaver*. Today she gives the fifth-graders a spelling pretest, saying the word and a sentence for it and then repeating the word. This week's words are root words, where the final letter must be doubled before adding some suffixes (such as occur, control, regret, patrol), along with words where the suffixes -s, -ing, or -ed have been added (omits, controlling, regretted). The practice test contains 24 words, and students check one another's papers for practice tests. Then they are to write each word they missed three times and do the next page in the spelling book, retrieve *The Sign of the Beaver*, and continue reading it.

Iris calls the fourth-graders to bring chairs to the empty area "for a quick review math lesson." Bringing chairs, books, paper, and pencils, the fourth-graders assemble. "My concern," she says intently, "came when I was going over some papers this weekend. You have to know this in fifth, sixth, and seventh grades, so I'm not picking on you. One of the first things you have to remember is this: If you're adding $\frac{1}{2} + \frac{1}{4}$, what do you have to do?" She writes the problem on the board. Jason excitedly says, "Change the 2 to a 4!" Iris asks which number. When no one responds, she says, "The *d*enominator. You can remember that because it's the *d*own number. Jason saw these two numbers and in his mind he realized he could use a four. Why?" Jason quietly says the words "common denominator." Iris smiles and says, "Yes, that's what it's called—a common denominator. An easy way to find them is to think about multiples. You can find a common denominator in your head, but today you have to do it on paper. How many of you asked me if you had to write this on it?" Four students confess they did. She teases Jason that he had also been asking her on Friday. She writes on the board:

$$\frac{1}{4} = \frac{1}{4}$$
$$+\frac{1}{2} = \frac{2}{4}$$

They agree the answer is $\frac{3}{4}$. Then Iris continues, writing this on the board:

$$\frac{1}{4} = \frac{1}{4}$$
$$+\frac{1}{2} = \frac{2}{4}$$
$$\frac{3}{8}$$

She asks, "Now is this right or wrong? Why?" When no one responds, she chides them, "Oh, *you* remember. You only add the *numerators*, not the denominators!" Following this, she asks, "What would be a good denominator if this were the problem?"

$$\frac{5}{6}$$
$$+\frac{1}{3}$$

They complete the problem, arriving at $\frac{7}{6}$ for an answer, and she asks what kind of number it is. With no responses, she says, "This is called an improper fraction. Why, Shawn?" He says, "It's more than a whole." Iris reminds them, "You can tell immediately, if the top number—the numerator—is bigger than the bottom one. So what we want to find out is how much this is in a *mixed* fraction. This is how you could do it."

"Once you get into this, it's something you'll do in your heads. Now, here's something *some* of you did on these papers."

$$\frac{2}{6}$$

$$+\frac{2}{6}$$

$$\frac{4}{6}$$

"By rights this is marked wrong because it's not in lowest terms. Remember how to look for common factors here?"

$$4 = 1, 2, 4$$
$$6 = 1, 2, 3, 6$$

"What's the greatest common factor to both?" They say it's two, so she asks how to return $\frac{4}{6}$ to its lowest term. Shawn says to divide two into each number. Iris directs them to return to their desks to correct the problems she circled—"Not all the ones that are wrong, just the ones I drew circles around."

On another day in mathematics Iris assembles the seven fifth-grade students and starts by saying, "Right now before we begin I want us to do some *mental* math. What's nine times eight minus two, minus ten, plus four, divided by eight?" She pauses briefly between operations. Bill responds, "Eight." Eight of ten say they were with her. She continues, "What's seven times six, plus eight, plus five, minus ten, divided by five? How many are with me?" Seven hands go up. "What's 56 divided by seven, times four, plus eight, divided by eight?" Joel responds, "Five." Continuing, Iris asks, "Do you feel you're beginning to flow into math now? Today we're going to review some division. I want you to do them in a certain way so you don't get into difficulty today, tomorrow, next week, whenever. We'll be doing problems like this."

$$60\overline{)563}$$

"Does this look familiar? Can we divide 60 into 56?" Bill says, "No." Iris asks, "So what's the largest possible answer we could have?" Joel responds quietly, "Nine." "The smallest?" asks Iris. Bill thinks it's zero. "So," continues Iris, "it's between these numbers, 0 and 9. What's a good way to *estimate* this?" Lacking a response, she continues, "An easy way here is to say what's six into 56?" Together they work the beginning of the problem:

$$\begin{array}{r} 9 \\ 60\overline{)563} \\ \underline{540} \\ 23 \end{array}$$

"Before we write this, we have to check what?" Joel says, "How much six times nine is!" Iris smiles and asks the group what the largest remainder is that they could have. The students say the problem is complete, and Iris writes a new one on the board.

$$23\overline{)549}$$

She asks them what the largest and smallest possible answers are, and they respond, respectively, 99 and 10. "So if you have an answer of 101, you're probably wrong," she points out. They decide to start with 20 to solve the problem.

Iris says, "Some of the books have you put a zero here because 20 times 23 is really 460, but if you aren't used to doing that, don't. Do it whichever way you're comfortable with. What number should we try now?" Bill suggests trying four, but they find four to be too large, so he suggests trying three. They complete this problem. Then Iris says, "Now we did that slowly and went through all the steps. What questions do you have? If you have trouble writing numbers, and some of you do, this is a hint for *you*. Turn your paper sideways and you'll have the little faint lines to help you keep your problems lined up. You might need two sheets of paper instead of one. That's okay if you do. You have to be neat and precise doing this because it's complicated enough. Once you do these several times you'll remember all these steps. First, make the box. Oh, should I start with an easy one first?" "Yeah," they softly urge. She says, "191, and divide it by 57. Work it out the way you should and let me know when you're done." Turning around from writing it on the board, she sees no one writing. "Oh! You're done already?!" she asks in a surprised tone. Bill says, "No, stuck." Others support Bill. Iris reexamines the problem she wrote on the board and says, "Oh, I see what I did! That's *not* such an easy one, is it? Let's do 157 and divide it by 21." She asks Bill, "What's the first step?" Put it down on your paper and see if you can go on from there." Iris solves the problem on the board as students work. Joel complains, "Oh, why did you do that? I was almost done, too." Briefly glancing at everyone's paper, Iris says, "Yes, and you all almost got it done right." She writes on the board 391 ÷ 62. Students say, "This is a hard one, right?" She says, "Yes." They murmur, "Oh." Iris continues, "What are you going to do if you're working at home and I'm not there to help?" Hunter has been working assiduously on the new problem. He puts down his pencil triumphantly. Iris asks, "How did you do, Hunter?" Hunter looks briefly at his paper and says he made a mistake. Showing it to Iris, he says, "See, I didn't put this *one* here." He has written:

$$
\begin{array}{r}
6 \text{ R}9 \\
62\overline{)391} \\
\underline{372} \\
9
\end{array}
$$

Iris says, "I'd have marked that wrong because I'd see it as six, remainder nine." "What kind of mistake is that?" Iris asks. Hunter says, "A *dumb* one." Iris contends, "All of us make mistakes. It wouldn't help you if I just said that's dumb. Instead, I'll say today, 'Okay, Hunter. What did you learn from that mistake?'" Hunter thinks he should look it over every time he finishes a problem. Bill agrees, and Iris says, "I think it'd be good if you worked some problems now. Please, please, please don't panic! It's going to take longer because it's new. You're going to be using *so* many brain cells! But don't give up. I want you to do the even problems, page 167." As they start, she assembles the fourth-graders for continued work on fractions, circulating occasionally to coach individual fifth-graders. Soon all are working at their seats on problems from the book, with a short homework assignment as well. Some brighter students in Iris's class are working at their own pace through the book, coming to see her only when they get stuck. After completing their arithmetic, they line up for lunch.

Following lunch, Iris reminds students to get their materials to go to Mrs. Dancey's room for social studies. They do so and begin filing out. Mrs. Dancey's class enters, find their seats, and get settled for science. Before they enter Iris slips on her lab coat covered with NASA patches. She begins, "Okay, in today's lesson there are some safety things. You're going to have to listen carefully and follow all of my directions or it'll be too dangerous and we'll have to stop. I'm not going to let any of you get injured merely because you're doing something dangerous. We're going to be starting our section on flight, and we'll be making paper airplanes, but what we'll do today will be a little different. I need someone who's a *great* paper airplane maker to help!" Chris volunteers, and he comes to the front with her. She stands in front of Chris, who is to give her directions to make a paper airplane, but he cannot see what she's doing. Chris tells her his directions. Chris wishes he could see what she's doing as he hears classmates' giggles. Iris follows the directions in an exaggerated fashion. Students giggle as she finishes with a large triangle with small flaps. Upon seeing it, Chris exclaims, "Oh no! That's not what I meant!" Iris smiles and says "Yes. Giving accurate directions isn't easy! Now some of you might have already formed a hypothesis about how well this will fly." Scoffing giggles are their soft reply. Iris continues, "Now, we need to set some criteria so we can decide if this flies." Shane suggests, "If it goes out a foot and then goes toward the floor, it's *not* a flight." Iris aims the unlikely triangle for a test flight. Students are surprised as it sails three feet and then does a nose dive. "It flies, it flies!" they softly say. Iris continues, "One of the most important parts of any experiment is the testing phase." Julia seems intrigued with the ungainly triangle and suggests holding it differently. Iris continues, "We can only make one change at a time. What if we changed four or five things? It wouldn't really be a test because no one could tell what was the important thing influencing the test. Julia has suggested one change, and I've heard three or four of you mumbling other changes." Iris says she'll change her throw and uses a smoother, longer motion to launch the triangle. A somewhat longer flight occurs. Chris suggests bending out the flaps—wings—a little more.

Iris distributes photocopied sheets with diagonal solid and dotted lines and the NASA logo printed between some lines and says, "I'd like you to make these planes now so you can test your own. You can see there are just lines on it. If you don't want to fold it on the lines you don't have to. Fold it as you'd like. Then put it on your desk so you can hear directions. But no testing until it's time. That's the promise I want. We *cannot* test 28 planes at once. Why?" Julia says, "They'd get mixed up." Iris asks why they'll be throwing them. Nathan says, "So they can glide, so we can try—test—them." Iris reminds, "When it's time for testing we'll test about five at a time. Any questions?" Moses believes they should test three. Iris reminds them, "You need to fold them, any way you want, NO cutting on this one. If you're ready, just put it down on your desk until everyone's ready." Angelo has been talking quietly all class period to no one in particular, and he now sends his plane on a small jaunt. Iris firmly says, "Angelo, outside to the bench." He leaves, sitting just outside the door.

Iris divides the group roughly in half and directs them to line up along the two long walls of the room facing each other. "Whenever you're ready," she says, calling upon the first five in each line to "Try not to aim up. Observe carefully. Here are some things to think about: how high it flies, how it lands, how far. If someone's plane lands near you, return it carefully." By fives, they test fly their planes, stopping once when a few renegade flights are launched. "We're *not* going to test any more until you follow the directions!" The last two people on each side test quickly their planes. Then everyone returns to their seats and Iris reminds them, "You may make one change—*one* change." Julia folds her wings a bit differently. Chris changes the nose shape, and all make adjustments. Then they retest the airplanes, observing and sometimes quietly cheering an especially long or high flight. Much quiet discussion and friendly boasting ensues—"Jack's went *all* the way up there!" "Did you see Bob's nosedive?"—as they return to their seats. Iris says she's not sending the airplanes back to Mrs. Dancey's room, so they need to write their names on them in a place that's easy to see and come back at day's end for them. They're to take them home to practice the same way; indoors, one change at a time. "What happens if you change the shape of the wings? What if you cut a part out? If you put a weight on it? The *world* record for a paper airplane flight is seven seconds. How close can you get?" She mentions books available about paper airplane folding and the paper airplane contests. Then she passes out a photocopied paper helicopter model containing directions to cut and fold it. Students return to their own classrooms. Later, Iris repeats this lesson with her own students, although no Angelo has to leave the room, criteria for flight are more clearly established, and the airplane Iris makes following a student's directions has somewhat larger wings.

At another time she's just returned from her Cleveland session with a new patch sewn on her lab coat about tomato seeds in space. She shares this with Mrs. Dancey's students: "Yesterday I was supposed to get the tomato seeds [recently retrieved from the LDEF in space], but they're still in California. They'll be mailed to us around March 13." Julia wonders whether they'll have them before spring break, and Iris says she believes so. Julia further wonders "whether it's too early to have a hypothesis about how they're going to grow." Iris says it isn't and directs Julia to write it down so she (Iris) can keep it in a safe place. However, Julia wants to share her thinking. She wonders what will happen to its roots since it's been in zero gravity. She speculates, "I'm wondering about the seed's natural fertilizer—the *nutrient*—in the seeds. If it's spent five years in zero G, I wonder where that nutrient went. Maybe it got all jumbled around and so only a certain part of it will grow well." Iris remarks, "That's interesting thinking Julia. Here's a notecard. Write it down and I'll put it in my grade book. That's one place where it definitely won't get lost!" Julia does, as Iris continues, "I told you something that isn't totally true. Remember the container the tomato seeds were in—we've been referring to it as the 'L-D-E-F.' Well, the NASA people say it 'L-Def' like 'L Deaf.' That's easier to say, isn't it? And here's a picture of the container when it was in space. The spaceship *Columbia* put it out there."

Following this, Mrs. Dancey's group continues working in small groups to write songs using space terminology. She tells the class that some people in Cleveland who work with NASA want to see their work.

Mrs. Dancey's class tries to use space terminology for words to go along with the music to Billy Joel's song, "We Didn't Start the Fire" while Iris's class writes rap songs using space terms. Iris's class completes the task first, probably because problems arose from the intricate rhythm and rhyme schemes in the Billy Joel song. Iris also had difficulty obtaining a tape of an instrumental-only version of Joel's song so they could sing their own words. They hope to turn the work into a videotaped production, and the process of writing the songs consumes several weeks, even though a few indoor recesses are also spent on it. During the time they discuss possibilities for verses, the groups refer to many space terms and the moon's geography and review the history of space flight.

On another day they closely examine plastic-encased moon rocks, compare them to similar rocks found on Earth, and read about rocks in reference books. Iris's class goes to help Karen Smith's second- and third-graders on another day, as described earlier. When school is over, children line up and leave in little clusters, talking about moon rocks and books, words and numbers.

Students perceive themselves to be learning several things in Iris's classroom. Walter begins by saying, "Well, I've been seeing that I can learn in different ways, not just by reading books and listening to the teacher. When I made that game I really studied the intricacies of the plot, and writing the song in science I had to listen to other people and cooperate, then use ideas and words about space. We also get to communicate with people at NASA. That's amazing that they're interested in what little kids learn. It also makes school more exciting when you have different things to do—a variety. I'm also learning a lot about how to follow directions and why that's important, to think for myself, to be independent and organized." At this point Walter interrupts himself and says, "Oh, that's not what you meant. . . . You mean spelling, reading, science, and health. Well, of course, we're learning *those* things, but we're also learning these sort of hidden things too because of Mrs. Robole. You know, when she comes back from Cleveland with new patches for her lab coat and posters and ideas, she's so excited that I can't help but get excited about science too!" Walter clearly sees the implicit curriculum at work in his class. Rather than a budding curriculum theorist, though, Walter wants to be an accountant.

Stephanie, on the other hand, speaks mostly about the overt curriculum when she says, "Mrs. Robole is absolutely great—awesome—in science about space, plant life, how the digestive system works, nutrition, and that stuff. She's the best I've ever had in science, and that's important because I want to be a veterinarian or maybe a lawyer. And in reading she explains the vocabulary to children, and we get to read lots of big, long thick books that looked so gigantic when you were little!" She also values Iris's sense of humor: "Maybe her humor makes teaching easier. Easier for students and for her. Students never think of her as a grouch. She doesn't get mad at you, but *you* know when you messed up." Iris also helps build Stephanie's self-esteem: "She's always giving me compliments about what I have on (like this teddy bear sweater my aunt knitted) and my work. But they're real compliments, not just phony words. You can tell the difference. And it's not just because I'm black. She does that for everyone. She's a teacher who thinks her students can succeed in life and always makes sure her students can do things needed in the next grade, like reading and math." Stephanie further claims that Iris has helped her become "tidier and more orderly in my work and thinking."

All students interviewed referred to science and reading learnings. Most also mentioned organizational skills and attributed their motivation to her.

The following year, an article appeared in the local newspaper spotlighting one of Iris's students, now in middle school, who won a national poster contest sponsored by Scholastic, Inc., and Aseptic Packaging Council. The prize went to Iris, who had submitted the poster, and her class. Many of Iris's previous students also won awards at the middle school science fair; indeed, almost all the awards were won by Iris's former students. With the award money, her class accompanied the poster's designer to the Columbus Zoo to see rain forest animals, and they are planning to buy some rain forest acreage in order to preserve it.

Iris's Practical Theory of Action and Her Solo Deliberations

Several beliefs are inherent in Iris's practical theory of action. One concerns developing a love of learning: "If they enjoy it, they'll continue to want to learn. They'll always do better in something they enjoy doing. They'll wind up with a positive outlook on learning rather than a negative one. Of course, they also have to understand that not everything in life revolves around things they enjoy, but I try to deal mostly with things they *do* enjoy." This theme is apparent in students' individual and group projects in reading and science, and it has not escaped the attention of Walter, Stephanie, and other students. Iris's students consistently score above the national average on the nationally normed test she is required to give in various subjects.

Related to this, Iris believes in in-depth projects because "if students are exposed to something of value long enough they can absorb it. If they hear, see, or read something interesting, they want more, and they're bound to learn it. That also eliminates most discipline problems."

Iris uses the metaphor of "teachers as entertainers." She says, "When the audience is appreciative I can do a better job. Now I hope you realize I don't mean the content is just fluffy entertainment. It has to be important content. It can be dealt with in entertaining ways, yet students can still learn."

Iris begins her planning by "knowing the students—what each finds interesting, difficult, and easy." She remarks, "I don't just cover stuff to get through it. I don't think in all my 18 years I've ever completed *all* the textbooks, but I don't think they'll even remember some of that unless it's interesting to them or they can use it a lot. So it's no big deal to get diverted by a current event that comes up or some particular issue or by an interest or difficulty students have. One positive thing about having the kids all day long is that I can decide on the spot to devote 45 minutes or so to an issue or interest that comes up. I can't ever tell beforehand what's going to come up or what will attract them intensely, so I have to juggle what we're going to do constantly. Maybe that's why I'm not a very good long-range planner other than knowing in general the next novel they'll read or unit they'll study in science or health." Iris is not unlike other teachers in this respect, as discussed in chapter 2.

As she learns about her students she plans many courses of action anew: "Each year's different for a particular group. Also, I don't like to continue to do things the same way. It becomes old hat too fast that way, and if *I'm* bored the kids will be." Iris's intellectual restlessness, worries about boredom, and desire for new knowledge explain why she has continued to take so many courses and workshops. The learning also affects her teaching. An obvious example is in her science lessons. Another is in the warm-up activities preceding mathematics lessons when she applies her learning about brain functions.

Her planning is complicated by the fact that while Iris plans she also has to attend to the graded course of study: "Deep down I plan for *kids*, but here's the curriculum—the graded course of study whose objectives I have to meet. I look at it once in a while to check on myself. Fortunately, most of it's pretty sensible, and I'd be covering those things even if they weren't there." She typically starts teaching with a very general plan in mind. She does not specify it beforehand; instead, she fills it in while teaching because she "wants to know *their* interests" and take them into account as she elaborates on the plan. She can be thought of, then, as a teacher who improvises.

Iris solicits assistance from students about some matters as she deliberates while teaching. For example, she asks about worthwhile projects in connection with the next novel and how to solve the problems of too few copies of the novel.

In terms of the implicit curriculum, Iris says she wants her students to learn independence, responsibility, cooperation, and a love of learning. Her overt goals focus mostly upon science and language arts.

In the following section, I describe Mapleton and Willoughby Elementary School. Then I present Mark Schaefer's teaching, practical theory of action, and deliberations about teaching third grade there.

Mapleton

Mapleton, a sprawling area accessible to an adjacent city on any of three different freeways, is made up of a series of small communities. The school system encompasses 127 square miles and serves nine villages or cities. The area is both urban and suburban in character. Mapleton residents are primarily blue-collar workers in the nearby city and its suburbs. Many families hold three jobs; each parent works as a custodian, maintenance worker, or clerk, and sometimes works two shifts. For instance, a child was recently overheard bragging, "My mom just got a new job at Burger King!" Fewer are secretaries, teachers, managers, or health care technicians. The economic recession has done away with most factory jobs in this region. Many families receive public assistance. State department of education data analyzed on a countywide basis reveals that Mapleton ranks next to the bottom, statewide, in both average income and proficiency test scores. Of almost 16,000 students enrolled throughout Mapleton in 1991, 13 were Native American, 127 were Asian American, 913 were African American, 59 were Hispanic American, and the remainder were Caucasian.

WILLOUGHBY ELEMENTARY SCHOOL

One small community in Mapleton is Willoughby, where modest one- and two-story homes sit on flat land amid large oaks, maples, and smaller shrubs. On most blocks are small brick apartment complexes where one-third of Willoughby's students live. Sparsely scattered among the residences are former corn fields that are being developed into still more blocks of houses. On one thoroughfare near the school is a strip mall. The supermarket and drug store are closed, their windows covered with plywood, but a bingo parlor, bar, and small used-clothing store remain in operation. Nearby a new discount store has attracted the business once done in the strip mall. Small churches of many denominations are in abundance in this part of Mapleton. Near Willoughby Elementary School is Cityheights, one of the most stable African-American communities in the county. Many Cityheights parents and grandparents who went to school at Willoughby now send their children there. A Cityheights resident explains, "We have a strong community. I feel I *belong* here. I grew up here, and I know everyone. We help each other in bad times, and in good times we laugh together." The other chief minority group attending the school consists of children from the Appalachian Mountains region of West Virginia, Kentucky, Tennessee, and southern Ohio. Also, a few Asian-American children attend Willoughby Elementary School.

The two-story brick building was erected in 1954. Its floor plan is a wide U. The first floor houses the office, library, gymnasium, cafeteria, music room, and lower-grade classrooms; the upper grades are upstairs. Colorful seasonal artwork decorates the hallways alongside some class projects about nutrition, local buildings, plants, and animals. Adjacent to the offices hang several awards. Most doors are closed. People pass one another quietly, talking in hushed tones or walking purposively.

Craig Bartlett, the principal, paints what he calls a "challenging" picture of the situation in his school. The students come from poorer families, and 48 percent are enrolled in public-assisted breakfast and lunch programs. Fifty percent of the families rented apartments at $350 a month in 1990, and many live in subsidized housing at $18 a month. A house costs $89,000. The community has a high mobility rate, and only 50 percent of current fifth-graders began school here; many leave and return several times. Mr. Bartlett says that evictions, families who move in with each other, and unstable homes account for much of this. Ten percent of students are raised by grandparents. Mr. Bartlett deals with 10 to 15 child-abuse cases in the school annually. Seventy percent of Willoughby's former students graduate from high school, and 15 percent go on for further education, although typically their parents have only completed eleventh grade, and fewer than 1 percent have completed college.

Although education may not seem to be Willoughby's highest priority, the high school around the corner from the elementary school unites the Willoughby community through its sports programs. Attendance at football games is particularly high. Parents also support the elementary school.

In a nearby coffee shop, local residents say they like to live here because housing is affordable and close to their employment and the community is safer than other nearby affordable areas. One local housewife who has four children at Willoughby believes the schools are better here than in the nearby city: "You know the high school dropout rate there is 50 percent. When we moved here from [there] Lenore was behind in reading and language, but she don't have a problem now. That show the schools are better here [sic]." The parent-teacher association has many members and holds a sale each year that raises $12,000 to $15,000 for the purchase of supplies and library books. Six parents volunteer on a regular basis, and parents recently supplied sufficient grocery store receipts to qualify the school for six computers in a promotion by a local store. The community does not frequently vote for raising property taxes that fund the school. As one old-time resident contends, "Once raised, taxes are never lowered. I can barely afford them now."

However, Mr. Bartlett is optimistic about the future. A new housing development is being built just south of the school where homes cost $80,000 in 1990. He hopes this will bring a more stable population than is currently attending the school. Unfortunately (for Mr. Bartlett and *this* school), as it turned out, these children rode buses to another school in 1991.

MARK SCHAEFER TEACHES THIRD GRADE

Mark and His Background

Mark is in his early forties and has straight graying blonde hair and a bristly mustache. He wears glasses and is of average height and weight. His typical daily uniform consists of slacks, a shirt and tie, and a pullover sweater. He always dresses the same to impart to students a sense of stability, he says.

Mark grew up in what he characterizes as a working-class neighborhood in Cleveland. He began college with the goal of becoming a dentist following his father's wishes. His own interests, however, lay in philosophy and social sciences, so he transferred to political science. Later he dropped out of school for a while to work in a small, family-owned manufacturing business and then to help manage low-income rental units with his brother. After he got married, he returned to college and changed his major to elementary education because he was attracted to teaching. After graduation, he claimed he'd stay in teaching "just until I get tired of it." He's so intrigued with his students' learning and his own thought processes, though, that I suspect it could be a long time before Mark tires of it.

Mark substitute taught in several school systems before taking a position in Willoughby, where he took over a fifth-grade class from a teacher who retired midyear. This is his eighth year of teaching at Willoughby. He has taught every grade level here except kindergarten and first grade, including both combined and single-grade-level classes. This is his first year teaching third grade. He enjoys teaching at Willoughby because he believes his background suits him well to do the job. He believes he can make a difference because "*anyone* can teach rich kids, but you really have to work and have something in your heart (or gut, or wherever) to teach here!" He has never missed a day of school due to illness. He says he thinks of himself as a Klingon (on "Star Trek"), a battler who has a positive outlook about winning each and every battle. Like the Klingons, he tries to be objective and is aggressive about dealing with problems.

It should be noted, though, that in the year following this study Mark had eye surgery for a detached retina. One day he returned to retrieve some materials so he could plan for his return. He tried to arrive when the students would be out of the room, but due to delays they were still there. Students crowded around him, hugging him and asking how he was. "You look cute in your play clothes," said one. Even though Mark tried to keep a distance from his students, it was clear they were fond of him.

However, Mark seems almost proud of his reputation as "Mean Mr. Schaefer." He thinks he earns this reputation due to his high expectations for good behavior in the classroom and when he has lunch or playground duty with second- and third-graders. He's against saying, "Oh, Joey, it's all right [that you can't read and don't know your math facts]. I still like you." He says, "I'd rather see Joey cry a little because he cares that he can't do his work. When Joey learns it, I'm *not*

Mean Mr. Schaefer anymore because Joey knows it and so does Mr. Schaefer. If they pay attention and study they *can* learn it. There's nothing wrong with these kids except that they haven't been taught. In fact, if you look at my test scores and papers you can see that they do learn it. If they think they can do something and then they do, they're on a roll and it spreads to other subjects. If they cry a little, that's good because I know they care enough to be a little frustrated and bothered about not doing well. If I can shore them up long enough so they can do it, they see they can and just take off. That's why I keep assignments pretty short, and I'm willing to test repeatedly—almost whenever a kid tells me he or she's ready to retake something they failed."

Indeed, he claims, "I'm a mean, demanding S.O.B. in a lot of ways, but pretty light in a lot of ways, too. I play classical music on the radio while they're working. But what gets kids really moving comes from within themselves, and there's individual variation about it. I have to touch them personally. Sometimes it takes a little sharpness and sometimes a little kindness. Every barb has to be equaled out with a pat on the back or they lose confidence and drive. It takes both."

He continues, "Achieving parity between the kids at Willoughby and other schools like Potomac and Chester means kids in my room have to work twice as hard to catch up. Otherwise we've denied them everything and they simply can't cut it. How can they compete with those kids to get into college and for good jobs? They can't. I have to convince them that learning's important and they can do it, and that's not easy when they've been doing overly easy and nonacademic work until they walk into my room. That's the beauty of having my former students come down and help these third-graders. They can get a real sense that they *can* learn and that it's important because they see kids they know from their own neighborhoods who know how to read and do math. So they get the idea that education is important, not because they hear a teacher preaching about it, but because they can see it in their friends."

Mark believes mathematics is important because "it's a way to introduce *systematic* learning and thinking. We develop learning and thinking systems in language, if there's an ounce of truth in linguistic theory, and language learning transfers. But the kind of thinking necessary in math is different. It's more systematic and linear, and kids need to learn both kinds [of thinking] to succeed."

In Mark's view, school curricula should focus on the academics. Toward this end, he believes in mastery learning and in keeping his feelings for students out of the picture: "My job's to teach them, not to love them. They have parents for that. They have to know someone cares whether they become *educated*, and I'm that person." However, he is clearly touched when former students come by his room to show him reports they've written and their report cards. Some also return to help him monitor and work with small groups working on reading or math facts.

The Classroom

Just outside the door to one classroom at Willoughby a bulletin board proclaims "Power Math Facts." Listed down its left side are students' names. Across the top are numbers through 12. Check marks appear in many intersecting boxes on the graph. A small cluster of students gathered around talking among themselves: "Yes!" "The sevens are history!" "Awesome!" "Hey! I made my fives!" "I guess I'll have to go for the sixes again. If at first you don't succeed, try, try again is my motto."

Immediately inside the door is a computer on top of a desk. Typically, two students sit here playing a game having to do with arithmetic. One plays the game while the other softly cheers or points out impending perils. A bulletin board behind the computer displays national symbols, and beside the bulletin board is a blackboard topped by the state and national flag. This is the part of the room where Mark does much of his teaching.

On one long wall are windows with bookcases below them containing flashcards and books. Atop the bookcases sit five plastic tubs where students place completed work. The long wall facing the windows contains blackboards and a bulletin board. Above these is the alphabet written in cursive letters. Just below Mark has nailed a thin wood slat with nails protruding at regular intervals. Clipped photocopied papers and a large tablet of chart paper hang neatly from them. A coat closet, more shelves, and a sink occupy the remaining shorter wall.

Scattered across most of the remaining space are 23 students' desks. Some are positioned in short rows or islands, others are separate, and still others are pushed against the teacher's desk. The remaining space contains the teacher's desk, five file cabinets full of photocopied worksheets Mr. Schaefer has constructed, two enclosed cabinets, a stereo system, a low round table surrounded by four chairs, and a small rectangular table with a chair at each end.

This year Mark has four boys in his room—William, Manley, Paul, and David—who are chronic discipline problems. This affects Mark's deliberations and teaching. Of the four, William's problem is most severe. He is supposed to be taking Ritalin, but at times his mother does not give him his medication before school. Mark believes William is potentially the most dangerous of the four because he's so out of control of himself, is tremendously strong for a third-grader, and is very violent at times. Although Mark has only 23 students this year, these four add greatly to his load. In the past he has also had students who were discipline problems in his class, but not this many at once.

Teaching and Learning in Mark's Room

Today, as on most days, children enter, remove their jackets, stow their gear in the coat area, and move to their desks to start their journal entries. Today's topics listed on the blackboard consist of completing two sentences: Something sharp is. . . . Something smooth is. . . . Some entries completing the first sentence are "pointed," "a tack," "a pin"; and the second sentence, "glass," "satin," "a mirror."

This year Mark writes beginnings of sentences or questions to answer because the class had difficulties earlier with more open-ended journal assignments. Later in the year, however, he makes them open-ended again. Some students enter later than others, dribbling in following their dismissal from the breakfast program. William enters, eyes full of tears. A short time later Mr. Bartlett enters and takes William out of the room after conferring briefly and quietly with Mark. Mark reminds students, "Today we have science and spelling tests, so I don't have any math sheets to hand out." It is unclear whether the few groans constitute objections to the presence of the tests or to the lack of math sheets. The loudspeaker pages Lillian to come to the office.

Mark stands near the blackboard in front of the room and leads the class in the Pledge of Allegiance. Then quickly he takes attendance and lunch count, writing the numbers on a small form and sending it to the office. William reenters, tears streaming down his face. He sits down. Mark continues, "Okay, please get out your math books and open them to page 35." Meanwhile, Stephanie starts crying softly, shoulders heaving and sighing. Mark goes over to her and hunkers down by her desk, saying quietly, "No, you're not, Stephanie. Everyone makes little mistakes. *I* make mistakes, *you* make mistakes. Hey! It's okay! Do you want to go to the bathroom and wash your face?" Stephanie's shoulders are no longer heaving, and she exits.

Mark returns to the blackboard, continuing, "This page deals with comparing numbers. We've done this before. When we compare numbers, we wonder if they're bigger or smaller, remember? The words we use to compare numbers are equal, less than, and greater than. We have signs. When we write *these* signs [pointing], they mean *these* words" [pointing again]."

On the board he's written:

= is equal to
< is less than
> is greater than

"In a number sentence when we say [symbol] we use words. We don't say '26 dash dash 26.' What does 'less than' mean?" Mercell softly says, "Smaller." He continues, "When we read *this* number sentence, 73<81, we don't say '73 arrow 81!' We say '73 *is less than* 81.' The arrow always points to which number, the greater or the lesser one? Now I'm going to move over to the other board." Stephanie reenters, and William starts surreptitiously moving his desk closer to Craig, who sits two feet in front of him. Eventually his desk front abuts Craig's chair, and Craig turns around angrily to see what is happening.

Mark continues, glancing nervously at William, "Now look at this board. I'll make up numbers that could be on the test. I'll write 84 and 36. What goes between them? Which way should it point?" Fred is called on and points his thumb toward the back of the room, in the direction of the 36. Mark goes on, "We're going to do two more, then you can do the book page. 47 and 52. I have to compare these. Which way does the arrow go this time?" Soft, angry mutterings emanate from William and Craig, clearly not about the lesson. When Dorothy is called upon, she points toward the front of the room, in the direction of the 47. Now Mark writes 32 and 87. "What's the first thing I do, Don? Craig, what do I do?" Mark writes the answer incorrectly, 32>87. "Is that right, Craig?" Craig says, "No, change the arrow." "Molly, which number goes here?" he asks, pointing to the small side of the arrow. Molly shrugs. "*Which* number?" he persists. Molly softly says, "The smaller number." Somewhat less patiently, Mark responds, "Yes, but what number, Molly?" She responds, "32." "Who can read it now: 87>32?" he asks and calls on Don. Don says, "Eighty-seven is greater than thirty-two." "Yes, I like the way you said that good and strong. Good job!" says Mark. At this point William and Craig hit each other so hard that it resounds across the room. Mark says loudly and firmly, "Okay, I'm going to have to take these two to the office, but I want you to get started." Lowering his voice, he hurriedly says, "Okay, children, I want you to behave yourselves. You know what to do; you know what page we're on. I'll have to be gone a few minutes, but I'll be back as soon as I can." After retrieving pencils and paper from desks, all are quiet as they begin working on page 35. Some complete their work before Mark returns and put it in one of the tubs. Then they continue their journals, get a stack of flash cards, or look at words in the spelling book. Manley sucks his thumb and completes four problems, occasionally getting up and wandering around the room. As Mark returns, he quietly reminds two boys to go see Mrs. Levinger (a special education teacher) for language class.

On another day the class's arithmetic lesson concerns place value, where children learn about expanded notation. At one point, after presenting an illustration of stamps in sheets, strips, and singly, Mark concludes, "And I describe this picture *this* way: 300 + 50 + 7. What do I call this? It's a type of notation." Dorothy responds, "*Expanded* notation!" Mark comments, "Great! That shows Dorothy was really listening yesterday because I bet no one ever heard that before." He goes on to discuss with students that things have places. Books go in desks, coats in closets. "Numbers have places, too," he continues conversationally and develops a chart on the board having three columns. At the top of each column he prints "Hundreds," "Tens," and "Ones," respectively. Students coach him about where to write each digit in 145, 409, 831, 473, and 367. On the assignment list on the board he directs the students to do numbers one through 36 (of 52) in the book. During the lesson he frequently asks particular students—Manley, Mercell, Stephanie, and Molly—whether they understand, and he remarks several times about how important it is to listen and pay close attention. At one point, for example, he asks, "Mercell, do you understand this? What number would you write to get this first answer?" Some quiet chattering can be heard around Mercell's desk, and Mark firmly cautions, "Now, I can hear someone telling her the answer, and you're stopping her from learning. *Don't* tell her the answer. Anyone else not understand?" Stephanie raises her hand. Mark continues, "All right, please look at question seven. I want to do it with you. In the number 473, what number is in the hundreds place? That's what this problem asks you, right, Mercell?" Stephanie firmly answers, "Four." Mark smiles, compliments her on speaking loudly, and says, "Okay, let's look at problem 17. In 367, what number is in the ones place?" Mercell replies, "Seven." Mark continues, "The last one we'll do together is number 27. What do the directions ask you, William?" William confesses he wasn't paying attention. Dorothy answers that they're looking at the tens place and answers the problem. The students begin work at their seats. Mark circulates, examining students' papers, conferring quietly, praising neatness, encouraging closer concentration, and reteaching some children.

This lesson was longer and in greater depth than the one about comparing numbers, and Mark confides he'd had to hurry through the ending of the latter one because he had to remove William promptly. On other days he introduces multiplication, addition, and subtraction with regrouping and word problems in which children have to discriminate among arithmetic operations to find a solution.

Following math they move on to reading. The school system has adopted a new basal reading series published by Heath; their consultant and the teacher's guide advise teachers to use all lessons with the whole class rather than with small groups. Smiling, Mark encourages students, "Read loudly, be proud of your reading!" They take turns reading paragraphs. Mark occasionally interrupts, directing Manley to calm down. As Mercell is reading, she reads that the character "brung" something. Mark exclaims, "What? She *brung* it? *Brung*? Do we say brung?" Mercell smiles shyly and says, "Brought." Mark sits down near the front of the room and listens as Clarissa reads. Students call out corrections, and Mark cautions, "Children! Now I'm tired of hearing that. *I'll* help Clarissa, but I want to hear *her* right now!" The class continues reading the story, taking turns. He does not typically follow the story with discussion questions because, in his view, "these kids don't normally pay attention long enough or well enough in late autumn to have complicated discussions. They're still struggling so hard just reading the words that it takes a lot of concentration for them. Maybe I can do that later in the year."

On another day he conversationally weaves some discussion questions in as students read. Today, he begins by directing them to get out reading books and their markers so they can slide them down the page to keep their place, and to turn to page 142. "This is called 'The Armadillo,'" he says. "I don't think they're found in Ohio except in zoos. Armadillos live in the South, and they mainly come out at night. They can roll up in a ball. They have a shell—not as hard as a turtle— but a shell." Molly starts reading, corrected occasionally by other children. When Molly entered the class this year she could not read and did not know the letters in alphabetical order, according to her summer school teacher. At the end of both first and second grades, teachers had recommended that Molly be retained, but because Molly's mother objected, Molly passed. After she completes a paragraph, Mark praises her and then says, "If you don't know what a weaver is, on the next page is a picture of a loom that a weaver uses. Now they use big machines, but they used to do it as they did in that picture. Cloth is really made out of many separate threads. You know that if you cut off your jeans in the summer you have some threads hanging out. A weaver weaves all those threads into cloth.

So the threads are weaved—" He smiles at his purposive mistake. ". . . *woven*—into a piece of cloth. Okay, Sandra, a loud voice so everyone can hear in the back." Sandra reads loudly, and then Alice reads. Mark stops the reading by saying, "Yeah, Alice. When he *realized* it, that means he knew it." William, Harry, and Clarissa read. He cautions Clarissa to slow down a little and then asks Amber, "What do those three dots mean?" Amber thinks they mean to stop, and Mark says, "They mean he's doing it again and again, row after row of weaving. They don't want to write it a hundred times. They just want to give you the idea that it keeps repeating."

Changing the subject, he asks Ted to count the number of paragraphs on that page. "Remember," he coaches, "when a sentence is indented, it's a new paragraph." At the end of Andy's reading, Mark says, "Okay, what does 'the cold grew more and more bitter' mean? That's funny. I think of *bitter* as a taste. What does this mean, that the cold is bitter?" William says, "You get chill bumps and you get real, real cold." Mark smiles and responds, "Right. I like the way you're paying attention." Mercell has a turn to read and then Stephanie. He praises each one.

Then he passes out a workbook page where students are to read sentences and insert the correct vocabulary words. He begins by having students read the words at the top of the page and briefly define them. For instance, William reads "Armadillo" and says, "It's an animal with a shell." Mark cautions Mercell to pay attention because "Jill [to whom she'd been talking] won't be taking the test for you. *You* need to be a good reader too! If we camouflage something, what do we do, Stephanie?" Stephanie says, "We color it." Mark asks why. William says, "So it blends in." Mark says, "Sure, like some army clothes, right?" The next word is *prey,* and Mark reminds students, "We all know from science that prey are the animals that other animals eat." A student provides an example. Mark continues to the next section of the page, where students are to draw lines between words that mean the same thing. He says, "What's another word for it? Those words are same-onyms—." Then he smiles and continues, "not same-onyms, *syn*onyms. Not cinnamon, *synonym.* Like loud and noisy. Below that, write a sentence for each word. We'll do our language in about ten minutes." Answered by groans, he cheerfully says, "Okay, instead we'll do our practice test in spelling."

On a third day, Mark directs the class to take out their books and announces, "Today we have a short little story to do and then some worksheets. Hey, little girl, everyone else is ready," he says to Lillian. After Tom reads, Dorothy goes; she can read "brontosaurus" but not "towering." As Dorothy reads, she comes across the word *crane.* When she finishes Mark arises from his chair and moves briskly to the chalkboard, where he begins to draw a construction crane and then overlays the bird crane on top of it. The room is as quiet as it has ever been, and children are watching keenly as Mark draws the cranes. William tells me the quiet and attention are because "the children are curious about how well he draws, and he's pretty good at it." Mercell reads and then Mark asks, "Sequel means what? Dorothy?" Dorothy says, "It means it's a story that comes after another story but has the same characters." "Boy! That's good!" exclaims Mark. "Sandra, what are characters?" Sandra mumbles through with a response the first time, and Mark chides her by mimicking her mumbling in an exaggerated manner. Then Sandra says loudly and clearly, "People in a story." "Great!" says Mark, "Okay, let's continue to read the story itself." William and Paul take their turns reading. Mark cautions the students, "Okay, let's look at this story carefully. It's the last one we'll read before the unit test." Kathy reads. He calls on Felicia, saying, "Felicia, loud voice!" She reads. When Fred is called on he doesn't know his place in the story. Molly reads, and afterwards Mark comments, "Oh, that's beautiful! Dorothy, what do you think about that?" Dorothy says it was pretty good. Mark exclaims, "What do you mean, *pretty* good? That was fine! Molly, I'm glad you've joined us. That's the best reading you've done all year! I hope you're proud." Molly beams shyly, and Mark calls upon Elliot, who does not know his place in the story. David makes a loud, rude noise, and much laughing ensues. After calming down, the children find the place again and complete the story. Then they do a vocabulary review worksheet for this story and others in the unit.

While the students are completing their reading worksheets, Mark hangs a chart containing a story in the front of the room. This story was written by his previous year's class. He says, "Okay, let's start wrapping up so we can start on writing our stories." "Gentlemen," he says to Manley and Paul, "I want your attention when we start on writing. Sandra, put your things away so you can give your full attention to your writing."

"All right," he continues. "I need everyone's attention. Pencils down, close your books. Eyes on this story up here." He points to the chart at the front, snaps his fingers several times, and asks again for their attention. "I'll keep the directions short, but this is your first story this year. Let's see. We started journals . . . let's see, the first week of school. But writing a story's different. As I've gotten older I've gotten better at it, and you will too. Do you know why? Because I've kept *trying*. I have two little girls up here still playing with things. Now, pay attention. I'll keep this short so you'll have more time, and I'll try to give you the best directions I can." Clarissa reads the story on the chart aloud, with other students making several corrections as she goes along. Margaret rereads it. "Now," Mark continues, "it gets easier to read a second or third time. What your story is going to need is a title. What's a title, Neil?" Neil replies it's the name of a book. Mark agrees, "Yes, the name of a story or book. See, on the chart paper I centered and underlined the title. Another thing you need is a beginning." He reads aloud the first sentence of the story on the chart. "What does that do?" he asks. William replies it tells you the character, the plot, and the setting, and then corrects himself aloud, saying, "No, not the plot but the character—Tom—that he's a rabbit." Mark reads the next two sentences and says they're the middle of the story—they tell something interesting about the character—that he has long fuzzy ears. "So that's the middle," he says. "If we have a beginning and a middle, what's the other part?" Students agree it must be the end. They silently read the entire story, and Mark asks whether this story has a happy ending. They respond that it does not. "Why?" he asks. "Because he can't hear well" is the response. "Well, okay, but he's alive. Maybe it's a little mixed, like most of our days, right?"

"Okay, stay with me here. I have a couple of things to remind you of and five things to do. If you do them well, you'll get an A. Can you understand my story? Is it neat? Now, you'll see here I changed some things. See? I skipped lines and crossed out mistakes, and then I wrote the new form above it. You'll reread yours and see some changes you want to make. Make them. But then if I turned it in I'd want to recopy it. Now, you have five minutes to think about your story. I advise you to keep your story to one you can write with one, two, or at most three characters because you only have the front and back of one sheet of paper for this one. Get ready by thinking about a beginning, a middle, an end, and a title. Then I'll tell you who your writing partner is. You can tell it to someone else out loud and be a good listener to their story. If you can tell a story to someone, it'll be easier to write it. While you think I'll put a paper on your desk. Just leave it there because I have specific instructions for heading your paper since this is your first writing sample for your folder this year. Hey, if your teachers didn't tell you last year, you already have a writing folder in the office. It'll stay with you until you graduate from twelfth grade. On Thursday, if we don't have an assembly or fire drill or something crazy, you'll have time after reading to go through it again so you can read each other's stories and tell what's unclear or messy. That person can help you be a better writer. You have five minutes now to think. Think of a story—a beginning, a middle, and an end. A title. Just let your imagination flow. Maybe put your head down to think, like Stephanie here is doing. Use your brain cells. Paul, if you can't manage this, I'll remove you from the room and you won't *get* to write a story. Okay, now just think. Use your brain cells." He circulates, distributing paper, and it is quiet as children appear to be thinking of a story. After about five minutes elapse, he says, "A story doesn't just happen. It's not your pencil that writes the story. It's not the paper. It's your brain, just like your math facts—your pencil doesn't do those, does it? Is there anyone who's not ready to start sharing your story with a partner now?" Two hands go up, but he continues, "All right, we'll start sharing stories now."

He quickly assigns partners and children move near one another. They talk quietly about horses, cats, princesses, and other characters. Some ask questions about the partner's story, and occasionally advice is given. Mark announces, "Okay, one more minute." He passes out additional paper and reminds students not to write on it yet. Next he has students return to their desks then calls for their attention. "Take a look up here. I need to show you how to head your paper. On the right-hand corner put your first and last names, not in jumbo letters, but neatly. Go ahead—NEATLY—up on the top right-hand corner. Remember, you'll be rewriting it on Thursday. Did I mention that?" Students say, "Yes." He continues, "Find the highest blue line. You're going to write on it Writing Sample #1 and the date like this . . ." He writes 12/11/90 on the board. He continues, "Look at what I write, and then you do it. I'll write it down here in bigger letters so you can see it and write it neatly. But don't you dare put it in the middle of your page!" Glancing at some papers, he says, "That's looking good. I like to see it. Yeah! Sometimes it's hard to listen to directions, but this is good. You'll have time to recopy it really well, but try to make it neat today. *Top* line, Paul. The top line is the line at the top—the very first one. Listen carefully. I'll tell you how to do your title. Be neat. It's just like in math. When you're neat you do your best work. Now, I want you to go down some blue lines. We want to skip two spaces. Where are we?" They say, "Third line." "Yes," Mark continues, "write your title, right. Now here you skip another line and start your story. You need to start over a little—we call that indenting. I'll pull a couple of people away to go read with Mrs. Samuels [the aide] for a while. You'll be able to work while some other people work with her." As students start writing, he circulates to help students spell words and with other problems. They continue this or meet with Mrs. Samuels until lunch, when Mark collects the stories and they leave the room.

Perhaps because this is the first time Mark has taught writing in this way, he wrote a detailed plan for the lesson, rereading it twice before school started. In his view, writing it permitted him to "examine it and think through all the steps before getting into the actual teaching." This is what he wrote:

I. Introduction
   • Show old big tablet story
   • Read story and tell how I planned and wrote the story
   • Story should
   1. Have title
   2. Have beginning
   3. Have middle
   4. Have ending
   5. Tell the reader something
   6. Be written so that the reader can understand your story as well as you do.

II. Give Assignment
   1. Take five minutes to think up a good story in your head. Go over your story silently in your mind to make sure it's one you can write down on one page of paper. Think of a title, a beginning, a middle, and an ending. Get all ready to tell someone your story quietly and listen to their story.
   2. Take five minutes to exchange stories quietly. Be quiet, storytellers and attentive listeners. (While you are sharing your stories, I'm going to pass out writing paper, but don't start writing yet. Don't even put your name on. WAIT for my directions.)
   3. Listen closely and head your paper exactly as I say.
      (a) First and last names in top right-hand corner.
      (b) On top line put: "Writing Sample #1 (12/11/90)
      (c) Now skip down three lines. Right on the third line write the title of your story.
      (d) Now underline your story title. Draw a line underneath the whole title.

4. Now write your story on paper so other people can read and understand it. Write neatly. Say everything you need to say so that people that read your story will enjoy reading it. I'll collect the stories before lunch. Until then, keep rereading your story and making it better.
5. On Thursday I'll pass out the stories so that you will all get someone else's story. You'll read each other's stories (some out loud) and talk about how to revise and rewrite stories with the help of a writing partner. Your writing partner will show you what's wrong or hard to understand about your story.
6. The last step will be to copy your corrected story neatly onto a clean sheet of theme paper and hand it in.

Mark divides the afternoon among social studies, science and health, and more mathematics. In social studies they continue their work with maps, where they are memorizing locations and names of the U.S. states. Students are armed with outline maps, crayons, and pencils; they watch Mark as he points to Texas, California, and the states surrounding Ohio and put their fingers on states on their maps. His goal for the next two weeks is for students to learn the names and locations of 12 states and by year's end to learn all 50. By now they have studied the world's oceans and continents as well as the major cities, rivers, and highways of Ohio. For 20 minutes children color and label ten states. Occasionally, they cluster in knots of ten and pore over the large pull-down map at the front of the room. Ted collects the papers.

Following this, children take turns reading a brief section about living things from their science book. On other days, they complete worksheets about the material they already read, take tests, plant seeds, and observe their growth.

After afternoon recess, students spend half an hour completing morning or afternoon work and placing it in the appropriate tub. Mark sees some students about making up tests on which they did poorly, and other students read silently or study math-fact flash cards. Margaret reads *The Borrowers* quietly to Kathy. Manley sucks his thumb and looks at the map. Molly turns over flash cards, quietly saying answers to herself.

With the day almost over, Mark says, "All right children, it's time for the fact tests." Desks get cleared very quickly; pencils are out. Five children enter from other classrooms to participate. With little fuss, Mark passes out different papers, each containing 100 math facts to different students, depending on which facts they have mastered. On the back of the sheets they write their names. On his signal they turn them over and begin writing furiously. After four minutes, he announces, "All right, four minutes." Some have finished and put their papers to the side and pencils down. These children are primarily from fourth grade and must pass with no more than three errors in four minutes. Third-graders have an extra minute, and while they work he quietly collects completed papers. As students finish, he writes their time on the backs of papers and collects them. At the end of the allotted time, he collects all papers. Now it is time to get ready to leave. The five visiting students return to their classrooms. Neil cleans the boards. Clarissa and Amber voluntarily straighten the flash cards while Mercell reshelves some paperback books. Then all get their jackets; a few retrieve papers from desks. Eight leave almost immediately, but most await a second set of buses that arrive in 20 minutes. While waiting, they study math facts, do homework, read silently, or chat amiably. On the way out David and Manley talk.

Of Mr. Schaefer, Neil says, "He's helping me get my math. And I'm prouder of my reading. He'll let me do things over until I get them right. It took me five times to pass my threes [in multiplication facts], but now I really know them. And I know how to study them. It's more work, but I can almost read now, too. We don't get to color and stuff, though. But we do in art. He's right about that. And I can color at home, but I can't learn how to read and do math there."

Mark's Theory and Deliberations

Clearly a part of Mark's theory is that the curriculum should focus on academics. By this he means primarily skills and content knowledge in mathematics and language arts. To a lesser extent, he focuses on factual knowledge in science, social studies, and health.

He wants to have proof of students' learning for their own use and for his information. For Mark, test scores comprise such proof, so he gives frequent tests from accompanying textbooks and that he devises. He looks forward each spring to administering the nationally normed tests required by his school system, and his students typically outscore other third-grade students in the system, although they do not significantly outscore students on a national basis. He will often give tests from textbooks and his own tests to individuals several times if necessary so they can prove their mastery to themselves and to him. When students can prove they know something, Mark believes it adds to their self-confidence, and that spreads to other subjects as well.

Related to this, Mark keeps assignments short "so their attention won't wander and so when first they see it, it'll look like something that's possible to do." He sets up few routines because "too many routines make school boring so kids lose interest in what they're doing." His routines consist of journal entries, arithmetic fact tests, and whole-class reading.

This year Mark's deliberations are complicated by several students in his class. Molly and Mercell work far below grade level, so he calls upon them frequently to ascertain if they understand what's going on, and he provides extra work for them. William's violent outbursts are dangerous and mean that "I decided to put myself between him and the rest of the class so he can't hurt them." Sometimes Mark has to carry him from the room while William kicks at him and hurls racial epithets his way. The discipline problems shown by Paul, Manley, and David are far less severe, and these boys control themselves on many occasions and, based on test scores, are learning a great deal. The remaining students are not as problematic regarding learning and discipline. Mark feels responsible for their academic learning and does not want to shortchange them merely because these other students are in the class.

Like many other teachers, Mark begins teaching most days with "a general game plan in mind. I fill in the details as I go along. I never know exactly which words I'll have to help them define [in reading] or how many [arithmetic] problems we'll have to do on the board before I think they really understand well enough to go ahead on their own."

SUMMARY AND DISCUSSION

For the most part, these three teachers are not unlike others who begin their planning with general ideas about how to proceed and then extend their sketchy preactive plans while actually teaching. Interactive planning appears to be a more significant aspect of these teachers' deliberations than their pre-active planning is. The reason for this is that they cannot always predict when reteaching or elaboration will be needed, when something will spark their own or their students' interests, or when other unforeseen opportunities and events will occur.

Fundamental to these teachers' preactive and interactive deliberations are their idiosyncratic theories of action, for they form the bases for and fuel the deliberations.

These teachers exhibit two chief commonplaces in their deliberations: one is their particular students, and the other is subject matter. However, they consider students more than subject matter and know volumes about their students. They appear to consider the milieu commonplace when thinking about students by considering community values and expectations.

Iris and Mark consult their school's curriculum policy—the graded course of study—occasionally while planning and augment or otherwise alter it if they believe it is necessary. They consult it to check up on themselves and to make sure the plans in their own curriculum align with systemwide expectations. Karen more often starts with children's books. None of the three begins planning with behavioral objectives or the graded course of study.

As this chapter demonstrates, teachers develop personal practical theories of action consisting of idiosyncratic sets of beliefs and images about what should be taught, how students learn, how to orchestrate lessons, and what materials to provide. These theories of action underlie teachers' curriculum planning and instruction in *their* classrooms. As a result, they also guide the overt and implicit curricula in each classroom. These curricula vary because teachers' theories of action are idiosyncratic.

The chapter further demonstrates that solo deliberation consists of a complex mental process by which teachers generate alternative solutions to perceived curriculum problems and then resolve them on the basis of their theory of action. For these teachers, more solo deliberation occurs interactively (while teaching) than preactively (before teaching). This occurs for different reasons. Iris waits so she can ascertain her students' interests, and on occasion includes them in her deliberations. Karen and Mark wait so they can see how the lesson unfolds and progresses. Additionally, Mark's class contains several disruptive students, and he cannot know beforehand when he will have to intercede. These teachers do not know in advance of teaching it how long each lesson will be since they do not always know how much elaboration or practice will be needed or how many interruptions will occur. These teachers begin lessons with a general plan in mind but no specific details.

Further, these three teachers have a high sense of their moral responsibility to do an excellent job. They value doing an excellent job over following the school's curriculum policy. However, what constitutes "doing an excellent job" is relative to each teacher's personal theory of action.

Finally, curriculum scholars and practioners might be better advised to use the term *solo deliberation* rather than the term *curriculum implementation* because the former process implies more mental activity than the latter. Teachers develop and redevelop the curriculum to such an extent that "curriculum implementation" does not sufficiently convey what occurs. Indeed, solo deliberation may be the most professional activity of teaching.

STUDY QUESTIONS

1. Give a specific example of how each of these teachers improvises. In what way can this be considered planning? Why does improvisation make sense?
2. Mark believes it is more difficult to teach where he does than where Iris and Karen teach. Debate that point.
3. Some might argue that one way to account for differences among these teachers is gender. I can find no evidence to support this interpretation. However, I can trace reasons for differences to social class between these two sites. Discuss this.
4. Develop a plan to teach a preservice teacher about improvisation.
5. A common administrative policy is that when observations are to be made of teachers, they are to have their lesson plans available to the observer. Comment on that policy in light of this chapter. What are some alternatives for teachers to demonstrate that they plan for their teaching?

NOTES

1. These cases and those in subsequent chapters were done in Ohio. It is important to understand the policy context because it affects both solo and group deliberations. Under Ohio law, school systems are to develop graded courses of study for each discipline and course and to redevelop them every five years. Once approved, the courses of study become the curriculum policy for each school system and mandate what teachers are to teach. Teachers may exceed but not ignore the goals stated in the graded courses of study. In states where other policies exist, the details of how teachers engage in solo and group deliberation may differ. However, the overall process of

deliberation seems transferable because studies of teacher thinking and planning and group deliberations done in many different locations show similarities. (See chapter 5 for more about this.)

2. I would like to acknowledge and thank the Department of Educational Policy and Leadership and the College of Education of The Ohio State University for granting me a three-month research leave to complete this part of my research.

chapter 4

Solo Deliberation in High Schools:

Three Cases

Like chapter 3, this one contains three case studies of teachers' deliberations and teaching and has an identical focus: the theory presented in chapters 1 and 2 as practiced in schools. However, in this chapter the case studies occur in high schools. I begin each case by putting it in the context of the school and its community, of the teacher and classroom, of the teacher's practical theory of action, of solo deliberations, and of the curriculum enacted in the school. Following the presentation of these cases, I discuss and summarize them.[1]

I developed these case studies by focusing on questions arising from the theory I presented in chapters 1 and 2. I did research daily in Maple City and Chester during a ten-week research leave[2] in the winter of 1993. I discuss my research questions and methodology in my research appendix.

Maple City

Maple City is the largest community in the Mapleton School District and is five miles across the district from Willoughby Elementary School described in chapter 3. Maple City was established in 1852. The growth of a nearby city has engulfed this once-rural area and begun to erode its unique qualities. According to residents: "Gone are the rustling corn fields and cows. Here are the housing developers. But it's a good place to live. I like it here. Little hustle and bustle, yet near the city. I can get anywhere downtown [in the bigger city] in just five minutes." According to the 1990 Census, 19,661 residents live in Maple City, with a projected annual growth rate of 30 percent. There is a junction nearby of several interstate highways, which makes the area attractive for the warehouses and distribution centers that are located here and that employ almost 1,000 people.

Motels, restaurants, and other travel-related businesses at interstate exits account for some other sources of employment, as do a nearby racetrack and shopping centers. The largest employer, though, is the Mapleton school system itself.

In 1991, the selling price of new, single-family houses in Maple City ranged from $75,000 to $375,000. Sixty-six percent of families own their homes or are in the process of buying them, 33 percent rent apartments or houses, and 1 percent live in mobile homes or trailers. The 1993 Maple City self-study report written for accreditation purposes typifies the bulk of the community as "squarely middle class." The chamber of commerce claims, "Probably the most important thing about Maple City is that it is a great place to live, to work and to do business." Citizens have tried to preserve its unique flavor despite its rapid growth, and the chamber points out that Maple City residents "are good neighbors. . . . It is a good place to be, and it's on the move." In giving the city's history, the Chamber reveals something of Americana: "Fire protection came to Maple City in the 1930s and the first high school football team began to play in 1930." They also extol the fact that the high school band was the first in a [then] rural school district in the state. The present Maple City High School was opened in 1970, replacing two former locations downtown.

MAPLE CITY HIGH SCHOOL

According to the high school's self-study report, in the 1992–1993 academic year the student population is 1,701 with a teacher-student ratio of 1:18. Of these students, 1,629 are white, 51 are black, 2 Hispanic American, 18 Asian American, and 1 Native American. In the school, 5.1 percent receive free or reduced-price lunch. Forty-four percent of graduates typically matriculate in some type of post–high school educational institution. Achievement figures are frequently a bit above national and state averages. Parents support booster clubs for music, athletics, and academics.

Maple City High School has a broad-based, comprehensive curriculum that aims to provide options for students that reflect the mission statement given in their self-study report: "To provide educational opportunities for all students which will enable them to be productive, responsible citizens after graduation whether they choose to continue their formal education, enter the job market, select a military career or establish a family." The curriculum consists of approximately 155 regular education courses and over 50 equivalent courses for students with physical handicaps, learning disabilities, and severe behavioral handicaps. Students may also participate in vocational programs at the Taft Technical School, where 34 vocational programs and related courses are available. Some Maple City teachers also teach their specialties at Taft. To graduate from the Mapleton high schools, students are required to have 19 units of credit, including three of English, two of social studies (U.S. history and U.S. government), one of science, two of mathematics, one combined unit of physical education and health, and one half-unit or demonstrated proficiency in consumer economics.

Maple City High School is a rambling, brown brick building on flat land in a suburban housing development near downtown. A large, airy multilevel commons area welcomes visitors. A display case contains athletic trophies, Tiger megaphones, and a large statue of a tiger (for the Maple City Tigers). Above it are team and individual photographs for basketball, football, and baseball. A poster welcomes students to 1993, and another invites seniors to a dance. At any time, about 425 students are in the commons, chatting, working on papers, reading, and eating at large round tables. Others are in classes or in the media center. Halls leading to academic wings of the building are brightly lit and clean, and people walk through them amiably. Here and there, brightly painted wall sections cheer for the school team. People here seem friendly and always ready to help a stranger find her way to geometry class or other places in the building and the community.

HASCAL LEGUPSKI TEACHES GEOMETRY

One corner of Maple City High School houses the mathematics department. Adjacent to the media center is a central study area surrounded by classrooms and restrooms. Down a short hall is Hascal Legupski's classroom, which is basically a large rectangle with chalkboards on the sides, 31 student desks, a teacher's desk, and three small bookcases. A flag hangs in the front left-hand corner above the teacher's desk.

Hascal and His Background

Mr. Legupski is in his mid-forties, six feet one inches tall, with a short brown beard and blue eyes. In addition to two periods of geometry, he teaches two general math classes, supervises a study hall, and teaches math at Taft Technical School. He reminds me some of Larry Bird, and today he has on a turquoise plaid shirt and navy slacks.

Hascal attended a small religious liberal arts college in a nearby state where he majored in physics. In retrospect, he sees that as a confusing time for him. He'd been the first in his family to attend college, and no one at home had discussed possible majors or careers with him. Lacking a sense of direction, he chose physics because an acquaintance was majoring in it. He taught with temporary certification for two years and then received his provisional certification. He was given a contract to teach physics and mathematics in southern Ohio and started teaching the year immediately following his May graduation. Then he moved to a more remote county school before starting to teach in Hough, near Maple City. After that, he stopped teaching for seven years while he studied at several colleges, universities, and a seminary. His contract had not been renewed early in his career in southern Ohio due to classroom discipline problems, he'd been told. His job teaching in Hough helped him resolve his classroom discipline problems. Until then, he believes, he was not a very good teacher:

Until teaching in Hough I just did whatever I had to do. Since then I've started developing my ideas about what's important. Students' thinking in a logical manner became important, and I developed my ideas about it more. Classroom control was important for practical reasons—I wanted to hold onto my job. But control isn't a natural ability for me. It's one thing I've had to work on here. One conflict I've had in the past is how you *engage* students if you have to control them. If you control them too much you set them up for game playing. Particularly for lower students—they don't feel they can ask you questions if you control them too much. They start thinking about the answer but not *how* to think about it so they can get the answer. Another thing I've tried to develop is a more realistic determination of where each student is. Two years ago we got a new department chair, and this one thinks my expectations are too high; he sees all my test scores. The expectation issue is a problem in the department. I don't want to lower mine too much, yet I find I have to reteach a lot of algebra and other mathematics these students *should* know.

Because Hascal wants to keep his job yet teach well, the expectation issue is a dilemma for him, although not for his former chair. "I found I've generally made a lot more assumptions than I should about students and what they actually know. It's a gradual process of filling in bits of knowledge where blanks were so I can make fewer assumptions about what kids already know. I've started emphasizing application and integration of ideas more, too."

Hascal sees planning to teach mathematics as simpler than, say planning to teach literature or social studies, because mathematics is objective and has logical sequences. The logic is particularly true of geometry, in his view. He says of planning:

In general in math the curriculum is set more or less by the textbook; I still use that model. One reason is that if I go farther than the book it upsets parents and the chairman. If I get *one* complaint from a parent, my chairman might see that as just a complaining parent. Two complaints might send up a red flag, but three would tell him there's probably a problem. So I try to stay with the book pretty much because deviating from it makes students and administrators uneasy.

The school system's text for geometry was adopted because of its fit with Mapleton's graded course of study. Hascal continues, "The organization of that textbook strongly affects my plans. I think about goals, but they're built in along the way. One problem I have is that I haven't taught this lower-level geometry class before, so I don't know what I can reasonably expect." He means he hasn't had many experiences on which to draw regarding typical problems students have in lower-level geometry and the sorts of lessons that work best. So, although he's been teaching at Maple City for 11 years, this is essentially his first year in this geometry course.

He reminisces that "a few years ago [at Hough] my supervisor asked me to write plans for a series of lessons. I did that, writing down what topics I wanted to cover, assignments, and so forth. I didn't think much of it then. But it did help me to be more realistic about the amount of time I had and what I could cover."

Teaching and Learning in Hascal's Informal Geometry Course

Geometry class begins today, as on most days, with students entering, taking seats, and chatting quietly. When most students have arrived, Mr. Legupski smiles broadly and has students pass in last night's homework. Then he eyes empty seats to take attendance. He confers privately with Sally who was absent yesterday. The juniors and seniors here are clad mostly in jeans, athletic shirts, sweaters, or sweatshirts and are well groomed and neat. A few girls have on skirts and sweaters, and one is wearing a green suit. They chat quietly about recently televised football games, movies they've recently seen, nearby murders over Starter jackets, other local news, worries, and aspirations for the future. Over the next ten minutes, the chatting crescendos and diminuendos as noise level grows and recedes. "Okay, folks, let's get quiet and take your notes out, please," he says, gesturing widely with both hands and smiling amiably. Students retrieve pens and notebooks or paper and quiet down. "Now, folks," he continues. "Okay, everybody, let's get quiet, folks, now, please. I hope over the next few days you'll go over these terms again. Take some time to review them if you aren't familiar with them, please do."

"A convex polygon—the book's definition is if you can put a rubber band about it and it would fit *tightly* it's a convex polygon. So this one *isn't*." He draws on the board:

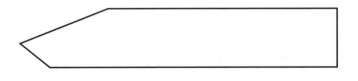

"And this one *is*":

"You also should know what a pentagon is, and so forth. When you name a polygon you name angles in order: *A, B,* and so forth." He draws on the board:

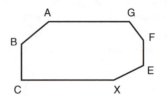

"Lisa, give me an example of consecutive vertices," he says. Lisa replies, "I don't know." Hascal continues patiently, "Now, Lisa, look at this figure. In this figure what are they? Read the definition to yourself, Lisa." She replies hesitantly, "*A* and *B, B* and *C?*" Hascal continues assiduously, "Okay, let's try someone else. Maggie? Okay, now, Maggie, read the definition to yourself. What makes *B* and *C* consecutive vertices? Do you know what consecutive *numbers* are?" Maggie smiles at him gently and then says, "Please call on someone else. I'm feeling real stupid right now." He continues, returning the smile, "Okay, Maggie, but listen up because I'll be back to you. What makes *B* and *C* consecutive vertices? It's not because they're endpoints of the same segment, it's because they're endpoints of the same what? Lester, what's *another* example here of consecutive vertices?" Lester responds, "*E, D.*" The chatting has resumed and begins to rise again. Mr. Legupski stands up straighter, takes a deep breath, stops smiling, clasps his hands in front of him, and says seriously, "Now, Mr. Perkins, give us another pair of consecutive vertices." He replies, "*X, E.*" "Now, Maggie," continues Hascal, smiling amicably again and gesturing with his right hand, "give us another pair of consecutive vertices." The chatting has diminished again, and Maggie answers, "*C, X.*" "Scott, turn around, please. Give us another pair, Andy." He responds, "*D, C.*" "Dave?" Hascal calls. "*A, X,*" says Dave. "Okay," says Hascal, "does everyone get the idea? Okay, folks, let's go on, then. Okay. Now, diagonal. A diagonal's a segment that connects nonconsecutive vertices. *AC* is a diagonal because it connects nonconsecutive vertices." To demonstrate this, he draws a dotted line on the figure on the board between *A* and *C*. Then he draws in the other diagonals as well. Lester asks, "Answerwise, are they the same answers?" Hascal responds, "They involve the same points but you list them differently. Okay, what we're going to do now is try to determine the measurement of the angles of a polygon and their relationship to the sides." He prints on the board: How are the sums of the interior angles of a polygon related? He says, "To do this we're going to form a chart." He writes Figure 4.1 on the board.

Lester has turned around and is talking about the football playoffs to Dave. "Lester, you got all of this down?" asks Hascal. "Yeah," responds Lester. "Good," says Hascal. "Now, if that isn't very clear, let's try a quadrilateral. He draws a kite-shaped quadrilateral on the chart on the line beneath the triangle, then 4, 2, 180°, and 360° in the pertinent parts of the chart. Charles asks, "Why's it called N-gon?" Hascal replies, "N equals the number of sides of the polygon. Now, let's draw the diagonal vertices of this polygon." He does this with dotted lines. "How many triangles do we have?" he asks. Lester says, "Two." As students respond, going across the line about the kite on the chart he writes the answers on the chart they're developing together. "Now," he continues, "how many degrees will we have here altogether?" Lisa responds, "360°." "Does anyone *not* see how we got there?" he asks. "Check!" says Lester. Two other students raise their hands. Hascal approaches their desks and quietly explains again. "Oh! I see," each of the three responds and smiles.

"Now, let's go on to a pentagon," Hascal says, returning to the board where he draws one. Then he turns around and says, "Len, Robert, let's get quiet. Len." Dave and Maggie quickly fill in the numbers for the chart. Andy asks, "How would you know where to start with your vertex?" "It really doesn't matter," says Hascal. "You can start anywhere. Now, let's try a hexagon. Okay, without doing any calculations, Jerry, how many will you expect to see?" Jerry responds, "Five." The class moves on to seven- and eight-sided figures in the same way, completing the chart as they progress. Hascal says of the answer about the number of triangles formed, "Now, Mr. Perkins, what will this be? Now, let's say we have a *ten-sided* figure. How many triangles will we find?" He glances around the room and Robert replies, "Eight." "Yes," says Hascal, "what's the pattern here?" Robert says, "Two less than the number of sides." Hascal asks, "Now, Ms. Kagan, if we have 27 sides, how many triangles will be formed?" Lisa responds, "25." They complete the chart for 10 and for 27, then he writes N on the next line and fills in the following box about the number of triangles formed. He asks Lester, "What will the sum

FIGURE 4.1 A chart for today's work

N-gon	Number of sides	Number of N-gons formed by diagonals of *one* vertex	Sum of $\angle$s in each N-gon	Sum of $\angle$s in N-gon
△	3	1	180°	1 (180°)

of the angles be?" Lester replies, "Six? Oh! I'm looking at the wrong line. No, $N - 2 \times 180$." Len blurts out, "Can you figure that out?" Hascal replies, "Not unless you know what N is. Okay. This is basically the postulate. What kind of reasoning have we used here? Is it deductive or intuitive or inductive? Folks, quiet!" The students are giggling because Len has just farted loudly, and it's a very smelly one. Patiently ignoring this, or perhaps unaware of it in the front of the room, Hascal writes on the board: Postulate: Sum of interior angles of convex N-gon $= 180(n - 2)$. "Lester," he says, "get control. Now, if you want to make some remarks either say them now or write them down, and you can show them to everyone in the hall. Do we know what the sum of all the angles would be of a regular convex pentagon?" He writes on the board:

$$\frac{180\,(n - 2)}{n}$$

"Okay, anyone not see where we got that?" Seeing no hands up he continues, "Okay, protractors and rulers tomorrow." As the class nears its end, the noise not only returns, but also increases. "Folks," he says, "let's get quiet for a minute. On this ditto I want you to do 1 through 17. And take a look at those book pages too." He quickly distributes the hand-printed homework assignment shown in Figure 4.2.

The bell rings, and all students exit except Martha, who's been absent a lot recently due to hospitalization. Hascal confers with her, cautioning her amiably but seriously, "My perception is it's going to take a *lot* of work on your part to catch up. I'm willing to help you any way I can, but I'm serious. It's going to take a lot of work." He also suggests she see the guidance counselor and promises to give her some extra homework if it would help. "Thanks, Mr. Legupski," smiles Martha as she leaves for her next class, and Hascal goes to monitor a study hall.

Other lessons follow a similar routine of collecting homework, solving some problems as a group about perpendicular bisectors, and interior and exterior angles. The class searches for patterns and constructs geometry-related postulates. In general, Mr. Legupski addresses the class amiably as "folks," but when the noise level increases sharply he becomes more formal and addresses students as Mr. or Ms. and their last name. He's usually at the front of the room near the board, although he frequently moves to students to confer with those who seem confused. On one occasion, as he begins explaining the homework on the board, the chattering reaches epic proportions. A not-too-quiet drone pervades. He says firmly,

---

Okay, now, shut up! I wonder how in the world you can do your homework if you aren't listening when I give these directions! Everybody got the idea? Then I want you to measure each of the three exterior angles for each triangle, then for each triangle find the sum of the exterior angles. And then construct a quadrilateral. Now, when you do this I want you to do a convex one, one that's *not* a square or a rectangle. Again, I want you to have an exterior angle at each vertex, measure each exterior angle and add them. Thirdly, repeat this for a pentagon—a convex one that's not regular. Once you've done this I want you to write out a sentence telling me the pattern to all this.

What does Hascal believe he's teaching these students? Obviously, he knows he's teaching geometry, but in addition he hopes they're learning "more about thinking." When asked what they believe they learn here, his students agree. Robert in particular (whose sister recently had math with Mr. Legupski and has become a social friend since graduating) goes on at great length about this and its importance: "Mr. Legupski really works hard to get me to *think*. I never realized before how disorganized my thinking was. And he really makes me go into depth about it, you know, really deeply." Robert continues somewhat tentatively, "We're also learning something else important, although you might not think it's important because it's not about math." "What's that?" I ask. He continues, "Well, I found out that gay guys are a lot like everybody else. They're nice, too, not just creeps or some kind of vermin." Julia adds, "Yes. I remember once in elementary school

FIGURE 4.2   Homework assignment

Use the diagram to answer the questions specifically (XY = AB, etc.)

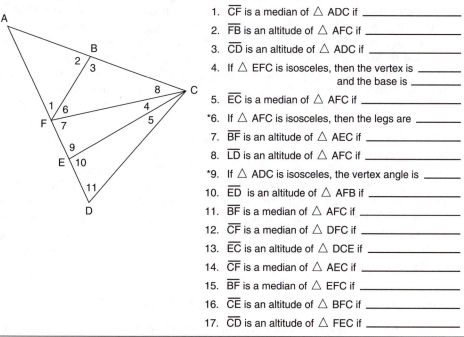

1. $\overline{CF}$ is a median of △ ADC if _____
2. $\overline{FB}$ is an altitude of △ AFC if _____
3. $\overline{CD}$ is an altitude of △ ADC if _____
4. If △ EFC is isosceles, then the vertex is _____ and the base is _____
5. $\overline{EC}$ is a median of △ AFC if _____
*6. If △ AFC is isosceles, then the legs are _____
7. $\overline{BF}$ is an altitude of △ AEC if _____
8. $\overline{LD}$ is an altitude of △ AFC if _____
*9. If △ ADC is isosceles, the vertex angle is _____
10. $\overline{ED}$ is an altitude of △ AFB if _____
11. $\overline{BF}$ is a median of △ AFC if _____
12. $\overline{CF}$ is a median of △ DFC if _____
13. $\overline{EC}$ is an altitude of △ DCE if _____
14. $\overline{CF}$ is a median of △ AEC if _____
15. $\overline{BF}$ is a median of △ EFC if _____
16. $\overline{CE}$ is an altitude of △ BFC if _____
17. $\overline{CD}$ is an altitude of △ FEC if _____

*You may (should) judge on the basis of appearance.

I had this black substitute. And I learned by the end of the day that she's a good, serious, smart person. I never knew that before. I'm not prejudiced or anything; I just never knew. I mean all you see on TV is rap stars and athletes, and they're not the most serious or smart people in the world! See, the same thing is true about Mr. Legupski. I want you to know he never makes a big deal about it, but we all know—he went on a march once or something. I'm real glad I got to take this with him. He's terrific." Julia adds matter-of-factly, "He's married, you know. To a guy." Robert continues, "I mean, when we were first assigned to his room, we [boys] made some pretty crude jokes about it at the beginning. We all knew he was gay, you know. But now I get real sick at those jokes and all the gay-bashing in the news, like in Colorado and that. I mean, what he does on his own time is *his* business. I've never felt uncomfortable in any way. I think I'm safer with him than almost all the girls are in some other classes." Julia agrees and they gossip a bit about men who make advances to attractive female students. Robert adds that he's learning "how to concentrate because sometimes it's so noisy in there it's hard to think like he wants us to." He speculates about the reason: "I don't think Mr. Legupski has taught this course much. I know he's taught Euclidian geometry, but not informal geometry, which *this* is."

I found it interesting (and somewhat humbling) that although I'd been in this classroom observing for several weeks, I did not know Hascal is openly gay until Robert brought it up. Hascal said he knew it would come up naturally in our work together, but he didn't want to make a big issue of it. In terms of teaching, he says this makes him feel "very different and probably under a microscope more [than heterosexual teachers]." Antigay comments by teachers and students before Hascal became known to be gay and being identified as different before acknowledging this contributed to this feeling in his view. According to Rosa Sherman, the assistant principal, a few parents call each year with requests to have their children transferred out of Hascal's class, but she points out that their reason is insufficient, so she doesn't make changes.

More to the point of students' opportunities to learn in this classroom, these students claim they see the benefits of meeting teachers who are a different race, gender, sexual orientation, and so forth. Julia says she wishes she'd had that substitute teacher for a longer time (although not wishing more illness on her regular teacher, she adds), and Robert wishes he'd had some Asian teachers and black male teachers. It seems that positive learning about tolerance for different people is one potential feature of the implicit curriculum for administrators to consider when hiring teachers and professors. It supports many schools' aims regarding multicultural education, and it might further that aim more effectively than the overt curriculum can. It is also matter for colleges of education to consider in recruiting students to become teachers.

Hascal's Ideas about Planning and What Influences It

How does Hascal think about and plan the curriculum of this informal geometry class? Clearly, the textbook affects his planning because it provides the basic organization and structure of the course, although he reorders the sequence somewhat. He thinks some fundamental things in geometry must be taught early, including some definitions and the logical approach mathematicians use in geometry. "They're like the ABCs in reading," he contends. In addition to the textbook, several other matters influence his planning and the enactment of those plans. One is his concern about control and that students here don't pay as much attention as he would like. He thinks this is a basic problem, so he tries to get them more involved by using "folks" when addressing the class and by asking questions of many members of the class. However, he does not want to control the students to the extent that they will not reveal their ignorance to him or ask questions. Clearly, Hascal has not cowed them to that extent, for several students in this lesson and others felt comfortable enough to ask questions. Concern about control has been an issue for him since he began teaching, as related earlier. Hascal enjoys the one-to-one reteaching that frequently ensues, and he thinks a lot about his question-asking strategies: "Sometimes I call on kids I know will be confused or who aren't paying attention or who *will* know the answer. That way I can reteach something or caution them if necessary. Every time I ask a question, it's not just a matter of *what* but also *who* to ask. I can make different points and have different outcomes by calling on different kids. But I don't always know in advance what questions I'm going to ask or who I'm going to ask. It depends on how attentive they are today and how well they are going in being able to deal with the material. I know what content I need to teach them that period, but I think I sort of plan it while I'm doing it." So, like many good teachers, Hascal can be thought of as an improvisational planner and teacher. That is, he plans interactively more than he plans preactively.

Hascal continues to reflect on many issues, such as how (and whether) to use sarcasm, how to respond to students, whom he should ask questions of, students' levels, and how much he "can legitimately expect of them—can they get there from where they are?" He thinks his supervisor might scrutinize him more than other teachers because of his sexual orientation: "I don't know if I *am*, but I *feel* as if I'm under a microscope." At any rate, he feels more vulnerable than some teachers might because his sexual preference differs from the mainstream, and it's public knowledge. For this reason, when his supervisor suggests he lower his expectations and pay more attention to discipline, he listens. As a result, his supervisor is another factor influencing his thinking, planning, and enactment of the curriculum. When teachers feel vulnerable, perhaps they are more strongly influenced by others' view than when they do not.

I now move to Chester High School to a class in drawing and another in Middle Eastern studies.

Chester and Its High School

This community differs sharply from Maple City. Although the two communities are on the same interstate highway and the nearby city's urban sprawl has affected each community's unique character, they share little else. Chester is one of the most affluent communities surrounding a nearby large city.

Chester's slick Chamber of Commerce pamphlet and professional-looking high school information sheet for college admissions officers characterize the community as upper middle class, suburban, and residential, with most residents engaged in professions and businesses and many working in the nearby large city. Chester's population in 1990 was almost 17,000 and was expected to double by the year 2000. The chamber lists primary occupations as professional and managerial, administrative support, sales, precision production, and craft. Like Maple City, Chester's residents strive to maintain its unique character in the face of urban sprawl from the adjacent city. Unlike Maple City, though, Chester is a fairly affluent area. According to a local realtor, homes in Chester in 1993 sell for $180,000 to $210,000, and little is available for less than $100,000, with an occasional home costing more than $1 million.

CHESTER HIGH SCHOOL

Parents here expect a lot of Chester's schools, but seem to be pleased. "My daughter graduated two years ago and was well prepared for college. My son graduated last year, and he's in college too, although he needs to bring up his GPA," reports one father in a local coffee shop. A nearby woman adds enthusiastically, "I wish I'd gotten the education my Cynthia's getting at the high school!" In November, the community had approved a bond issue to build a new high school. Due to overcrowding at Chester High, the board requested additional money to add a wing so they could avoid double sessions during the two years needed to build the new high school. In February, the community turned down this second bond issue, perhaps because they were weary of being asked to raise their own property taxes so soon. (However, I should point out, on the same day all bond issues in the nearby communities failed, except one to support expanded police services.)

Built in 1972 and added to in 1982, Chester High School is a large, sprawling light brick building. Its wings join one another at surprising angles, yielding small, oddly shaped courtyards and study areas throughout. These angles are echoed by the banks of lockers placed at odd angles in some areas near the roomy commons where students eat lunch. Some halls are lined with greenhouse-type windows, which permit views of the courtyards and adjacent fields. The carpeted halls are brilliantly lit.

Chester High is a four-year high school. This year almost 2,000 students attend school. Of them, 1,755 are white, 151 Asian American, 43 African American, 10 Hispanic American, and 4 Native American. In a typical year, over 99 percent graduate. Graduation requirements contain 18 units of credit, including 4 of English, 3 of social studies, 2 of mathematics, 1 in science, and a half each in health and physical education. Advanced placement and honors courses are available in literature, biology, chemistry, physics, computer science, and American history. The 1992 class took a total of 116 advanced placement examinations. This class also had two National Merit Scholarship finalists, and nine commended students; the class was recognized for academic achievement in other ways as well. They were accepted in more than 79 colleges and universities.

Students here chat mostly about the same issues they did in Maple City as they walk to classes and visit over lunch in the commons, although Chester's students are more likely to be overheard discussing college applications and wondering which colleges are best for them. Adjacent to the commons is a display case containing many shiny athletic awards for the Chester Cheetahs, and banners proclaim support for upcoming Cheetah contests, promising glorious victories. Morning announcements on the public address system also congratulate students for awards in recent arts competitions.

JILL RICHARDSON TEACHES DRAWING

Jill and Her Background

Adjacent to Chester High School's commons area is the art department, where Jill Richardson's classes meet. Art rooms differ vastly from other classrooms—they virtually reek of creativity with their rich smells of paints, oils, clay, pastes, and different kinds of papers, odors more pungent than the aroma of floor wax, books, chalk, pencils, and erasers typical in other classrooms. Jill's room is no exception, although it is neater than many art rooms, perhaps because it has ample storage room and because Jill insists that students clean their work areas before departing for their next class.

Jill, who is about 50, has taught art for over 15 years, with seven years in elementary schools, one in middle school, and more than a dozen at the high school level. This is her fourth year at Chester High School. She's from a conservative farm family where women were not supposed to go to college. Nonetheless, she attended several nearby colleges and universities as a night school student, took classes in summers, and attended workshops to increase her ability and understanding both as an artist and as a teacher. "You gotta keep up with both!" she says firmly, and she continues her education to this day. This year, Jill got married, and her students are happy for her.

Jill is petite, with long brown hair she pulls back with a colorful scarf or large bow on some days and lets flow freely on others. She typically wears slacks, a blouse, and jacket. Perhaps because she is small, but also because of her individualized teaching practices, it isn't always easy to spot Jill in the classroom. Her students ask the visitor, "Looking for Mrs. Rich?" and point her out. She's usually sitting near a student talking about his or her work, although she typically begins each period more formally with about five to ten minutes of instruction before it is time for production. She says she tries to follow the discipline-based art education ideas. Her aim is to "formally incorporate art criticism, art history, and aesthetics in ways for students to get credit. I take seriously the things I present. Art production is important, and students are excited about it, but I want them to be able to make good decisions and be less confused about what they do." She further encourages each student to develop a "creative voice":

What students bring to class is very important. I have to (and *they* have to) recognize their own creative thoughts. Sometimes as a result I've changed requirements for a project for students. I guess sometimes I feel guilty because I think I should have more of a whole-class instructional approach like other teachers, with less emphasis on individualization, but there's no opportunity to produce in most other classrooms. This is the only opportunity for them to express themselves visually, generally between elementary school and graduation from high school, so it's important—no, *crucial*—for me to balance the whole-class presentations with plenty of time for their individual, creative production.

When talking about her practice, Jill speaks ardently and intently, with great spirit, enthusiasm, and commitment.

Jill's room is a long rectangle with a small square alcove by the door to the classroom. On several bulletin boards and cabinet doors are posters in her calligraphy about elements of design and how to analyze a work of art:

What do you see? Describe (in your own words). What is the representational subject matter you see? Note any nonfunctional use; identify the work of art, using references if needed. Be objective.

How is the work of art organized? Study how the artist used each element and principle of art.

What do you think the artist is trying to say? Explain what is "happening" based on the first two steps. (Use *your* intelligence, imagination, and courage.)

What do you think of the work? Does the work succeed or fail? (Perhaps it succeeds in some areas and fails in other areas.)

Also around the room are baskets, sculptures, and many interesting "found" objects such as bones, brilliantly colored leaves, and rocks. Built into one long wall are storage cabinets that hold students' work or various kinds of papers and cardboard, paints, brushes, brayers, clay, art journals, magazines, and other materials for students' productions.

Tables with adjustable tops and stools form a large U around the center of the room. Higher tables with high stools are outside the U, and Jill's desk, filing cabinets, and art books are in a small space along another long wall. This term a group studying installations has built one about the experience of prejudice and placed it in the small square area adjacent to the door. Passersby can view it from outside the art room through small slits, and many frequently do. During the term Jill and her students erect an arrangement of several items in the center of the room, to use as subject matter for drawings.

Jill's Ideas about Planning and Their Influences

Jill describes planning and teaching as a "terrible (as in awesome) responsibility. It's *serious* business to plan and teach!" Typically, she plans the full year's sequence of major themes, topics, and art techniques by breaking the year into big chunks of time, estimating roughly how much time to devote to each theme, and then filling in details as she goes. She keeps looseleaf notebooks for each course she teaches, adding pages of ideas she develops each year and writing notes to herself about what worked well and what to alter. She's excited and influenced by new developments in the art world, such as deconstruction and installations, and she frequently tells her students brief stories about shows she's attended or read about in art journals.

Another influence on Jill's planning this year is Chester's policy of moving toward outcomes-based eduction (OBE) in anticipation of Ohio's probable move toward such a policy. In her view, this will be difficult, because many of the examples of OBE she has seen come from science and mathematics, where objective answers are considered outcomes because of convergent thinking. Fewer examples come from writing or the arts, where a primary goal might be (as in Jill's case) to develop an individual creative style. The OBE policy appears to be in conflict with her primary goal and perplexes her. She joins a group of students and teachers to consider the conflicts and she seems hopeful about working it out by year's end:

> OBE *could* work in our favor. If we [in the art department] write our exit outcomes, which really are our goals, it can make a great deal of sense. The way the administration sees OBE means we're going to have a chance to work creatively with the schedule and with the idea of outcomes. They don't seem to see outcomes narrowly like behavioral objectives or something. That's good, because then the arts have a chance. Maybe it'll even open up other possibilities for us to work across disciplines. I see a lot of interlinkages, and so do other teachers and the students. Really, what they're saying is we need to have reasons for everything we do. No kidding! I agree, and I *do*. It gives us a chance to work with students' ideas and to meet students' needs. We're already doing a lot of it, but I guess *they* just want to see it on paper.

The guiding principles that she has adopted into her practical theory of action come from discipline-based art education (DBAE). However, she is as concerned with students' visual art production as with their learning about art criticism, art history, art theory, and aesthetics. It is her aim that students incorporate DBAE ideas into their ideas for their art productions by making better decisions. She is aware that art is difficult for many students because they are used to courses where right and wrong answers exist, rather than those where they are to integrate ideas from class into their thinking and productions. She wants them to think and talk in depth about their art work. Jill thinks this will enrich their thinking, help them to integrate ideas, and allow them to become more conscious of their individual creative voices. "You have to integrate it into a whole," she says of DBAE. She also believes Harvard's Project Zero is valid. She sees differences between the way she enacts DBAE and what she's read and heard about it, particularly at a national conference she recently attended. What does Jill's work look like in action? I describe that in the next section.

Teaching and Learning in Jill's Class

The graphics project in Jill's drawing class is to design and print a business card, letterhead, and envelope. Thirteen students are in this class. Four are from Japan and will return there after their parents' work in Chester has been completed. She begins class today by confessing through a gentle smile:

> I want to apologize to you today. I didn't get to go over your papers as much as I would have liked. I had a meeting to attend, but tonight I *will* go back through them, and I'll clean up the art room. This work today isn't necessarily for a grade. Today, I *could* show you a videotape or lecture to you about the theory of relief printmaking, but this time I want you to experiment first. Then when I do show you the video later in the week, it'll be more meaningful.

She pauses while students retrieve blocks of wax or linoleum, knives, and brayers. "You'll have to share the printmaking tools," she says. "Follow the same process I showed you yesterday." Jenna approaches to ask, "How do you transfer the design to the linoleum?" Jill sits at Jenna's seat to demonstrate, and six other students gather around to watch the process. Joshua later transfers his incorrectly; thus, when he prints it, the design itself is backward. Students transfer their designs to wax or battleship linoleum and then laboriously cut them using various knives. As they do so, Jill circulates, chatting with each student: "Oh, I like this line. How do you think it'll print?" "This texture is marvelous here." "This shape really catches my eye. Why is that?" "Wow! I really like all those skinny angles you're using. They have a nice unity to them."

A student from another course who has a pass from study hall this period is working on one of the high tables outside the U on an oil pastel drawing. He has another student hold the portrait up for him so he can see it from a distance.

Jill announces to all, "The only thing I need from you today is your design for your business card. You did a *super* job with them! It'll be real interesting to see what you do with the *large* linoleum later when we do illustrations."

As the class is ending, Jill says, "Time to put your tools away." They do so, wash their hands, place their projects in their storage bins, and line up. "Have a super day," she says warmly. "You guys did a good job. You have a lot of patience cutting those blocks. It isn't easy, is it?"

On her way to her next class, Jenna tells me she is taking this course because of Jill. "You can talk with her about everything: current events, racism, *her* experience as a student, art shows, and personal problems. And I wanted to study a different medium. I took painting last year. She's really interested in art and in us. You can tell."

Next day, the class begins with Jill asking students to retrieve their projects and a piece of black board as she calls their names. "There's rubber cement. And the typewriter's over there if you need it, and I have some black pens. That's for the first 15 minutes. Then we'll watch a video. It's really good. We'll be doing some printmaking. This tells about it and gives you some language to use when you're doing it." Then she asks if anyone has anything for her to photocopy or reduce. "Remember, this is due today, and if you don't have it, there *will* be points taken off." Robert asks, "Mrs. Rich, could you reduce this so I can use it on my card?" She collects his project and several other items from students, then leaves for the photocopy machine. Students position their business cards, letterheads, and envelopes on the black boards, then rubber cement them. Jill returns, reminding them, "Okay, you have about five more minutes." Students request more time. "I'm trying to do a *really* good job!" says Nikki. Jill seems convinced and says, "Well, I think we might have a communication problem about this project, and it might be partly my fault and partly yours. So, I'll tell you what. We'll go ahead and watch the videotape today, and if you're done you can start on printmaking tomorrow. And if not, you can have another period or part of it with this. Okay? Is that fair?" Students seem relieved, and Jill sets up the monitor and VCR. In five minutes, she starts the videotape about woodcuts, tools, how to use them to make a wood block, and how to print it. A few students continue mounting their projects, but most take notes. The videotape explains that the image must be reversed from the drawing in order to make an identical image. Joshua interrupts his notetaking to exclaim softly, "Aha!" The videotape then goes on to caution viewers about other potential pitfalls in the printing process, such as how to make prints overlap correctly when using multiple plates for a print with several colors. When the 20-minute tape ends, all students seem attentive. Alex remarks that she did some of that last year as a freshman in the general introductory art course. Jill smiles, nods her head in agreement, and says, "We're going to be doing a reduction print. Wood engraving is cutting out a negative image, carving it in relief. In the video they showed three main printing techniques. You'll have a quiz on this on Friday. Tomorrow bring your notes with you and some writing—your writing or a friend's. We'll be doing an illustration related to it." She collects the black pens and completed projects.

On his way to his next class, Joshua explains why he's taking the course: "So I can understand what I'm doing when I do art. Mrs. Rich is great! She's wonderful. I can talk to her about all kinds of important things: my [dismal] grades, the news, why we have bad race relations in America, what college to apply to."

On Thursday, she begins class by saying, "Jenna, you were taking notes during the videotape yesterday, and so were a few others. For a few minutes we're going to review a little for tomorrow's quiz. Then we'll start thinking about the piece of writing you brought and about an image it contains and what would be an appropriate illustration for it. So get out your notes and let's get this review done. Think of a question to ask the class—one you think you might see on the quiz." Jenna asks, "Like vocabulary?" Jill responds, "Sure, anything from your notes." Jenna asks, "What's a brayer?" Robert responds, "The instrument you use to ink your block." Nikki asks, "What's meant by 'registration'?" He calls on four students, but neither he nor Jill accepts their answers. Two students confess they don't know. Jill coaches, "Remember how they put little light marks on their paper and then positioned it carefully on the block before burnishing it?" She demonstrates with a woodblock. "When you put a *second* color on you have to know where to place the block. That whole process is called 'registration.'" Jim asks, "Plate?" Anne responds, "That's what you carve into." Sarah asks, "What are three types of printing?" Brad responds, "Relief, reduction, and uh. . . ." Jill closes the brief review by saying, "I'll review again *very* quickly before your quiz tomorrow, but *you* study your notes tonight, too." Then she directs them to think of an illustration to create from the piece of writing they brought. Almost everyone has remembered to bring one. They scan them for a few minutes and then chat with a neighbor about the images they plan to create before obtaining paper and pencils. They draw for ten minutes and then put things away. Class is over for today.

On Friday, as promised, Jill very quickly reviews a few terms and then distributes the quizzes shown in Figure 4.3.

On Monday, Jill begins class by saying:

There's a lot of negative space in these designs. I'd like you to fill it. Oh, and you did real well on the quizzes. The information was easy because it was just stuff I said in class or you saw on the video. So it shows you were listening. The reason I do that is so you have the information before we start printing.

She calls students' names individually to retrieve their projects. Then she circulates and passes out their quizzes. Well over half the students have gotten all the questions right, and the remainder have received either As or Bs. Students also obtain magazines, scissors, and rubber cement. They look through the magazines for interesting and suitable textures to use in the empty spaces of their designs, cut the textures out, and place them on their designs. Now Jill is moving around the room, conferring with individual students on their juxtapositions of different textures and the shapes and lines in their designs. After about ten minutes, she says, "In a few minutes we'll go over that quiz. I recorded the number you got right because I wanted to see if everyone's ready to go on to printmaking. Anybody have anything for me to photocopy?" She takes four students' projects to the copy machine as students continue to work on their designs. Upon returning she says, "Let's get your quizzes out now to go over them. If you got 100, please just be quiet for this review." As she finishes, students begin jabbering, none too quietly. "Just be quiet for about five minutes here and we'll

Identify the printmaking tool shown below.

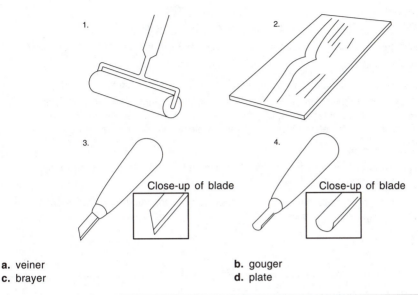

1.
2.
3.
4.

Close-up of blade
Close-up of blade

a. veiner
c. brayer

b. gouger
d. plate

Match the descriptions of printmaking concepts in the right-hand column with the terms in the left-hand column. Write the correct letters in the blanks.

a. registration

b. intaglio print

c. silkscreen

d. relief print

5. _____ The ink is on the surface of the block not in the grooves.

6. _____ The ink is squeezed through a cloth screen.

7. _____ The ink is in the grooves of the block.

8. _____ A system of placing the printing plate in the correct position so the colors fit together on the printing paper.

9. Suppose you are cutting a piece of linoleum to prepare a block for printing. In which direction should most of the cuts be made?

  a. toward the artist
  b. in circles
  c. away from the artist
  d. zigzag direction

10. A block must be held firmly with one hand while you cut. Where must this hand always be placed?

  a. on top of the other hand cutting the block
  b. behind the blade and behind the path you are cutting
  c. in front of the blade

FIGURE 4.3 Graphics quiz (*continues*)

11. Our inks are water-based. You clean with

    a. water and soap   **b.** gasoline

    c. turpentine   **d.** nail polish remover

12. What step must you take in preparing relief blocks to have the design print correctly?

    a. color the design red   **b.** carve the design in reverse

13. What are the two basic methods for creating multicolored relief prints?

    a. (1) Create blocks for each color, (2) Create one block, print copies in one color, clean the block, cut the block and print the second color (color reduction), etc.

    b. (1) Cut the block for each color, (2) Color the block with two colors and cut.

14. What is a monoprint?

    a. A print made from a surface with ink on it. Only one print can usually be made.

    b. A print made with one color.

15. To create unity in a design similar lines and shapes are repeated many times creating a rhythm that relates the theme of the print.

    a. true

    b. false

GRAPHICS PERIOD _____   NAME _____

    FIGURE 4.3 (*continued*)

be done with this. Anybody miss the first four?" Probably because she remembers a few have confused the gouger and veiner tools, she holds them up for all to see and reminds students of the differences. "Did anyone miss the brayer? And the plate?" The jabbering resumes, and she asks, "Could I have it quiet in here?" She reminds them of item 8, perhaps remembering their difficulty with the idea of registration on Friday. A student interrupts to ask, "What about 5, 6, and 7?" "We'll get to them," says Jill, smiling. As she returns to item 8 about registration the jabbering has become a din. "What is *registration?*" she perseveres. "Remember when they were using different plates on the video? And they put little marks on it?" The talking increases in volume, and she says, "Would you rather we do this at the end of the period and you can continue your work now? I really want all your attention so you'll know these well when we start doing our printing soon." A student turns on the radio to a classic rock station at a low volume, and students resume their work on their designs. They seem relieved and happy to be working on their projects again, perhaps because they see the work of this class as producing art, not learning material for a quiz. Several students say this and that they enrolled in the course "to *do* art, not to talk about it or write about it." Jill continues conferring with students, helping them look at what they are doing and think about why they are doing it. She asks questions such as, "Which way do you like these textures best? Why?" Ten minutes before the period is over she directs students to put their projects away. Then she resumes reviewing the quiz. There is now relative calm in the class, and students are clearly taking part by asking relevant questions when they are confused.

After class Soshi and Michelle work to impress upon me the extent of rapport Jill has with the class. Soshi says, "She's great at helping you a lot, and she's not *shocked* if you cuss. She asks you not to do it again and to think of another way to say it, but she's not shocked." Michelle agrees, "She seems interested in my work and makes me really *look* at and *think* about what I'm doing. You can't just slap things together and call it art, you know. You have to have an idea and a plan about how to get it to look like your idea." They further remark on what they're learning from Jill. Soshi says, "That art's important and takes hard work." Michelle argues, "Art doesn't just take hard work. It takes a lot of thinking and looking, too. I also am learning that adults can be fair, some of them listen to students and change their ideas about what to do, like she did today. I mean she didn't make a big deal about it like being embarrassed because she thought we beat her or something. I guess she just saw we really wanted to do our projects, not go over that dumb quiz. So she figured 'Why fight city hall?' and had us do our projects. Then in the end, she still got to go over the quiz, so nobody lost anything. We just did it in a different order. And that's smart. That's why we respect her."

Students design illustrations for another two weeks and then make multiple-color prints of them. They find it's necessary to simplify some parts because it is difficult to cut fine lines and close details into their blocks.

This year 30 of Jill's students from various courses and the art club win awards in a statewide competition. In previous years her students have also won more of these awards than the students of most other art teachers in Ohio. Some would argue this provides ample evidence of positive student outcomes, but Jill is concerned about how to meet Chester's new OBE policy. Eisner (1969:5-9) argues about such objectives:

1. they tend to overestimate the degree to which it is possible to predict educational outcomes;
2. they tend to treat all subject matters alike regarding the degree of specificity possible in stating educational objectives;
3. they tend to confuse the application of a standard and the making of a judgment regarding the appraisal of educational outcomes; and
4. they have tended to imply that the formulation of objectives should be a first step in curriculum development and hence have confused the logical with the psychological in educational planning.

Eisner further argues that how a person formulates educational objectives is not simply a question of technique but relates to one's conception of education, and he distinguishes between instructional and expressive objectives and the ways they function in curriculum planning. I agree with his points, but I would add that teachers' practical theories of action comprise one important part of how teachers conceive of education. I believe Eisner's article is relevant to Jill's solo deliberations about how to contend with the new Chester policy, and I have given her a copy of his paper. I turn now to the final case of this chapter where James

Kennedy teaches a small seminar using a computer simulation. This year's focus is on Arab-Israeli conflict.

JAMES KENNEDY TEACHES SOCIAL STUDIES AND COMPUTER SKILLS

James Kennedy's class in a computer laboratory is far from the art department. The laboratory is a starkly white rectangular room with 14 MacIntosh SE computers on tables around the perimeter. Four tables have been pushed together in the center of the room, so students have plenty of space to meet and to work. This course has several phases to it. In a first one, students have opportunities to learn about the history, geography, and culture of the Middle East. At the beginning of this term, James accompanied his government classes to Washington, D.C., for the presidential Inauguration and some seminars, so a substitute teacher begins the first phase. When he returns, he resumes teaching the first phase, presiding over study hall, teaching his government classes, and coaching junior varsity wrestling.

James Kennedy and His Background

James grew up in Cleveland and attended Cleveland State University. He says he "wanted to be a home boy for a while." He was a wrestler in high school and later transferred to Ohio State University because of his wrestling interest and because he'd read about an exciting change in wrestling coaches there. In high school he had also always liked history. He says he was "a good student in high school with over a 3.0 average, but not valedictorian material. Academics weren't the *most* important things in high school life, but neither were they unimportant." He was fairly bright and enjoyed school; it was no struggle to go to classes, and he had good relationships with his teachers.

As an undergraduate in social studies education he remembers himself as a "kind of go-to-class, get-credit type of kid." He had a few options in his program, such as the choice of two cognate areas in the social sciences, and he selected political science and geography. He was also in a work-study program and remembers that he was a somewhat aimless undergraduate until he took his social studies education methods courses, where he really enjoyed the two professors who taught them. He also recalls that he spent a lot of his college career at the Ohio State student recreation center. "Then destiny stepped in," he says rather dramatically, "when in my junior or senior year I met my [future] wife in a training room there. She was a gymnast and I was a wrestler." When he graduated in June, she still had another year to complete. "Things fell into place for a chance to obtain a graduate assistantship in sports administration, so I scurried around, took the GRE, and applied to the program and for the assistantship. That assistantship finally did come through, but very late, but I was sweating whether I would do it if it didn't. We were married at Christmas, taking classes at the same time."

Following the completion of his master's degree in sports administration, a job opened in Cleveland running an athletic club. Several people warned James against taking the job, but undaunted, he applied and was offered the job. He and his wife were attracted to the idea of returning to Cleveland, so he accepted the job. However, he realized almost immediately the job was horrible; with extremely long hours and many responsibilities, this job was simply the wrong one for him. Simultaneously, he and his wife realized they had enjoyed life near Ohio State University more than in Cleveland, so in November he resigned, and they returned to Columbus. James substitute taught in many nearby high schools almost every day. He was hired as a long-term substitute teacher in Chester with the understanding that if the upcoming school tax levy passed, he'd be hired as a regular social studies teacher. It passed, and this is his seventh year at Chester High School.

James's Thoughts about Planning

James relies heavily on the notebook accompanying the simulation for his planning of much of this course. He was on the committee to redevelop Chester's graded course of studies for social studies (described in chapter 7), and he recalls, "I had the simulation notebook in front of me as I wrote that part of the graded course of study. It's *so* worthwhile, there's just no reason to alter it much. When I *teach* it I update it some every year through current events, but there's no real reason to deviate from their plan. Over past times I've learned some better ways of doing things than when I first taught it, and I know what I need to emphasize now because of what kids have trouble with, its potential, and how to realize it more effectively than the previous times. But, what would I change from the manual!" Following the simulation itself, he teaches more about computer skills in a brief unit he designed. He employs what he sees as some of the most useful computer skills because he sees them as "important—no, crucial—for these kids' futures."

James's notebook that accompanies the simulation is one and one quarter inches thick. It contains an overview, technical information, and many materials to photocopy and use as handouts or for reference. The first page says:

You and your students should regard this notebook essentially as a reference book. The book contains information on the schedule, the "steps of play," or things the students can or cannot do, technical information dealing with how to communicate, and background information on the countries, characters, and history of the simulation. You should expect to consult this manual at various times *throughout the entire exercise*.

Immediately, however, there are a variety of tasks that need to be addressed. Some of the most important things you will need to become familiar with include:

Subject Matters:
   What is our team assignment? (chapter 2)
   What is the scenario for this term? (chapter 2)
   With whom may each of the roles communicate? (chapter 1)
   Who are the people and what are their interests? (chapters 4 and 5)
Technical Matters:
   How do we communicate? (chapter 2)
   How do we prepare messages? (chapter 2)
   What is our ID and password? (chapter 2)
   How do we send messages that we have prepared? (chapter 2)
Process Matters:
   What should we do first? (chapter 1)
   What are we suppose [sic] to do this week? (chapter 1)
   Can we do this or that? (chapter 1)
   What are our options? (chapter 1)

Nowhere does the manual state that teachers *must* follow the advice in it. It does have many statements about how to keep the simulation going interactively among so many different schools:

Week One:
   Immediately sign on to the computer and automatically enter the AIC conference.
   In order for a school to be assigned a team(s) and become part of a simulation, the school must do two things:
      1. Transmit a message to MARKUS MUELLER confirming the number of teams you anticipate and your preference(s) regarding team assignment, and,
      2. Respond to the Discussion Item in the AIC Conference.
YOU WILL NOT BE ASSIGNED A PLACE IN A GAME CONFERENCE UNTIL BOTH OF THESE TASKS ARE COMPLETED.
Week Two:
   Team assignments will be sent out at the beginning of week two to those schools that have completed the two tasks from week one. The SCENARIO will be made available in an item in the AIC Conference. Some new role profiles and profile updates will be made available as items in the AIC conference. Each team is to submit a PRESS RELEASE reacting to the scenario.
Week Three:
   Each role is to TRANSMIT one message to someone on it's [sic] part of the COMMUNICATIONS MATRIX. Team matrices should be retrieved by using the appropriate VIEW command. (See page 1:18) (Interactive Computer Simulations Laboratory, 1993:1)

This simulation is one of several developed at the University of Michigan in its Interactive Computer Simulations Laboratory. The manual states the program's goals:

The Arab-Israeli Conflict Simulation is a political and diplomatic role-playing exercise. Its purpose is to immerse participants in the dynamics of national and international politics—and thereby help them to become aware of the complex nature of political reality. ICS [Interactive Computer Simulations Laboratory] enables students to experience actively, rather than observe passively, complex political activity. The goal is to make learning both profound and enduring.

James agrees with these goals and comments, "The amount of students' identification with their roles seems to vary some from one term to the next. It's unclear to me why that is, but sometimes they seem to almost feel things that happen to their character either in the simulation or in the real news in a very personal way. Sometimes they also seem to take it to heart when the country or group of people they represent has something happen to it."

He sees his role here "basically as a facilitator to make sure everyone is comfortable with the technology. The simulation teaches everyone the basics of telecommunications." Indeed, at times it is difficult to decide whether this course is about computers or about social studies because it is so well integrated.

Mr. Kennedy got interested in simulations through a nearby college. Chester High School was approached by the county's educational consortium to participate in a computer simulation project about the U.S. constitution with about a dozen schools in the area. The nearby college invited one teacher from the social studies department of each school to attend a one-day workshop about the project. Because James taught the U.S. government course, owned a computer, and was known to use a spreadsheet program for his grade book, Chester selected him. At the workshop, he says very animatedly,

I met Edgar Taylor [the director of the simulation laboratory] and Clancey Wolfe. They were very creative people and they knew computers as well. I was very impressed with their simulation, so we [at Chester] decided to go with it. At first, I had no class because we made that decision too late to get it in the schedule, so I recruited students out of study halls and gave up my planning period. We had some bumpy roads learning the technology, and at first we had just two computers and a phone line for a modem. I figured we could do a better job if we had advance notice and time, so we proposed it as a senior elective and added it to the computer lab. We started with two computer simulation courses a semester, and it got as high as nine or ten sections. One year I was department chair plus teaching nine sections of computer simulation full time. We revisited the graded course of study [see chapter 7]; there was a big push from the state department of education for more economics. So we rewrote the curriculum to offer computer simulations as an elective, and each spring we determine which simulation or simulations to offer.

I still use it because the content is taught in a very nonthreatening way. There's a kind of evolution to the course, and then it's *there*. Students tell me it's absolutely the most important course they ever took.

Realistically, I know the course is not for everyone, but it fits students who don't like sitting in a desk and being talked to. It's technologically nonthreatening, yet they can gain skills helpful for the future, primarily in telecommunications and word processing. They see they *can* do it, and pretty quickly.

The Computer Simulation Program James Uses

Because this simulation figures so heavily in James's planning, I examine its background and basic features in order to understand his practice. The Arab-Israeli computer simulation was the first one developed by the Interactive Computer Simulations Laboratory. Edgar Taylor, its director, originally taught a face-to-face course about Arab-Israeli conflict at the University of Michigan, and in 1974 he developed it as a computer simulation course. In 1984, it was piloted in secondary schools. Next the laboratory developed several other simulations as well. Each year they update the notebook accompanying the simulation. For example, in 1993, they replaced information on the George Bush administration with that on Bill Clinton's team.

This simulation is more complicated than many curriculum materials. It has four interrelated components: background information and handouts for students and teachers, information about how to use the simulation, the network that coordinates the simulation, and a news group for teachers to use to ask each other questions and trade information.

According to Edgar Taylor, schools involved in the simulation this term are located in Michigan, Alabama, Illinois, Ontario, Korea, Japan, Italy, Germany, Belgium, Mexico, Britain, Okinawa, Israel, Iowa, Ohio, Kansas, and North Carolina, although some of these are involved in simulations other than the Arab-Israeli one. Some schools in foreign countries are probably either "American" schools or schools on U.S. military bases. The simulation is one way for those students to remain in contact with other students "at home."

Entities represented in the simulation are the United States, the Occupied Territories, the European Union, the Palestinian Liberation Organization, Israel, Jordan, Saudi Arabia, Syria, Egypt, and Lebanon.

Teaching and Learning in James's Class

The class is split evenly among male and female students, juniors and seniors. Of the class-level split, James says,

I think the juniors might be working a bit extra hard so the seniors don't show them up. That's good, a little friendly and productive rivalry.

We'll see how they work together as they get into the actual simulation. I think they'll do fine. They're a more sophisticated and motivated group than some I've had, and they seem smarter, and especially for a first period class they seem well prepared, energetic, and a good group for this course.

Ten juniors and seniors have enrolled, and most are taking the course, as Ralph is, "because it looks interesting." Tony says, "Students told me you learn a lot but it isn't a boring read-the-book, listen-to-the-teacher, regurgitate-it-all-on-tests kind of course because of the computer simulation part." Carol agrees, but confides, "I thought this would be useful because I want to be a news reporter after college."

James, who is about five feet, seven inches tall, is wearing black slacks, a white shirt, and a tie today. He's 34 years old, has dark hair, and usually seems happy, energetic, and businesslike. He begins this first period class at 7:25 A.M. by saying, "In this course you'll learn basics of telecommunications with a computer. You'll be sending out your *own* messages, and you'll have a partner. Don't *one* of you take it all over; work *together*. Both of you should. That way if one of you is absent you can still send your message."

Then he turns to today's lesson, continuing the first phase, which introduces and reviews the history, geography, and culture of the Middle East. Students have thick photocopied handouts, and they occasionally underline or write on them. James walks them through the handout, pointing out significant matters. James conducts the review in a conversational manner, and students' responses are brief. "Yesterday we talked a little about the Balfour Declaration. What was that about?" Ralph responds, and James continues, "Yes, what about the Zionist conference 20 years earlier?" Edward says, "The Holy Land was sacred to all these different groups, and they kept having meetings to try to figure out how to settle the land issue—everyone wanted it and no one wanted anyone else to have it." James continues, "And what was the philosophical position of the West?" Carol says, "It shouldn't belong to any*one*." James responds, "Unless?" And Carol replies, "Unless it's also available—accessible—to others." "After World War I, who controlled this area?" asks James. Edward says, "The Ottoman Empire." "Yes," says James, "but we can't forget there were all these sects and groups of people wanting to control this. And that's what happens here. So you have Arabs against Israel, Jew against Moslem, but also Arab against Arab because they divided up the remaining land after partition. The next document and the McMahon Conference happened next. *In effect* they said that the British are encouraging the Arabs to overthrow the Ottoman Empire. One concern was that they would destroy the Holy Land as a way of getting even. In the meantime, unknown to the Arabs, what did France, Britain, and Russia do?" No one responds, so he continues, "Okay, this is when they decided to partition it up with some spheres. So on the one hand they're saying, 'Yeah, go ahead, overthrow the Ottoman Empire and we'll help you,' but partitioning was going on. President Wilson wanted freer choice. What was our role in World War I?" Ralph responds, "Late entry." James continues, "Yes. We had many fewer casualties. What was our role?" Edward says, "We were a long-time neutral." James goes on:

When Wilson gets into the war, here's what the British and French wanted: they wanted us to go in and reinforce. But Wilson said no, we have different goals there. *They* wanted to divide it up and we wanted freedom of choice there. I'm on page 4:37 of the handout toward the middle of the quote in bold type. Now, this is a significant number—more than 10 to 1, Arabs to Jews. This isn't important to commit to memory, but if you were an Arab at that time would you be very happy? So, Hitler starts in Germany (later on the page), and the Jews' numbers swell, and we get into partitioning. What does that mean, Jay?

Perhaps caught off guard, Jay responds hesitantly, "Separating into spheres of influence?" "Okay," says James, "What's going on as Jews are moving in?" Jay replies, "Take over jobs." "Yes," says James, "and what is your role as an American Jew?" Edward says, "Send money." James continues:

Are you going to have a difficult time convincing American Jews that Jews have been persecuted and need a homeland? They send money and buy land. Move along here to page 4:38. Now, here's the next important thing. Great Britain is designated by the League of Nations as the country mandated to set up a government. Remember, they were interested in partition. Later, they go to the U.N. and say, "Maybe we're moving too fast here. We need to slow this down." And you can imagine what the Jews felt! *Whoa*, you betrayed us! Two options were taken to the people of Palestine. One: shared power and a national council where Jews and Arabs would make decisions together. Not quite a federal system, more a confederate system where only a few powers would be held by this council. Option 2: partition into three entities—Jews, Arabs, and international. So, the Jewish people who make up less of the population are to be given more of the land. So the Arabs are going to balk and hold out for more land and thinking, more time and they'd get more land, when the U.N. decided, and the next day Israel announced its independence. So on the *next* day, Arabs go to war, and what happens?

Carol says, "Kick butt!" Tony asks why this happened. James says, "Israel has always been keen on self-preservation. They have an army; the Arabs aren't as technologically advanced. Later, Egypt started to become more advanced and the Camp David accords were signed (getting ahead of ourselves), leading to what?" Edward responds, "Sadat's murder."

James goes on, "Egypt had 53 million people—3 million less than France, 4 million less than Great Britain. Anyone want to hazard a guess about Israel?" When Tony queries, "Half a million?" James says, "Four million, roughly a tenth. Saudi Arabia is second, Jordan about the same as Israel." Carol wonders, "What about Iran and Iraq?" James responds, "They don't participate in this simulation. They were never major players. When the Gulf War started, what was it about?" Edward reminds everyone, "Kuwait." James continues, "Remember, when we sent the Patriot missiles there, why did we send them?" "Israel," replies Carol. "Why?" asks James. "It was geographic. The Scuds were going there," says Carol. "Look at the map. Where is Israel? Why did Saddam Hussein send the Scuds there?" asks James. Edward says, "Holy War." James continues, coaching them about the upcoming simulation,

---

All the things happening right now can be used in your simulation, but remember this. It's just a simulation. It doesn't have to duplicate reality. You need to *create* a reality based on history, our fabrication, so to speak, creating your own path. Hopefully, part of the past will surface such as the 400 Palestinians recently being kicked out of Israel. Don't get preoccupied with *peace*. There's a term called "state craft." Anyone ever hear that? We are *so* far from peace here that we can't bring it about at all soon. What the diplomats are trying to do is move beyond this state craft to figure maybe we'll have peace in some decades. And don't get preoccupied with *war*. Yes, you'll have to threaten sometimes and make alliances. So we'll be making some small steps toward peace. Have all of you read through those documents [in the handouts]? If you haven't please do. This is just a whirlwind tour to highlight significant events. It probably has a Western perspective. In our next phase we'll learn some about the computer and develop some national goals depending on the country Michigan assigns us."

On the next day James continues the review in much the same manner, talking briefly and students responding curtly. However, today James starts by reading part of an article in the local morning newspaper reporting that Israel would provide its recent deportees with cellular phones to ease their consultation with lawyers. He also says students are to turn in a folder with at least 20 articles about the Middle East, including comments. It is due two months from now, on March 19, but he adds, "You can certainly turn it in sooner!" At the end of this period he says, "One question, before we wrap it up here for today. These are our choices. I've never made a request to Michigan before, but if you had a *choice*, which country or group would you want us to be? Personally, I have no great desire to play the U.S. because last semester's class was the U.S. Do you have any strong notions of what you'd prefer if we could have a choice?" Carol offers, "The European Community," and Edward, "The PLO." Edward's suggestion is met with some enthusiasm by others. James closes by saying,

---

All right. That gives me *something* to go on, but I'd like you to give it more thought. I'll ask you again tomorrow. Here's what else you'll need to be thinking about. What I need to know is who you'd like to have as a partner. At first, I didn't ask students this. I just assigned them, but some pairs didn't get along. So you need to write me a note and say who you'd *like* to work with and who you *can't*. But you'll put me in a bad position if you give me only one choice. For the next two days we'll be watching *Exodus*, then on Monday we'll practice on the computer about its keyboard, some of its commands, and how to boot up the disks. Then we'll still have a chance to work.

For the next two days they watch an abbreviated videotape of *Exodus*, taking notes and talking briefly about events leading up to matters depicted in the film. Some also trade titles of novels they are reading about the Middle East.

During a second brief discussion many seem to support assuming the role of the PLO. For the most part, students have written notes saying they could work with anyone in the class, so he makes the assignments. They learn how to turn on the computers, boot up disks, and then play several computer games to familiarize themselves with the computer's keyboard and commands.

On Monday the class learns they have been assigned to be the PLO for the simulation, and students rejoice. They also receive a message from Le Monde, the voice of the Michigan simulation laboratory that provides the "truth" for the simulation by setting its conditions. They find the message confusing, for (unlike what is occurring in the "real" world) it tells them Israel has permitted the 400 recently exiled Palestinians to return. James also asks them to read about the various PLO roles included in the simulation with their partners. They are to decide which role they would like to assume. He warns them that while being Chairman Yasir Arafat might be attractive, it also demands great responsibility. Students work cooperatively, discussing various roles but also eavesdropping on other pairs. In the end they arrive at a cooperative decision about which pairs will assume which roles. No pair has volunteered to be Yasir Arafat, perhaps because of James's warning. James asks which students consider themselves to be hard workers. Edward is the only student to raise his hand.

On Tuesday they move to the next phase: the simulation itself. James formalizes role assignments agreed upon yesterday. Edward and Ralph and another pair volunteered to be the same character. Perhaps because of Edward's intense participation, James assigns them the role of Yasir Arafat, and they agree good-naturedly. Following this discussion, students immediately obtain their disks, and James begins by saying,

---

Let's turn computers on and get booted up. We need to send a message. If you have your original disk you had last Friday, you need to get rid of all those games you played on Friday. Throw 'em all away. Let's see if you know how to do that. That's your first step. How we doin'? Let me know when you're done. If you've done all that, open up template and see if you've passed your first test. Let's see how you do. We're gonna send our first response to an Item, so let's call it RES Item 2. Okay, how we doin' here?

He stands behind students as they work on their computers, looking over their shoulders and occasionally coaching someone. "*Now*, if I were gonna send this file for you, I'd know what it is," he says. "We're going to do three things today: ask for clarification from Michigan about Israel accepting the return of the 400 Palestinian exiles, send out a press release, and write Message Number One to Michigan. If you're sending out a press release you have to become the reporter. They want us to respond to a brief question: 'Is a resolution to the Arab-Israeli conflict in sight?' I downloaded this from Michigan before you got here today." He continues that his voice is a little off today, probably because of a cold he and his son share. Indeed, today James wears a warm Chester sweatshirt, and his son is with him for this first period class, after which James takes him to a nearby day-care center. At any rate, James confides somewhat huskily, "I hope I can get through all of this today with my throat the way it is. Let's start by you taking ten minutes to think about their question and write a response from your point of view." He directs Carol to send Message Number One. She starts thinking and composing her thoughts and ultimately sends this message on the computer:

On February 10, while reading over Item 14, we were quite surprised at the statement explaining that the Israeli government had allowed the 400 Palestinian exiles to return from Lebanon. We were under the impression that this conflict had not been completely solved, and that only about one-fourth of the refugees had been allowed to return. Since the Le Monde is our "bible," are we to assume that for the purpose of this simulation the Israeli government has backed down and allowed the Palestinians to come back? We would greatly appreciate a response to our confusion to this important matter.

Eagerly awaiting your response,
Nayef Hawatmeh of the PLO

James discusses strategy, how to work within the simulation, and its rules. For instance, he starts today by showing students his notebook. He says, "Information about other countries and characters are in here. Hopefully, others are staying in character, so they're referring to these materials. You can't ever tell, though. Now, remember, what happens if we see something in Le Monde?" Tony responds, "It's reality." James directs students, "All right, now I want you to get to your own computers." Pairs of students move to computers, dragging over chairs so they can see the screen together. He continues, "Go into Sent files and open it up; then open up the Action Form Template. Now, folks, I don't want us to write on this right now, but on the right column there's a scrolling symbol. Scroll it all the way to the top of the Action Form. Now, folks, look at the top of the form. This is the area my last class was weakest in. This is a way you can actually *do* something in the simulation." "Oh," he says, interrupting himself, "what's the big news from Israel today?" Myrna responds, "One-fourth of the Palestinians are allowed back in." "For how long?" continues James. "A year," responds Myrna. "Letting another country admit them, maybe, knowing it's only for a year?" queries James. "What's Israel's motivation here?" Edward says, "Avoid U.N. sanctions?" James continues, "Now, when you take action, it goes out to your mentor and security officer at U. of M., who would approve or not approve the action. Questions about the action form?" No one has any, and he continues, "At that point you need to close this file down and open up your transmit sheet: Mubarak." Tony asks, "Where's it at?" Another student shows him quietly as James continues, "You have to change this to our country and your character's name. Any time you have to send anything out, the first thing you have to do is say who you are. Usually most of your transmits go to only one or two people. Scroll down the bottom and see the list of code names. Those are all the people Mubarak can communicate with. *You'll* change these countries and code names now that you know who you are and that we're the PLO. Let's close this down. Now, get a sheet of paper so you can write down the directions for how to turn on the computer and send messages."

Students return to the large table for notebooks and write at the top of a page, "How to go on-line." Then all students cluster around James's computer. "All right," he says. "We turn the computer on. What we need to do is, if the hard disk drive is closed, we have to open it, so we double click to do that. Then we find and open the ICS folder. ICS stands for Interactive Computer Simulation. You double click to open it up. At this point, we're gonna open up the AIC double micro. At that point it asks what you want to do now. So then we'll open up the ICS. Now, when it opens, the first thing it does is ask you to capture this text. It's vital to save this. Does anyone in here have the same initials?" No one does, so he says, "Good. Okay, what we'll do is put our initials and the date. So just put February 2 and your initials. What we'll do with this eventually is just put it back in the saved folder. We've already opened up the macro, so we select it. What's the most obvious thing to do? The one that's highlighted is what the computer wants you to do, and if you hit the return key. Under *normal* circumstances, you'll then type in AIC: and the game number you've been assigned. It's usually 1 through 6. So here we go. We're now in Join ICS:AIC1. Now, today, the games haven't been turned on yet, so it'll dump us back to the beginning, but it says there are new messages for me." He quickly tells students how to download them in order; then he checks messages on the screen and reads them aloud: "I'll do my best to put Chester in the thick of things, Edgar." James types back, "Edgar, Thanks, James." They view other messages and James asks, "Who's got a disk ready to go with a disk of yesterday's messages we should send?" Myrna does, so James coaches her about how to transmit them, with classmates gathered around watching. Myrna sends the messages and then drops them into Sent files. Before ending the transmission, Ralph says he also has a message to send, so James coaches him through the process as well, although Ralph remembers a few of the steps Myrna followed. This time, other students are quietly chatting and reading. "Anything else to send?" asks James. With no responses, he teaches Ralph how to hang up the telephone link to end today's transmission. Students leave for their next classes. On the next day, the game begins.

For the next eight weeks a routine develops: Students enter, obtain downloaded messages, cut them apart, and pass each to the pair who has assumed that role. The group agrees to adopt a peaceful stance and work together toward inclusion in a peace conference. They share and discuss their messages. James reminds them on several occasions to be sensitive to the fact that others, such as the Occupied Territories, also believe they speak for the Palestinians. On occasion, a pair may send but receive none in return. However, for the most part, when a message is sent a reply is received, if not immediately, within a few days. Students typically refer to the simulation notebook's communication grid to determine with whom can they communicate in terms of other characters and countries and those characters' titles. Then partners discuss strategy, compose messages commenting on events within the simulation, and try to make alliances. Finally, they run the spell-check part of the program. Supervised by Mr. Kennedy, one student usually transmits everyone's messages in a frantic few minutes at the end of the class period. For example, early in the eight weeks, Yasir Arafat sends this message to the European Community:

Greetings President Mitterand!

It gives me great pleasure that Israel has decided to allow the Palestinian deportees back into the country. Could this be a sign that Israel is finally showing a willingness to compromise? Now that it is legal for Israelis to talk with Palestinians perhaps the negotiations can continue and hopes that you and the rest of the EEC help back these talks.

Inshallah,
Yasir Arafat

Arafat sends this to Lebanon:

Chairman Berri,

Greetings from the PLO. The political climate is changing here in the Middle East. The recent victory concerning the Palestinian deportees shows progress for our cause. We honor you and your position on the situation. You are truly our brother.

In the past our organization has been based in your country and you showed us support for the notion of a PLO representative at the forthcoming peace conference.

Inshallah,
Yasir Arafat

Edward Said sends a message to Rubenstein of Israel, whose reply seems belligerent, so Said comments on the unproductive nature of such statements and receives this message in return:

Said, PLO

First, I would like to apologize for my last message, for I did not think it had an agressive tone. Second, I would like to start having talks with you. I can assure you that I will do my part in the negotiations on the settling of your homeland. The Prime Minister also agrees with me on this. I can say personally say that we are considering to let you use some of the land [sic].

Rubenstein,

Israel

Future messages continue to be belligerent one day and calm (but misspelled) the next. The Said pair discusses whether this is a planned strategy on Rubenstein's part or if the waffling is due to arguments between members of the Rubenstein pair. The Said pair decides to try to maintain their own position whatever they hear from Rubenstein. Further, several receive messages implying that the PLO and especially Yasir Arafat are terrorists.

The group also decides Arafat's reputation may be hampering the PLO's move to initiate movement toward peace talks and their inclusion in them, so they develop a press release, added to during the eight weeks:

On the third Monday of last November I was fortunate enough to be able to meet with Yasir Arafat, the Chairman of the Palestinian Liberation Organization. On this cool sunny afternoon I talk to the man about his life. He lived his life feeling that Palestinians had a right to their own homeland and when the Zionists were permitted to have one his desire for a Palestinian state was magnified. At the age of 18 the war between the Arabs and Israelis raged. Arafat had been living in Jerusalem and was forced to flee. "My family walked through the village of . . . Deir Yassan . . . what a massacre! Finally we reached Gaza. We were exhausted and destitute [sic]." It was upon his arrival that he dedicated his life to the establishment of Palestine. Now at the age of sixty-three Yasir Arafat is wiser, more experienced, and still working for his cause. "I have worked for Palestine all my life and with the support of my Arab brothers I feel the establishment of a homeland for my people is inevitable." Stay tuned to further editions of THE LIFE AND TIMES OF YASIR ARAFAT.

One day during that eight weeks, Chester has a snow day and school is canceled. On the next day, before class begins students talk about how they spent their free day—studying for a trigonometry test, fretting over another student's operation, and reading for various projects, including the one for this class. James shares the sledding adventures he had with his son. Class begins with James saying, "Things are really starting to roll hot off the presses now! Usually things that are private messages get personal attention. I've already seen one private message that'll stir some emotion, but don't get carried away. We'll do the press releases first. Carol, will you serve as town crier of the day?" Carol says, "Sure." She reads the first press release and then asks whether she should read the one the PLO sent recently. James responds, "I think everyone basically knows the content of that one," so Carol reads the other five press releases. James continues, "When the press release goes out you normally get a message saying the NSA (national security agent, appointed by Michigan as one of its staff members) received it. If you get a personal message, I've found the easiest way to respond is merely to respond. You won't use the reply. Due to downloading time, you'll just send a new message. In the future I'll cut away these little tags that the messages were received. I'll get some little glue sticks here. The message I think'll upset you is from Israel to Said." He reads aloud the threatening message, which says:

We do not wish to have any confrontations with you. We ask that you remove yourselves from our lands and the talks from the UN delegations. If you do not, we'll be forced to take action against you. We do not wish this, but if we have to we will be ready.

Rubenstein

Edward erupts, saying, "What're they gonna take action against? *We* don't even have a country!" James continues, "What I want you to do today is look at our goals so that everything we do will be aimed at those. Write down what you think are the most important goals so we can have a discussion tomorrow. Folks, next week is Michigan's break week, so they ask you that you not send anything then." Students reread goals stated in the simulation notebook and then begin writing their own. The Said pair responds to Rubenstein by critiquing the tone of his message yet again; they wonder if Rubenstein is schizophrenic because of his recent wavering from peaceful overtures to belligerence. They send out the only message going out today. Then they return to the large table and write their three goals. "You'll really have to be ready to send everything *this* week because the mentors won't be there." Students gather belongings and leave for their next class.

On another day, James begins class by selecting Todd as the town crier of the day. Todd reads the Occupied Territories' request for the PLO to engage in terrorist activities. James suggests continuing to "look like the good guys by using great restraint." Todd continues that the Clinton administration today called the recent press release from the Occupied Territories concerning eight deaths in the Gaza Strip a hoax. The Occupied Territories claimed they were shot to death by

Israeli militia and called for retaliation. The Clinton administration stated it was "simply a lie." Students notice the item about the shooting was not from Le Monde, so they decide it was probably suspect and talk for a while about strategy. James says, "The Golan Heights is an area wanted by Syria and by a Palestinian state with some agreement about no arms to be acceptable to Israel. It might be a way to create an armistice so countries won't keep rearming, which is a financial drain on many of them." He announces that he won't be here tomorrow because of a statewide wrestling meet and that the substitute teacher who started the class for him would return. He makes sure Todd and Edward know how to download messages for the class and reminds everyone to work on their articles and make sure they know how to sign on. "That's a testable item before the end of the nine-week grading period," he warns them, before sending everyone to the computers. Students work again in pairs and send messages to various people about the Occupied Territories' claim. Near the end of the period he talks about high-speed modems and their use in the statewide lotteries as well as recent changes in computers, their costs, obsolete functions, and innovations. Students send messages, gather belongings, and go to their next class.

On Monday, upon his return, he begins class with more news from the Occupied Territories, which have now developed more involved plans, including a new proposal dealing with Palestinian rights. He says,

"Those are *other* Palestinians writing that, so you should read it and develop a response. What would you feel about Israel withdrawing from the Gaza Strip and turning it over to the Arabs? In the paper this morning it said the Arabs weren't in favor of it because it would create tensions among the Arabs, so it was thought of as a trick. And this morning President Clinton and Prime Minister Rabin announced they'll give part of the Golan Heights back to Syria. So what looks good on the surface is sometimes lots more complicated. So maybe we need to start preparing ourselves and others for self-rule so it won't be anarchy after some kind of peace plan. That gives you an idea of what is happening in the real world. Be sure for the simulation to respond to the serious peace plans other groups have suggested, such as the one from the Occupied Territories. One word of caution, though: We have eight days until the nine-week break and nine people to quiz about signing on. I told you a week and a half ago you could do it as many times as needed if I had time, but we're running out of that kind of time now."

Edward takes the quiz and receives a 95 percent. "You could have done that a bit quicker," says James. Carol has already taken the quiz and received 100 percent. Myrna also takes the quiz and gets a 95 percent.

Things continue relatively normally. Students enter and leave; one student a day is the daily town crier; James discusses current events in the real world; messages are sent and received about planning a peace conference. Then, one day in May, James enters from hall duty and says dramatically, "You're being set up. You're being set up. You're *absolutely* being set up." Jordan has suggested the PLO undertake small terrorist activities against the U.S. Sixth Fleet. "We have to take action if we want to control our own destiny," he continues. "Maybe we have to say something like the U.S. is not really interested in peace, so they should keep their bathtub toys out of our area. Jordan is organizing a boycott of all U.S. products. They'll use this second message [calling for a boycott]. If you react to the first one [about terrorism] you need to explain to them. Maybe you should send the whole thing out for world opinion. Send it out the same way you received it. You let all know about what you've done about denouncing terrorism. Someone in the delegation has to turn just to the Arab nations. *Everyone* needs to denounce what Jordan's doing. The Sixth Fleet is absolutely powerless to act unless Israel is attacked. So the Sixth Fleet isn't really a threat. You're going to be manipulated—Jordan will deny everything." Students get into their pairs at a computer and send out both private messages and a press release questioning whether Jordan is trying to sabotage upcoming peace talks.

The group meets and decides to continue to have a peaceful and positive attitude in all messages, but to add a public relations element through some press releases. For example, Berri communicates to Hawatmeh of the PLO, who replies to Berri:

Mr. Berri,

I understand that in the past you have had reservations about supporting the Palestinians in our fight for independence. I sympathize with these reservations, for you have given much to us and unfortunately we have give little in return. I am writing this message to ask you to review your present opinion of the Palestinians and listen to our present goals with an open mind. At this time, the PLO hopes to re-establish Arab states diplomatic and financial support for the PLO and their commitment to goal [sic] of Palestinian state, the PLO also hopes to overcome the standard which bars our organization from an active role in Middle East peace talks, hence becoming recognized as the sole representative of the Palestinian people. The methods the PLO plans to use to achieve these goals are one of a peaceful origin; we realize that violence will only complicate this delicate situation. I would appreciate any support and understanding you could provide for us; however because of past grievances, I can understand your hesitance. Please respond to this and let me know of your reaction.

Always in peace,
Mayef Hawatmeh

They work until the bell rings signaling the end of the period, and Edward hurriedly transmits the messages.

In the end Arafat is invited to an uneventful peace conference where virtually no progress is made. Edward says he learned through the simulation that "peace is going to take *decades* to achieve there, and I don't think there's much the United States can do to hurry it up. If we did it would just lead to problems like Nassar's murder. And I practiced word processing and learned a lot about telecommunication. That's exciting." Carol agrees and adds, "What's happening in Bosnia is probably something that'll also take a long time to resolve, but the world seems to want a quick fix. It just doesn't work like that. These problems have a long history and take a long time to work out because of hatred, memories about what's happened to your family, teaching of hatred, and traditions. I agree with Edward—telecommunications is *really* exciting! I was a little intimidated at first, but *not* now, and that's good."

As I followed this case, I became interested in how and why other teachers used this simulation, so I sent eight questions to teachers involved in this simulation via a facilitators' news group. A few teachers responded. One teaches at an overseas U.S. military high school where the simulation is offered as a course in itself to tenth- to twelfth-graders. She likes it because in her view it gives students an opportunity

> to learn about and use skills of the "real world," to be self-directed, to make their own decisions, to "think on their feet," to learn to work through these conflicts using their own thoughts and decisions, to communicate with schools all over, and to be successful even when they are not told exactly what to do and what not to do. Some really eat this up, others ("the sheep") never catch on.

She reports she was hired to teach this and many other things and that she teaches seven different classes a day. She ends her response with an enthusiastic, "I LOVE IT!!!!!!!!"

A teacher in Canada, at a public high school where the simulation is offered as a part of an elective senior advanced course in twentieth-century world history, believes that the chief purposes of the course are

> to learn more about the Middle East, to realize and hopefully understand the intricacies and frustration involved in diplomacy and conflict resolution, to apply the skill learned through the action form to other historical events (e.g., Cuban Missile Crisis, Gulf War, Vietnam) and to learn more about using computer technology. The major skill I can see is the ability to think (while this may sound simplistic, they had to look at a situation, resolve their understanding of it, and communicate that to their contacts). The other major skills developed dealt with clear communication (in diplomatic language), and the ability to initiate action as well as reacting to it. An understanding of all sides in the Middle East was, at least partially, achieved. I like the interaction that is obvious as the

simulation moves along. I also appreciate the depth of understanding the class seems to develop about the situation in the Middle East. They now seem to be more willing to look at all sides of a situation rather than basing a decision on one line of reasoning.

Whereas the teacher at the overseas school was hired to teach the simulation, this teacher heard about it from a history consultant and was asked to try it if interested. After being promised support about computer use, this teacher agreed to try it, confessing to having been "a computer illiterate when I started." Like James, this teacher's first class was small, with just nine students, and the first time through the simulation program was not as active as possible, "but as I became more comfortable with the programme, my succeeding classes became much more so." As a final note, this teacher says, "The class took ownership for the simulation as evidenced by their reaction to messages and press releases received. If they were threatened or insulted THEY were threatened or insulted." A third teacher in Iowa echoes these themes, but heard about it from a teacher at a state convention and decided to use it. This teacher particularly liked the amount of involvement required of students.

Some themes, then, are common among teachers using this simulation. It is typically offered to seniors, although some juniors also take it. These teachers perceive its strengths as involving students in decision making, developing thinking skills, learning about computer applications, and learning more about the Middle East as well as conflict resolution. Students in James's class would agree. Perhaps the main idea here is that *students*, not *teachers*, use this simulation. It should be noted that students in James's class did not "wear" the culture of the Middle East in the simulation. Although they applied historical events on occasion, their thinking had a Western perspective.

Following the actual simulation, a three-week debriefing period takes place during which students shed their simulation identities and discuss them and other matters with one another. Several students from Chester make plans with those from nearby states to attend concerts, and the Jordan team denies having tried anything underhanded in the simulation. Of the simulation debriefing, James says, "It was fun. They did a pretty good job of responding to it and writing to one another. A couple of schools weren't involved in it at all, but that's fairly normal. I think some teachers don't see its value, so they ignore it, and that's too bad, because it's valuable."

Finally, in the last three weeks of the term, James teaches them about some uses of computers other than the electronic communication and word-processing functions he developed in their unit. They make posters advertising a meeting at the high school and learn how to use a spreadsheet to display data. For the latter project they construct a spreadsheet to display data using statistics on Chester's baseball players obtained from the coach. James begins by passing out a sheet about each individual player to each student. In alphabetical order by

TABLE 4.1 Summary: Components of these teachers' curricula

Teacher—Elementary School (chapter 3)	Major Elements of the Explicit Curriculum	Major Elements of the Implicit Curriculum
Iris	Space exploration and other science matters Language arts, mathematics, and health	Science is important The scientific method Working independently and perseverance are crucial in learning and success Self-confidence Some knowledge is objective; other has to be constructed
Karen	Language arts Mathematics, health, science, and social studies	Many exciting, important, and humorous things are contained in children's literature Language arts, particularly reading, is important Some knowledge is objective; other has to be constructed
Mark	Mathematics Language arts, science, social studies, and health	Questions have objective answers Someone of their (working-class) background can go to college and be a teacher Hard work pays off Men can be as concerned about children and education as women Mathematics is important Basic knowledge is important Self-confidence

Teacher—Secondary School (chapter 4)	Major Elements of the Explicit Curriculum	Major Elements of the Implicit Curriculum
Hascal	Geometry, some remedial algebra as needed	Logical thinking Gay people can be as good as straight people Hard work is necessary and pays off
Jill	Visual arts: graphics, drawing, printmaking, painting, art theory, and art history	Creative thinking is important A unique personal style in art key to success
James	Uses of technology, skills needed in those uses Reasons for and the nature of the Arab-Israeli conflict, related history and culture	Technology is useful for learning, organizing, and communicating information It's important for people to learn how to work together and to do so Self-confidence Men can be caring parents

Chester baseball player, they take turns reading aloud the data on their sheet as all enter the data on the spreadsheet. They end class by comparing players' statistics and storing the data, and then James dismisses them for the summer. In this final section of the chapter I summarize these cases.

SUMMARY AND DISCUSSION

I began this chapter with a case study of Hascal Legupski, a geometry teacher. Partly due to pressure from his department chair, Hascal plans by referring to the textbook adopted for this course. However, because his expectations are higher than the rest of his department, he has to reteach some algebra and basic arithmetic on occasion. Students say they learn geometry, thinking skills, and tolerance for people who are different from them by taking this course with Hascal. Jill Richardson, the teacher in the second case, teaches drawing in a high school in a more affluent town. She emphasizes developing individual creative styles, techniques of drawing, and use of various media. Jill plans by deliberating about discipline-based art education, current trends in the art community, and what has worked well in the past. James Kennedy teaches social studies in the same school. A significant outcome of his teaching is computer applications as well as learning about the Middle East. During the simulation itself, James's plans revolve around the simulation notebook, although he's also very attuned to current events in the Middle East. Following the simulation he plans by referring to a unit he developed about other computer applications. Table 4.1 summarizes what students in the elementary case classrooms (in chapter 3) and in the high school classrooms (in this chapter) had opportunities to learn.

The three high school teachers talk more about the content they teach and less about the students and milieu than do the three elementary school teachers in chapter 3. Jill and Hascal, however, do talk about individual students. All six teachers discussed their personal conflicts about planning, their frequent selection among many alternatives, and other features of solo deliberation. At the risk of being overly reductionistic, I display some elements of their planning in Table 4.2.

STUDY QUESTIONS

1. To be sure, not all teachers are as excellent and professional as the six depicted in chapters 3 and 4. Some seem to be satisfying mandated curriculum objectives, keeping their noses clean, and collecting their paychecks. Students seem to learn little in many classrooms and are bored and impatient. In keeping with the spirit and theory of this book, explain what can be done about this dilemma.
2. How do Hascal's feelings of being different influence his practice? What else influences his planning? How do these interrelate?

TABLE 4.2 Characteristics of these teachers' planning processes

	Salient Features of Planning	Major Influences on Planning
Karen	Starts broadly with examples of children's literature. Mostly plans interactively	The nature of each children's book. Iris's ideas about science
Iris	Starts with understanding her students. Develops general plan, elaborates interactively	NASA space workshop ideas. Karen's ideas about children's literature
Mark	Starts with goals about mathematics and language arts; elaborates interactively	Discipline problems. Students' possession of few language arts and mathematics skills
Hascal	Starts with textbook	Department chairman's view of expectations. Students' not possessing prerequisite skills. Feeling different
Jill	Starts with theory of DBAE. Consults and updates notebook of ideas	Impending outcomes-based policy. 42-minute periods
James	Primarily starts with notebook accompanying program he uses	The program he uses and its schedule. 42-minute periods

3. Compare and contrast Hascal's methods of control with those of Mark Schaefer (chapter 3). What accounts for these differences and similarities in your view?

4. What does Hascal's case imply about whether homosexuals should be permitted to teach?

5. Compare and contrast Jill's and Iris's practice. What accounts for similarities and differences?

6. Compare and contrast Hascal's and James's reasons for heavy reliance on curriculum materials.

7. Just as social class affects practices described in chapter 3, the same is true in the cases in this chapter. How does this occur?

8. The organization of the middle school differs from that of both the elementary and the secondary school. How might this organization influence the deliberation practices of the middle school teacher and cause them to be different from what was depicted in chapters 3 and 4?

9. Which of the six cases in chapters 3 and 4 troubles you most? Why?

NOTES

1. As is true of other cases, I have changed names and some insignificant details to mask identities.

2. I am grateful to the Department of Educational Policy and Leadership in the College of Education at The Ohio State University for granting me a ten-week research leave and to students, teachers, and administrators in Maple City and Chester who collaborated

with me in this research. Without this support it would have been impossible to learn what I did. These people know who they are and have received a copy of the book as well as earlier drafts of pertinent parts of chapters to check their veracity and whether I maintained their anonymity.

part **III**

Group Deliberation

This part of the book contains three chapters that present the theoretical literature and examples of how people develop the curriculum in groups.

chapter 5

Group Deliberation about the Curriculum

$\mathbf{I}$n addition to solo deliberation, a second occasion for curriculum deliberation is group deliberation.[1] Whereas solo deliberators develop an *individual* construction of their reality, group deliberators develop a *social* construction of their reality through a quest for intersubjective agreement. Hence, the social construction of meaning is a major focus of this chapter. Later I discuss in greater detail four interrelated characteristics pertinent to group deliberation: (1) simultaneity, (2) the social dimension, (3) normative interests, and (4) conflict. In this chapter I discuss each separately and also point out some interrelationships. In a third section I discuss the issue of the lack of linearity in deliberation. I close the chapter with a summary. Chapters 6 and 7 consist of case studies exemplifying many points made here.

THE SOCIAL CONSTRUCTION OF KNOWLEDGE

Group deliberation is a process making sense as the group seeks agreement, which is the foundation of the social construction of knowledge. During curriculum deliberation a group develops a set of agreed-upon (tacitly or overtly) interrelated ideas, values, and norms. The group focuses on beliefs and values about the content of schooling—what should be contained in the curriculum, its sequence, and organization. This process brings to the surface individual competing normative interests. Conflict among these interests ensues inevitably, tying the group together as it examines alternatives closely.

The primary feature of the everyday life through which we move is its social character. Each of us is one person among others, and we are bound together through the common influences we share, through work, and through trying to understand others and have them understand us (Schutz and Luckmann, 1973 and 1989). This everyday life has meaning to us through our culture (Bernstein, 1976:141).

Schutz contributed heavily to these ideas about our participation in the world. In Schutz's view, we interpret our life. Although the world has sense and meaning for us, we typically take it for granted. Our interpretation is socially derived because we live in the world with others, and thus our plans and actions mesh with those of other people, as when we work with them in curriculum deliberation. Obviously, we do not create such interpretations on our own. Some interpretations are handed down to us by our parents and teachers. Our language itself embodies interpretations. Through our lifelong interactions with others, we acquire and develop interpretations (see Schutz and Luckmann, 1973 and 1989). Schutz refers to *personal* views (such as teachers' theories of action) as "subjective" (see also Taylor, 1977). When groups deliberate to develop a curriculum, they actually create both a text and a subtext. The text is the curriculum they are developing, and the subtext is the set of agreed-upon norms and social rules for proceeding. The text and subtext are highly interrelated, as they influence each other greatly.

One way to think about solo deliberation is that it involves an individual (and hence, in Schutz's terms, subjective) construction of knowledge. That is, teachers experience many phenomena—events of their lives, professional discussions, coursework, reading about their subject matter, and teaching itself—and are constantly working to create meaning from them. This process lies behind the development of their theories of action. However, this process cannot be totally an *individual* one, because other people take part in our experiences and influence them. For instance, Mark Schaefer (chapter 3) and a third-grade teacher-colleague, Alan Root, recently had a brief discussion about their practice of having their students maintain journals:

MARK: I'm thinking of canning the journals. I want to use the mornings for math, and the kids come in at such odd times because of buses and the breakfast program. It's just a mess to do first thing in the morning.

ALAN: I use them first thing after lunch recess, and that works well for me. They come in and have something to do immediately to start the afternoon, and they know it because it's routine. Language is *important* for our kids!

MARK: Good idea. Maybe I'll try that. The kids *do* need their journals because of their low language development when they come into third grade here.

As this vignette illustrates, Mark reconsiders his idea to stop using journals as a result of his brief exchange with Alan. Mark and Alan frequently share ideas and materials they have developed; they look around in each other's rooms and ask what the other is doing. There is a friendly rivalry and some cooperation between them. Mark finds that it motivates and influences his work. To date, Bess, the other third-grade teacher, has not included herself in these exchanges, although in 1992 this school's third-grade test scores zoomed from last to first place among third grades in this school system. Mark believes it is mostly a result of this friendly rivalry between him and Alan, and even Bess has become motivated as well. All three trade worksheets and focus more on the content of mathematics (and more recently on language arts as well). Mark believes that focusing on it more and providing more extensive practice—with some of the practice as homework—have made the difference. Also, in 1993 the school system purchased a computer-based individualized mathematics program, and in 1994, $500 worth of mathematics manipulatives after sending these third-grade teachers to workshops to learn how to use them. While $500 is not much money for math manipulatives for three classes, the three teachers decided to order several different sets of items and to rotate their use.

Group deliberation follows processes similar to those of solo deliberation. However, in group deliberation, knowledge is built through group processes while developing the curriculum. It is *social* because individuals in a *group* develop a policy such as a graded course of study, a curriculum guide, or curriculum materials for an entire school system. Individuals bring with them their idiosyncratic (subjective) practical theories and normative interests. Thus conflict is likely to occur due to inconsistencies between them. While the group is engaged in a common purpose, these practical theories inform each individual's view of that purpose, the commonplaces, the roots of the curriculum problem, and its potential resolution. During the group process of developing the curriculum, a minisociety forms about values, the nature of knowledge, and ways of operating. By closely examining alternatives and engaging in conflict, the group reaches agreement.

When individuals meet, they could remain an aggregate rather than an actual group with a unique minisociety, as I have suggested. This might be particularly true if, as frequently happens in group curriculum development, they were appointed to the group by administrators. This is one reason for attempting to solicit volunteers rather than appointing members.

What are some important characteristics of a group? Cartwright and Zander (1953:48) argue that groups engage in frequent interaction, define themselves as members, are defined by others as belonging to that group, share norms about common interests, have interlocking roles and goals, identify with one another, find the group and its work to be rewarding, and act cohesively toward the external environment. These characteristics pertain in an ongoing group that is interacting and reaching agreement. McGrath and Altman (1966) add the characteristic of commitment to the group's task. I think commitment is germane because people develop it through the process of reaching agreement. Forming a group involves sharing norms about common interests, or, in my view, of developing agreement among individuals. Individuals cannot possibly act as a group until this occurs, even assuming that each individual still has his or her (subjective) practical theory of action. Because of this conflict between the group and the individuals in it, much group deliberation revolves around how to approach the task, given the various positions, particularly early in the process when people are starting to understand both the nature of the task and one another. This is why normative interests and conflict are so pertinent to group deliberation and, paradoxically, why the process of coming to agreement is so crucial. Obviously, conflict is less likely if the group has a common position from the outset, as evident in Cross's (1992) research.

In endorsing cooperative inquiry, Reason (1988) advocates an approach similar to deliberation. He argues that cooperative inquiry, like deliberation, is based on participation, a holistic perspective, evolutionary knowledge, reflective subjectivity, and knowledge in action. He suggests several skills necessary for cooperative inquiry, and I believe they are relevant to group deliberation as well: paying close attention to the experience as one takes action, managing anxiety that arises out of conflict, a genuine examination of the world, and working collaboratively on a complex task with a group of peers. People's experiences in groups are filled with tensions that arise from conflict and from questioning the world and the nature of knowledge. These tensions could easily provoke stress, which is deleterious to deliberation, as I discussed in chapter 1.

In her research about deliberation, Jung (1991) found that a major interest of the group she studied was the avoidance of conflict. Eisner (1990) more directly asserts that Americans tend to shun ambiguity, and that this is the most important factor inhibiting change because intolerance of ambiguity stabilizes society. Peck (1987) describes conflict-avoidance tactics practiced in groups. They range from fleeing the conflict through scapegoating, to resorting to the authority of the organization, to building a dependency on the leader and ignoring the existence of the conflict, to fighting and the formation of coalitions. Smith and Berg (1987) agree with Peck that groups cannot function effectively until they stop dwelling on simple conflict resolution and instead pay attention to groups and how members interpret the experience of group life (in an effort, I think, to reach agreement among group members). In Smith and Berg's views, a group and the individuals in it will not thrive unless it allows for the conflict or the ambiguous reactions evoked by group life. Puglielli (1994) found that the perception of difference (of virtually any sort) inhibits group work. Moreover, conflict plays the positive role in deliberation by virtually forcing deliberators to examine alternatives meticulously.

How can a group entertain conflict in productive ways so the conflict does not thwart its deliberations or destroy the group itself? One way to manage the anxiety of group life that arises from conflict is to change the perspective on group life from conflict to paradox. Smith and Berg (1987) identify three major categories of paradox inherent in group life; they suggest people can manage apparent conflicts by identifying the paradoxical links among them. This permits people to intellectualize the conflict and thus separate themselves somewhat from its emotional impact.

Smith and Berg's first category of paradox includes ideas of belonging related to identity, individualism, and involvement. In each case, group members may experience anxiety when struggling with what they have to sacrifice of themselves to belong to the group (and hence reach agreement). Through paradoxical reframing, people can see themselves as both creating and being created by the group. A group can become a group only if its members express their individuality, and so expressing individuality is important in forming a group. In this process of creating and being created by the group at the same time, conflict is supported. A safe emotional environment is created in which members feel they can make controversial statements. They understand their own practical theory of action and are able to express and defend it but not hold onto it rigidly.

A second category of paradox concerns engagement related to trust, disclosure, and regression. In each case, anxiety is intense because such issues emanate from the hidden, rarely acknowledged side of group life. Each person struggles with how open to be, how much of their inner self to reveal, and how far to go in suggesting a novel idea or one that seems at odds with others' ideas. This occurs as the group moves toward a willingness to trust and disclose. However, the person has to know the group well in order to feel sufficiently safe to risk personal disclosures. Paradoxically, the acceptance of oneself in the group depends upon the acceptance of everyone else. Group members need to view both themselves and other members as competent and as having an investment in the group. So, one paradox is that unless people feel comfortable in the group, conflict can probably not surface; yet, only genuine colleagues who trust each other can initiate, entertain, and resolve the conflict. People who do not value their own views, those of others, or the group's decisions may not raise contrary points of view. Thus it is crucial for individuals to become a group and to learn about one another. One clear example of this occurred recently in Chester (see McCutcheon in Marsh et al., 1990) where a group was redeveloping the curriculum for gifted and talented students. When I raised the matter of conflict as an interpretive lens, several rejected it because, in their view, "Other people on this committee are some of my best friends." Conflict is possible only among people who know and respect one another. Without such affinity, people are likely to disengage rather than feel comfortable enough to raise a contentious point.

Finally, a third category of paradox concerns authority and dependency. These paradoxes center around (1) individuals' struggling with the dynamics of influence, such as how to have a voice in the group, (2) how to speak with authority but not arrogance, and (3) being willing to compromise but not about absolutely everything. This category suggests the necessity of being a careful and reflective listener. One should word ideas thoughtfully, reflect deeply on values and ideas, and attend to supporting the group process as well as helping the group develop ideas. One should also help people understand the benefits of conflict in deliberation.

In both solo and group deliberation, an individual's work is purposive and therefore rational. However, merely because it is rational does not mean it is dispassionate. Because individuals and groups care deeply about their work, it is also passionate and thus frequently hotly debated in groups. Secondly, while groups may aim for holism, knowledge created in a group is selective because it is impossible to attend to everything simultaneously. Thirdly, both individuals and groups accumulate knowledge over time and develop a sort of cognitive map of organizations, which Sackmann (1992:140–142) separates into four overlapping categories. First is dictionary knowledge, comprised of sets of words and definitions, the content of situations (such as what constitutes a problem), and the semantics and signifiers acquired in a specific cultural setting. Part of shared meanings hinges on shared words and definitions. Second is directory knowledge, which concerns common practices and processes (such as how problems are solved). A third category is recipe knowledge, which is based on judgments and prescriptions for improving matters. Sackmann's fourth category is axiomatic knowledge, which includes reasons and explanations for the causes thought to underlie a problem or event. I think these categories may form an interesting basis for analyzing what occurs during deliberation.

Because a group is simultaneously becoming a group and solving a curriculum problem, groups take longer to solve problems than do individuals (Anderson, 1961; Fox and Lorge, 1962). Group deliberation may appear to be highly disorganized, particularly at the onset, because it is developing the subtext (group agreement) and text (curriculum) as it is becoming a group that is learning about one another and trying to define the problem and approaches to treat it. One significant benefit of group work is that it typically generates more alternatives and develops more creative solutions than individual work (Thorndike, 1938), perhaps because conflict arises from differences among individuals' subjective theories of action.

Social construction of knowledge and reality (Berger and Luckmann, 1966) occurs so frequently and naturally, and we are so immersed in it, that we take the process for granted. As a group engages in the process of discussing various phenomena, a coherence evolves between an individual's meanings, those of other members, and those of the group. In just this way, a group developing the curriculum develops its own meanings, language, processes, views about how to improve the curriculum, and explanations of matters underlying difficulties. In both solo and group deliberation, the curriculum developed is likely to be idiosyncratic since it grows out of that particular individual's or group's efforts and agreement and because it is tailored for the setting. While conflicts among people holding different normative interests are inevitable, it is important to continue to deliberate and keep the group's purpose in mind in order to resolve the curriculum problem under consideration.

It is useful to examine the nature and origin of group culture. Groups should be kept under 20 members to permit the face-to-face contact that allows people to become sufficiently well acquainted to develop trust. In this way, risks can be taken and conflicts develop. Large groups can be broken into subgroups to permit more intensive interpersonal interaction, as exemplified in the case study in chapter 7 about the development of a social studies graded course of study for the Chester school system. Two other important characteristics of groups are that they meet on a regular basis and that they share an identity or sense of purpose (also true of the case in chapter 7). I believe they develop that identity as they come to agreement about their social construction of reality. Ridgeway

(1983) suggests that each small group has a unique character recognizable to its group and to outsiders, and I agree.

In the case of curriculum deliberation, small groups are usually subunits of larger organizations, such as schools or school systems. These intermediate groups have the potential to influence both those larger organizations and individual teachers. The face-to-face interactions of these small groups form the context for the group's social construction of knowledge, which is important to individual members, to the group, and also to the entire school or school system.

Given the nature of group deliberation, group members should be people who can tolerate ambiguity and conflict and who are active listeners. They should question each other to clarify and extend ideas and should occasionally summarize each other's ideas before elaborating upon them. Further, they need to be people who can keep in mind the group's purpose and work toward that end. People who are arrogant or who personalize disagreements would probably not be as helpful in collaborative work. Finally, curriculum development by people who are genuinely interested in it is ideally the best. The best group would be one that consists of those with different practical theories but expertise in at least one of the commonplaces Schwab (1978) mentions.

The case I present in chapter 7 clearly exemplifies the development of agreement in group deliberation and its relationship to the curriculum developed.

FOUR CHARACTERISTICS OF DELIBERATION

There are four interrelated characteristics of deliberation particularly relevant to group deliberation: simultaneity, the social dimension, normative interests, and conflict.

Simultaneity and the Social Dimension

Simultaneity is the occurrence and consideration of several matters at once. In group deliberation, both the development of the curriculum and the group's development itself occur at the same time. That is, as they develop the curriculum, the group also establishes how its members will talk together; defines what kind of language it will use; and decides the most compelling issues, how the priority of issues is determined, how aggressively to argue for a point, and other similar matters. Additionally, each member appraises the others and learns whose ideas are valuable, powerful, consonant with their own, or in opposition to them. This is an important *social dimension* of group deliberation, for through it the group arrives at its particular knowledge and reality (see Berger and Luckmann, 1966)—a group view rather than idiosyncratic individual ones.

Since I have already discussed the social dimension subtext of group deliberation, I turn now to normative interests and conflict.

Normative Interests and Conflict

In group deliberation, each individual brings an idiosyncratic, "subjective" theory of action, as discussed in earlier chapters. People discuss many matters, including the commonplaces. Core beliefs from teachers' theories of action are inherent in them: the nature of the content, of the students, of the milieu, and of the teachers who will be using the curriculum. Aspects of one person's theory are likely to disagree fundamentally with another's. This is clearly exemplified in chapter 6. In many cases, those practical theories the individual wants adopted as part of the group's platform comprise a deliberator's normative interests. Teachers believe it would be easier to teach if the curriculum policy being developed or the materials being adopted were congruent with their own practical theory. Further, teachers believe their own theory is valid because of their direct experience with it. Thus they assume it would be in the group's interest to adopt it. Another normative interest might be an individual's desire to be promoted (perhaps to supervisor). Such an individual would like to gain the attention of an administrator present at the deliberations. These competing practical theories and normative interests conflict, forcing deliberators to examine alternatives closely. Conflict drives the deliberative process as individuals strive to move from personal (subjective) interpretations and platforms to one arrived at by the group. The case study of reading-textbook adoption in Mapleton in chapter 6 exemplifies relationships between personal theories of action and normative interests, and between interest and conflict. Is the conflict that arises in curriculum deliberations necessarily deleterious?

Nye's (1973) position is fairly representative when he considers conflict to consist of negative hostility between individuals or groups because, in his view, it can tear apart individuals in groups. Thus, he suggests avoiding and reducing conflict. To Nye, some people have a greater tendency than others to remain subjective, to select certain features of their surroundings for attention and to ignore others, to be rigid in adherence to their own subjective views, and thus to restrict their perceptions and thoughts to only certain approaches or information. I believe that subjective selectivity is prevalent. This reductionism is probably also involved when teachers construct their practical theories of action. Selective attention applies in particular to curriculum matters because of the lack of absolutes in education. However, I do not believe social conflict is necessarily deleterious because people in a group setting are forced to examine alternative positions more carefully than when deliberating alone or when unanimity exists. I would like to describe another position about conflict.

In contrast to Nye, Dahrendorf (1959) argues that conflict has several positive features and outcomes. In his view, it can establish unity in a group. The interdependence of antagonistic individuals whose positions conflict can actually "sew" the group together as they discuss their subjective idiosyncratic positions and closely examine alternatives. It prevents group disintegration and leads to group agreement. Moreover, in Dahrendorf's view, conflict can lead to pressure for innovations, creativity, and change, thus deterring the complacency arising from too much stability. In the long run, conflict in deliberations will not disappear, and it actually has great merit. As people resolve their differences, they construct knowledge and create agreement together.

ON THE LACK OF LINEARITY
IN GROUP DELIBERATION

Organizational theorist Senge (1990:12) describes systems thinking as his "fifth discipline":

> It [systems thinking] is the discipline that integrates the disciplines, fusing them into a coherent body of theory and practice. It keeps them from being separate gimmicks or the latest organizational change fads. Without a systemic orientation, there is no motivation to look at how the disciplines interrelate. By enhancing each of the other disciplines, it continually reminds us that the whole can exceed the sum of its parts.

Senge (1990:73) goes on to argue that reality is made up of circles, and when we see straight lines, we limit ourselves as systems thinkers and misunderstand reality. In his view, the nature of our language shapes our perceptions. The subject-verb-object structure of Western languages prepares Westerners for a linear view. Also, I think we view time as linear. Senge contends we need a language of interrelationships, a language comprised of circles, and systems thinking can yield this, for by using it we will no longer view the world as fragmented or in a linear manner. He urges us to perceive the whole rather than individual pieces.

The flawed linearity of Walker's (1971) naturalistic model described in chapter 1 may result from the linearity of language and its influence on his thinking as well as his linear thinking about time. Deliberation is simultaneous, with the process of both coming to agreement and developing the curriculum itself occurring at the same time, and so it is important to think about deliberation in nonlinear ways in order to understand it.

Senge further argues that our most powerful learning comes from direct experience, but organizations present the dilemma that "we learn best from experience, but [in an organization] we never directly experience the consequences of our most important decisions" (1990:23). Because organizations are frequently fragmented, it is important to help people see the whole of the enterprise and interrelationships among actions. A manager makes a decision, for example, and then workers are to carry it out. This may be particularly important in curriculum development where plans are made to develop knowledge, skills, and disciplines throughout students' school years and sometimes across several disciplines. One way of achieving this is to develop the curriculum by collegially constructing and sharing a genuine vision to prevent fragmentation. Just as it would have been impossible to build an AT&T, Ford, or Apple in the absence of shared vision, it is also unlikely a school system can educate in the absence of a genuinely shared vision. Senge believes a shared vision uplifts people's aspirations as the individual sees his or her work as part of a larger purpose embodied in the organization's products or services.

SUMMARY

In this chapter I have taken the position that group deliberation consists of knowledge that is built out of a process of group agreement. Because individuals hold different normative interests, this process is likely to involve conflict. However, conflict helps the group generate and examine alternatives closely, knits the group together, and in fact adds to the knowledge. How the group functions is probably as important as curriculum development itself in group curriculum deliberation. They interact, as Senge's work implies. As a result, members and leaders should support deliberation and understand it to develop agreements, tolerate conflict, and reflect on their normative interests.

STUDY QUESTIONS

1. In your own words, what is meant by the social construction of knowledge? Intersubjective agreement? What roles do they play in group deliberation? How are they achieved?
2. In what ways are solo and group deliberation interrelated?
3. What are some essential features of forming a group? What skills of group members might be most helpful in supporting group deliberation about curriculum?
4. What makes it difficult for large groups to engage in deliberation? What advice would you have for leaders of very large groups? Why is that good advice?
5. Why is group deliberation not likely to be unidirectional or linear?
6. What characteristics of groups are *most* related to deliberation in your view? Why?
7. What tips would you give and follow about how to create a healthy group environment where deliberation can prosper?
8. Group deliberation is probably best understood by engaging in it. Engage in it, keeping a reflective journal about how it does and does not resemble what I described in this chapter.
9. Analyze what Len did as the group leader in this case. Contrast and compare his actions to Judi's (chapter 6).

NOTE

1. I am indebted here to Gary Best and William Pasters for their thoughtful comments on an earlier version of this chapter and for their suggestions about reorganizing this chapter and extending my reading.

chapter 6

Adopting Reading Textbooks in Mapleton

I begin this chapter by discussing how adopting textbooks is a curriculum decision. I present other researchers' work about the extent of use of text material in classrooms and my own research into how teachers use textbooks and reasons for the extent of that use in an elementary school in a school system similar to and near Mapleton. Then I portray the process of group deliberation educators employed in Mapleton to adopt a new reading series, especially its conflicting interests. I close the chapter with a discussion and summary.

TEXTBOOK ADOPTION AS A CURRICULUM DECISION: THE EXTENT OF USE

For more than 60 years many teachers have relied heavily on textbooks as instructional tools. Inherent in these textbooks and their accompanying supplementary materials are goals because they contain and exclude particular sorts of skills, knowledge, and values. Thus they have the potential to greatly influence both the overt, the implicit, and the null curriculum.

In 1931, Bagley found that students in U.S. schools spent significant portions of the day on formal mastery of text materials. This still seems to be the case. Davis, Frymier, and Clinefelter (1977) found 78 percent of the fifth-grade curricula they studied to be associated with textbooks. Studies sponsored by the National Science Foundation indicated that science, mathematics, and social studies teachers rarely used the inquiry techniques of the curricula developed in the late 1960s to early 1970s. Rather, they relied on textbooks for the basis of the curriculum (Stake and Easley, 1979). These studies are but a few indicating a pervasive reliance on textbooks for curriculum decisions, and they support

Talmage's assertion (1972:21–22) that the textbook serves as the "arbiter of the curriculum of a school system."

This is particularly troublesome because the seven textbook companies with the highest sales are owned by large corporations whose motive is profit, not necessarily advancing sound educational approaches. Further, three states (Texas, California, and Florida) adopt textbooks on a statewide basis, and thus have a profound influence because textbook authors and editors sometimes modify their wares to qualify for adoption in those states (Black, 1967; Bowler, 1978), thereby ensuring large sales. As a result, the values held by textbook adoption committees in Texas, California, and Florida can influence curriculum on a national basis. The widespread use of textbooks, the profit incentive for publication, and the influence of three states on textbook content raise questions about how and why textbooks are used to the extent they are, the nature of the curriculum that results, and whether textbooks are appropriate vehicles for determining the curriculum.

THE NATURE OF TEXTBOOK USE: THE RESULTANT CURRICULUM AND REASONS FOR TEXTBOOK USE

A few years ago I examined textbook use in a local elementary school near Mapleton. In nine of ten classrooms studied in this elementary school, teachers relied upon the textbook, teacher's guide, and accompanying materials almost exclusively for ideas about what to teach and do during lessons. These nine teachers did not typically follow suggestions in the guide for enrichment activities, for they believed, as one teacher said, "we have to cover the *basic* material." Many of the enrichment lessons were more creative, open-ended, or active than were the activities presented in the basic part of the lesson. Most of the curriculum was passive, calling for convergent thinking, two-dimensional paper-and-pencil work characterized by filling in blanks (written and orally); it almost never involved students' personal experiences or interpretations. The general pattern of lessons was a teacher's lecture (or reading aloud) followed by recitation and practice in workbooks, in textbooks, on the board, or on worksheets. Homework consisted of reading parts of textbooks and answering questions on worksheets about the content. The curricula these teachers enacted differed greatly from those Karen, Iris, and Mark (in chapter 3) and James and Jill (in chapter 4) enacted.

After a search at central office, none of us could locate the school's policy, but teachers believed that since the school system had purchased the books, they were morally bound to use them since they did not want to waste taxpayers' money. Several also felt they had been subjected to pressure to use textbooks by peers who talked to the principal if they deviated widely from them, even though the principal took no action on the reports. The one teacher involved in this study who did not follow the textbook decided to transfer to another school system at the end of the school year. He did so largely because he believed the active learning he used in his practice differed so greatly from those of the other teachers that his students would have difficulty in subsequent years adjusting to the more rote work. Parents requested that teachers send books home with students on weekends, which may have added to the belief that textbook use was expected. Further, state law in Ohio dictates that textbook adoption be tied to the curriculum policy of each school system, and so these textbooks adhered closely to that policy. As a result, these teachers believed it was easier to use textbooks in order to meet the curriculum policy than not to use them. One teacher commented, "A great deal of information is gathered in one place for the kids and for me in these books." Another added, "They wrote a lot of good practice exercises for kids to do." A third said, "I know I have to teach *this* stuff. They've got it all nicely organized, so I might as well use it." Some of these teachers also believed that since they were written by experts, the textbooks must be worthwhile and trustworthy. "Look, a university professor authored this math text. It *has* to be current and sound!" said a first-grade teacher.

Moreover, these teachers were concerned about the articulation of the curriculum from one grade level to the next and believed the textbooks took care of this problem. They also felt the textbooks kept the curriculum uniform among all classes at the same grade level and indeed wanted all students in any one grade level to be exposed to the same ideas and materials, assuming the students would absorb this material.

The widespread use of textbooks in this school near Mapleton is also due to the backgrounds of its two previous principals. Neither had any elementary school teaching experience, and both referred teachers to teacher's guides of textbooks as the bible of teaching. Every teacher who'd been at the school for at least five years could cite many examples of this in almost all subjects. A teacher confessing a need to learn more about teaching reading, for instance, was directed by the principal to "go to the book storage room and pick up three or four teacher's guides for reading books. Study them. They'll show you how to do it quicker than any course at Ohio State can."

The curriculum in this school was organized by discrete academic disciplines along the lines of subject-matter-specific textbooks. Some teachers recognized this problem. For example, in one faculty meeting they were deliberating about the language arts program. A teacher asked, "Are we going to let the textbook authors dictate that we have separate lessons in reading, writing, spelling, and English?" When no one addressed this issue, she let it drop. Teachers rarely related a lesson from one discipline to that in another. Most student activities were of the paper-and-pencil, fill-in-the-blanks variety, calling for convergent thinking and "right" answers. Virtually no high-level thinking skills, such as analysis, interpretation, synthesis, or criticism, were required to do the tasks in these classrooms. Students did not construct knowledge here—they acquired it.

Textbooks appear to control the curriculum in these and in many other schools and classrooms based on the beliefs of teachers, administrators, and parents, as expressed here.

Apple (1981) discusses why such extensive use of textbooks is harmful and even dangerous by claiming that packaged curricula such as textbooks "de-skill" teachers. That is, they take responsibility for curriculum planning away from teachers. In my view, this occurs because, by adopting the ideas in teacher's guides, teachers deny their own practical theories of action and let others do the deliberating and weighing of alternatives about lessons. The teacher's guide provides all the "answers." Apple (1981) argues that the emphasis on skills is one reason why such packaged materials have caught on. Schools are increasingly held accountable by parents and the government for producing measurable outcomes. In his view, the consequences for both teachers and students of this form of education include diminishing the craft of teaching because the teacher no longer needs to plan a curriculum or individualize instruction. A commercial publisher plans a curriculum in explicit detail and the teacher's role is merely to execute the plan. Many packaged materials even specify what a teacher is to say (down to the exact words) and do. They relegate the teacher to the role of classroom manager. An extreme example of this can be found in the 1962 edition of the DISTAR reading kit's teacher's guide:

> Follow the presentation as closely as possible. Don't improvise on the presentation materials. . . . Don't introduce variations of the instructions. Don't wander off onto other tasks. Don't use the material as a point of departure for free-association teaching. And above all, don't become involved in lengthy explanations. The directions for each of the tasks are designed to explain by showing. Resist the impulse to "tell" the children. Chances are they won't have the faintest idea what you are talking about; you will unfortunately demonstrate that you cannot be relied on to clarify, that you only confuse. (Englemann and Bruner, 1962:12)

Since 1962 the authors of this guide have softened their tone somewhat, although the materials are still scripted. Clearly, textbook adoption decisions are important because textbooks control the curriculum in many classrooms because teachers deny themselves opportunities for solo deliberation when they accept what the guides say to do.

I now describe the case of the adoption of reading textbooks in Mapleton. In order to understand the context in which this occurred, readers are encouraged to refer back to chapter 3, Mark Schaefer, and to chapter 4, Hascal Legupski, both of whom teach in Mapleton.

ADOPTING A READING SERIES IN MAPLETON

A group of almost 40 people is deliberating adoption of a textbook series. The group consists of representatives from each school in the district and a teachers' association representative. The superintendent has appointed Judi Marienthal to lead the process. Judi has no training in curriculum development, but she does have training in human relations and educational administration. Her training and the respect many teachers have for her are two reasons why the superintendent says he appointed her. Judi says she sees her role as making sure the process follows the district policy and moves along speedily enough to ensure the new curriculum materials are in teachers' hands when school opens late next August.

The group meets after school, convening several times just after 4:00 in a large, dark room at central office to deliberate about which series to purchase. They follow the process developed in 1988 by representatives of the administration and the teachers' education association, shown in Figure 6.1, and the Mapleton curriculum/adoption study shown in Figure 6.2.

Leading this group is Judi Marienthal. Judi is in her forties and has a master's degree in educational administration and some training in human relations. In an effort to understand the thinking underlying what was said in the meetings I observed, I interviewed three teachers, Robin, Lauren, and Audey, who seemed very active in meetings and representative of views held by many members of the larger group. Robin teaches at Apple Lane School, where the faculty is developing teaching strategies and a curriculum based on the philosophy of open education. They use a whole-language approach to the language arts, employing children's literature and many writing activities in the curriculum as Karen Smith, described in chapter 3, did. Robin says, "Students learn how to be at home in their language by *using* it. We shouldn't artificially separate reading from writing, spelling, grammar, and so forth. They should all be integrated because when kids talk they're also learning something about listening, reading, and writing, and vice versa. These are all communication skills, so they *are* the language arts because that's how we communicate—through language. We shouldn't teach word-attack skills. English goes *against* phonics rules more often than it follows them. Students learn how to read by reading a *lot*. That way kids generate their own rules as they generalize about reading, not by memorizing and applying someone else's rules on worksheets and then transferring those to reading when they're reading stories and novels." Robin's practical theory, which concerns a whole-language approach, is evident in the contributions she makes to the group's deliberations. This practical theory also constitutes Robin's interest because it will be easier to implement a series adhering to this view than one that does not. It is in her interest to adopt a series based on such a perspective, such as the Holt series from Holt publishers being considered does.

Lauren has a somewhat different view. She believes that "children need exciting stories and factual articles to read. Kids here have very low language ability. I think it's because of their homes. I bet they rarely get to talk much at home. They don't go to the public library. We need good things for them to read and discuss so they will read them and practice language use."

Audey volunteered to work on this committee because she's interested in eventually becoming a supervisor or administrator. She recently completed a master's degree in mathematics education and thinks this committee will also help her understand reading better. Audey says, "Reading and math are really the most

THESE PROCEDURES WERE DEVELOPED IN COMPLIANCE WITH THE COLLECTIVE BARGAINING AGREEMENT, SECT. 1702.2, PGS. 111–112

INITIATE ADOPTION STUDIES:

Select content areas to study for adoption, based upon the Five-Year Curriculum Review and Adoption Cycle.

Make budget request for each content area, based upon Five-Year Curriculum Review and Adoption Cycle. Upon notice from the Superintendent/designee giving budgetary approval, call for committees.

A. MEMBERSHIP (each functioning committee):

1. Identify chairperson for each adoption study, designated by Superintendent/designee.

   ADOPTION COMMITTEE [To be filled in as appointments are made.]

   CHAIRPERSON: Judi Marienthal

2. Mapleton Ohio Education Association designee appointed by the President of the association.

3. Representative from each school, selected through the Building Curriculum Committee.

   a. High School: one bargaining unit member representing the subject area or affected course.

   b. Middle School: one bargaining unit member (per grade level) in the subject under study.

   c. Elementary School: one bargaining unit member per school representing grades K, 1, 2 and one bargaining unit member representing grades 3, 4, 5.

4. Notify publishing companies of content areas being studied.

B. COMMITTEE FUNCTIONS:

1. To review and recommend for adoption textbooks and/or instructional materials deemed essential to effective instruction in a given program and/or course.

2. To communicate to the affected building staff membership and administration via the building representative(s) about the identified task.

   Committee members are also responsible for finding an alternate if they cannot attend a meeting.

3. To communicate from affected staff membership to the study committee via the building representative(s) about the identified task.

4. To communicate in writing to and from the Central Curriculum Committee via the Study Committee chairperson/designee.

FIGURE 6.1 Procedures for district study committees: Textbook/ instructional materials adoption, October 19, 1988

5. To make adoption committee closure presentation to Central Curriculum Committee via chairperson or designee prior to presentation to the School Board.

6. To develop building level implementation procedures for Board approved adoptions by each building representative in cooperation with the building principal/designee.

C. COMMITTEE MEETINGS AND OPERATIONAL PROCEDURES:

1. To hold initial organizational meeting after school to establish timeline and process under which committee will operate.

   A tentative schedule of meetings and overall scope of the task to be accomplished shall be determined at the initial meeting of the district adoption committee and copies will be provided for each committee member.

2. The agenda shall be the responsibility of the chairperson of the committee.

3. Minutes of the meeting shall be distributed to all committee members and all members of the Central Curriculum Committee.

   The teacher's association designee will assume this responsibility.

4. Committee members will develop/adopt an evaluation instrument and use it to individually review text/materials under consideration.

5. Committee will screen and narrow selections to best 2–4 series, if possible.

6. Presentation meetings by publishers MAY be scheduled for all teachers and/or for the committee.

7. "Finalist" materials will be available for preview in the buildings for all teachers who teach the content area under consideration.

8. Teachers who choose to review the materials MUST complete a brief evaluation form for each series. If three series have been recommended, a teacher must complete a form for each of the three to have his/her "vote" count.

9. The study committee will collect all evaluation forms, tabulate them, and send out a formal notice of the results to all affected teachers.

NOTE: A procedure will be established for providing equity among staffs who have an imbalance of teachers who teach the subject (to be agreed upon ahead of time by the adoption committee).

10. The adoption committee will submit a formal recommendation to adopt a given series and/or appropriate instructional materials to the Central Curriculum Committee. The committee chairperson will submit the recommendation to adopt, which shall include the materials to be included in the adoption and shall identify the grades and/or courses which shall be included. Adoption recommendations must be in compliance with the approved budget.

   (See RECOMMENDATION FOR ADOPTION form.)

FIGURE 6.1 (*continued*)

D. ADOPTION PROCEDURES:

1. Adoption recommendations and sample materials will be submitted to the Board for perusal prior to formal Board action.

2. Board will take action on recommendation.

3. Director of Curriculum will initiate purchasing process. Schools will receive notice of what has been ordered for each building.

E. IMPLEMENTATION PROCEDURES:

1. Implement the use of the materials through in-service and/or other support activities deemed desirable or necessary. The adoption committee should address this issue and establish a procedure for working with each building representative in cooperation with the building principal or designee.

2. Following the Five-Year Curriculum Review and Adoption Cycle, a new committee will be formed to review outdated texts/materials.

PROPOSED TEXTBOOK AND SUPPLEMENTAL MATERIALS ADOPTION POLICY

Philosophy

The selection of educational materials, including textbooks, will be in accordance with state law. Textbooks and other educational materials will be used as tools for implementation of the curriculum and will assist the educator in attaining objectives specified in courses of study. Every effort will be made to select the best materials available recognizing that even the best have some weakness.

Objectives of Educational Materials, Including Textbooks

The primary objective of educational materials, including textbooks, will be to support the goals of the curriculum. Current educational materials will be available for teacher and student use at each grade level and for each course of study. Educational materials, including textbooks, will be selected to:

- Complement the educational philosophy of the Mapleton School District.

- Address the educational needs, competency levels, and learning styles of students.

- Provide factual information in relatively equal amounts for opposing views of controversial issues.

- Stimulate student and teacher interest in subject matter being presented.

- Insure access to a wide variety of ideas for students and teachers.

- Represent current educational trends as well as successful traditional methods of instruction and teaching styles.

- Fit the annual appropriation for textbooks and materials as approved by the Board of Education.

FIGURE 6.1 (*continued*)

164

Responsibility for Selection of Educational Materials, Including Textbooks

The Mapleton Board of Education is legally responsible for adoption of all textbooks and must adhere to Ohio Revised Code #3328.08. The Board also has the ultimate responsibility for all other materials used in the district's classrooms.

The certificated staff has professional responsibility for textbook selection. The master agreement provides the means for certificated staff input into curriculum and textbook selection.

The community has a responsibility to the students of the district to see that community values are fairly represented in materials chosen. Therefore, the Superintendent will inform the Board of the formation of any textbook study committee and the Board will appoint a board member(s) or community representative(s) to serve on the committee.

While district-wide textbook adoptions are not required, they are encouraged to promote educational equity, continuity of program, and financial efficiency.

Selection of educational materials not requiring formal Board adoption will be made by professional staff members through the PPbS [Professional Personnel benefit System] system.

Material requiring formal Board approval, justified through PPbS, or on file in a teacher lesson plan will be considered suitable. Any material not meeting these criteria, which the teacher believes may be sensitive, will be discussed with the principal or his designee prior to presentation.

Criteria for Selection of Educational Materials Including Textbooks

All educational material will be considered on the basis of:

1. Overall purpose—should address the objectives specified in each course of study and reflect district philosophy.

2. Student needs—should be challenging but address general learner needs, such as physical and emotional maturity, skill level, and learning style.

3. Teacher needs—should be compatible with and adaptable to a variety of instructional styles and preferences.

4. Community needs—should reflect high ethical and moral standards that foster respect for all people.

5. Authoritativeness—should reflect highest standards of professional field including background, education, experience, reputation, and previous work.

6. Authenticity and scope—should be reliable, complete, objective, and of sufficient depth and breadth to cover material and be appropriate for grade and age level use.

7. Content—should be well organized and follow a logical sequence. It should be interesting and aesthetically pleasing.

FIGURE 6.1 (*continued*)

8. Technical quality and cost—quality should be commensurate with the cost and appropriate for intended use.

9. Durability—should complement existing materials and be flexible enough to adapt to further use.

Record Keeping

The selection committee's criteria and evaluation sheets for all selected material will be kept on file in the district's central office for all district adoptions. Recognizing that much compromise is required to achieve agreement on materials selection and that there are not perfect materials, both strengths and weaknesses of the selection should be included.

FIGURE 6.1 (*continued*)

important parts of the elementary school curriculum, no matter what anyone says. If I can demonstrate to the administration that I know a lot about these two subjects I think I'll have a better chance at such a job than if I just show them I'm only knowledgeable about mathematics." She believes children learn to read "by applying different word-attack skills to unfamiliar words, so children need to have a healthy dose of phonics, context clues, rhyming-word families. They also need a *lot* of practice reading interesting stories." Her practical theory, which rests on children memorizing and practicing these skills as well as by their reading interesting material, is evident in her contributions to group deliberations. It is in Audey's interest to adopt a series stressing reading skills because such a series would be easier for her to implement than one with a vastly different approach, and she favors the Harcourt Brace Jovanovich series. Because of her career advancement aspirations, it is also in Audey's interest to learn more about reading and language arts and to demonstrate it to administrators.

At one meeting, scheduled near the completion of the committee's work, Judi places examples of all materials being considered on large tables around the room's periphery. She and I arrange the materials by publisher so supplementary materials (including colorful puppets, audio cassettes, books of various sizes and shapes, charts, workbooks, and tablets) are beside basic texts for each. Judi puts potato chips and dips out on another table, makes coffee, and sets out cups, creamer, and sugar. Then she places copies of the beliefs and recommendations statements the committee has developed in previous sessions on tables in front of the 40 chairs in the room. At 4:00 P.M., 35 teachers begin to enter. Some are chatting excitedly with colleagues about how the day went, sharing teaching tips, and commiserating about difficulties. Most deposit their belongings and obtain coffee or walk down a narrow corridor to a soda machine, returning as still others enter. Judi reminds them in a businesslike tone to look at the materials on the tables so they can vote soon. Most have already started doing this. They talk quietly and munch chips or sip soda or coffee as they look through the materials and make comments: "I like these stories. They're actually exciting for a change."

We recommend the following program for adoption by the Board of Education as instruction material for use in the Mapleton Schools:

PROGRAM TITLE: _____

COPYRIGHT DATE: _____

PUBLISHER: _____

CONTENT AREA: _____

Materials of the program selected by the committee for use in Mapleton Public Schools are listed on the attached page.

This program was selected for use over other similar programs because: _____

_____

_____

_____

_____

_____

_____

_____

_____

The program has been selected for adoption in the following subjects/courses or grade levels:

_____

_____

Committee members:

Chairperson: _____   _____

_____   _____

_____   _____

_____   _____

FIGURE 6.2 Mapleton public schools curriculum/adoption study recommendation for adoption

"All of these little separate books are gonna be a problem for some people. I don't have any idea where *I'd* store them in my room." "This series has lots of good stories about minority kids. I like that." "I don't think these big books are stiff enough to stand up by themselves so the first-graders can see them, and I'm sure not going to hold them up!"

At 4:20 Judi asks everyone to sit down and "have a look at the beliefs page they developed previously," shown in Figure 6.3. Almost immediately Audey raises her hand, is recognized by Judi, and says, "I don't like number seven. I don't think we agreed to that. I think we said 'reading strategies' *not* 'literature study.'" Although Robin doesn't agree, many others do, and Judi says she'll make the change and get it to them through school mail. Then she asks teachers to get ready to rank the books by publisher, contending, "Thirty-five heads are better than one!"

Audey wonders whether teachers would accept the kind of testing included with the Holt series: "It's so subjective. Can most of our teachers do this? Will they [the administration] make us write a test?" Judi reminds them of the state law in her reply, "You must test the pupil performance objectives in your graded course of study," and then she quotes from the Holt teacher's guide about their philosophy on evaluating students' progress. Audey grumbles softly, "We aren't ready for that here in Mapleton." Robin claims a willingness to go to *anyone* in the district and argue that by using Holt's program all the pupil performance

FIGURE 6.3 Reading adoption committee, K–5

BELIEFS AND RECOMMENDATIONS

Having struggled together throughout the 1988–89 school year in an attempt to develop and form a district philosophy and set of beliefs about the teaching of reading, we offer the following ideas for consideration and discussion:

BELIEFS

1. There is no one "correct" way to teach reading.

2. Students are more likely to acquire reading strategies when the teacher "models" effective read-aloud and think-aloud strategies.

3. Students can become strategic readers with positive attitudes about reading when the teacher explains when, why, and how to use a reading strategy.

4. Good reading instruction takes students beyond the skills and motivates them to read on their own.

5. Providing students with time and support for silent reading gives all students the opportunity to involve themselves in reading for sheer pleasure.

6. Providing time and support to share and discuss reading helps students better understand what they have read and, often, motivates them to read more.

7. Ability grouping is not essential when the instructional focus is on literature study. The teacher has many options for whole group and/or skill group instruction.

8. Reading, writing, and language arts skills and processes ought not to be viewed in isolation, but rather seen as inextricably intertwined.

objectives can be covered: "I'd love to go to the school board to explain this." Lauren remarks, "It's a political choice," without elaboration. Robin disagrees, "We have to choose *the best program*, not just make a decision we know the board will approve." Lauren claims this is idealistic. Robin, shaking her head, mouths "No!" emphatically.

Judi says, "Holt really scares me to death. It's so different. But this is a democratic process. I just worry that we're not ready for it here in Mapleton. Remember, you're representing the 90 percent of teachers who aren't here." Lauren adds, "One poem section [in Holt] really concerned me. I don't like their selection." Judi reminds all that "your job will be to explain this all to your teachers in your building." Cynthia remarks, "The trade books with Heath . . . they're *contrived* trade books. Do we get class sets? Five copies? One? What do we do with them?" Robin, who's majoring in language arts education in graduate school, seems frustrated and mumbles. Cynthia suggests, "I could see in-services about how to use trade books." Robin agrees, "Yes, that would be crucial. I think it's pretty clear they're the future for teaching reading." Judi puts a halt to the deliberations, saying, "Okay, we're ready to vote now."

Teachers are to vote 1, 2, or 5 for each of the four books highest on the list they ranked at previous meetings. Judi has weighted the voting in this way so a clear-cut recommendation is more likely. A lower score is a better score here. Their average of votes by publisher is:

Harcourt Brace Jovanovich: 2.29

Holt: 2.47

Heath: 2.81

Houghton Mifflin: 3.26

Judi chuckles, "Oh. If we adopt Houghton Mifflin we're going to have to learn how to say it." She quips an aside to a small sneezing and rasping group, "Boy, you guys are in great shape today. At least you're all sitting together. Does misery love company?"

Judi directs everyone's attention to the recommendations paper she is distributing so they can decide on in-service later. The paper lists the following:

1. The district will take a leadership role in providing ongoing in-service at the district and building levels over the next two years.
2. Training will be provided so that each building will have one or more teachers trained to serve as resident consultants for the adopted program. Released time will be arranged when at all possible.
3. The district will provide opportunities for parents to understand and appreciate the reading program.
4. Each teacher must take an active role in learning about the new adoption in order to implement the program efficiently and effectively.
5. All teachers will teach the goals and objectives in the Board-adopted Reading Course of Study. However, teachers will be encouraged to

explore and practice a variety of methodologies and personal styles in teaching reading.

6. Teachers and/or buildings who do not wish to use the adopted reading materials must develop and submit for approval their instructional plan, which will include specific materials to be used.

Robin points out and strongly advocates item 6 on the list: "I *don't* think that would be too onerous. I think we at Apple Lane might do that if a reading-skills-approach textbook is adopted. That would *destroy* our program!"

The remainder of the meeting is devoted to deciding on dates and times for presentations to teachers by the publishers' representatives of the three top choices. Judi reminds people that no one *has* to go to these meetings. Then they briefly consider what teachers are likely really to want to have out of the different materials: textbooks, workbooks, tests, supplementary readers, manipulative materials. They decide that textbooks and workbooks will be ordered for everyone. Other materials can be added at the building level. However, Judi acknowledges it would be unrealistic to purchase everything because next year is a mathematics textbook adoption year. Thus, it would be a good idea to be conservative in ordering since money will be needed for that adoption as well. She says "We probably will all get the textbooks, tests, and workbooks and maybe the trade books, but not the cutesy stuff." At 5:00 P.M. everyone gathers belongings, loots the materials display with Judi's approval, and heads for home.

During the following week the three meetings are held in the two high school auditoriums at which publishers' representatives make presentations. Judi says about half the eligible teachers attend at least one meeting. In each case the representatives claim that their program has solved virtually every problem teachers could face in teaching reading. Copies of the proposed materials are delivered to each building. Following those meetings all teachers are to evaluate the three eligible books and to vote by June 2 for the one series they most favor. Mapleton teachers vote to adopt the Heath series, and the board approves their decision. This is not surprising in that the Heath series is not centered entirely on a reading skills approach or on a whole-language approach.

SUMMARY AND DISCUSSION

Textbooks play a large role in determining the nature of the curriculum in many classrooms, so adoption of textbooks is an important matter. In this case, the teachers brought their practical theories of action to the meetings and applied them to the task. These theories informed the group's deliberations. It was in these teachers' interests to adopt a reading series congruent with their own practical theories because it would make teaching easier. If the materials fit their theories they would not have to transform them as much as if the adopted materials differed widely from their theories. Because teachers' practical theories are idiosyncratic, differences among them can lead to conflict. If deliberations are permitted to continue, the ensuing conflict can be helpful in weighing alternatives. For this reason, it is important to have different positions represented in group deliberation and to allow deliberations to continue so ideas can be elaborated upon and weighed.

One social rule this large group appears to have developed is to have members raise their hands to speak, deferring to Judi to maintain order fairly. Judi's actions may have influenced the group's process and decisions in several ways. In the interest of moving the process along speedily, Judi sometimes halted deliberations prematurely, as when she called for a committee vote when they were deliberating intensely about the consideration of various texts. This action appeared to short-circuit the group's deliberation. This may mean issues were not considered as thoroughly as they might have been if the deliberations continued. Perhaps Judi was the victim of stress because of the impending deadline to make a decision. At any rate, as a result the group had little opportunity to socially construct reality. Moreover, Judi did not want to have the meeting last too long, given that several group members were ill, all had already worked a full day, and they would do so again tomorrow. Judi may have further affected the decision by revealing her own temerity about the Holt series. An understanding of the deliberative process and skills in group leadership is important in facilitating group deliberation. Judi appeared to know neither skills nor process and didn't claim to.

Another factor that may have impeded this group somewhat was the set of procedures drawn up by the union and the board of education. These procedures were developed to promote a fair process for adopting curriculum materials, but they may do little to promote adopting excellent materials. This seems to be a clear example of the influence of unions on the curriculum that Eisner (1980) cites. Judi's primary focus was on following those procedures, perhaps partly because of a lack of training in facilitating group curriculum development through deliberation.

Solo and group deliberation interrelate because teachers' solo deliberations help them formulate their practical theories, which they apply in group settings such as this one. They are further interrelated because the group's decision will influence solo deliberations. In this case, the decision involved how much and what to alter about the reading materials. Robin and colleagues at Apple Lane School will have to alter the adopted Heath series to reflect the whole-language approach they are devising, or they will adopt a different text and argue its merits to the board. They ultimately chose to do the former because they already own many supplementary trade books to use with the Heath series. Audey says she will have to develop more worksheets to supplement Heath's skill pads about phonics, dividing words into syllables, and other skills she believes will help her fourth-graders with word attack. Lauren doesn't think much alteration will be necessary. Mark Schaefer (chapter 3) used the Heath series the following year by constructing worksheets about contractions, devising extra vocabulary sheets, and employing some paperback trade books he's acquired over the years. For him, "it works fine because it's so bland and middle of the road that anyone could use it. The Heath text is pretty good." He also subsequently forms small (untracked) groups so students will have more turns and so they will be more visible to him and thus increase his opportunities for individual work. Despite the suggestion that teachers use the Heath series with the entire class for efficiency purposes, this practice of teaching with small groups works well for Mark.

STUDY QUESTIONS

1. Locate and talk with a teacher who relies on textbooks heavily. What statement does the teacher make about why he or she does this? What other factors in the setting might support this teacher's reliance on textbooks? What is the nature of the curriculum there? How does it result from this reliance?

2. Analyze the questions and activities in three textbooks for the same grade level and discipline. What might students learn through them? What implicit curriculum accompanies them?

3. How might the Mapleton policy about procedures for textbook adoption have interfered with deliberation? Locate a similar policy from a local school system and consider its potential influence on group deliberation.

4. Give an example in this case of the relationship between interest and conflict.

5. How are solo and group deliberation interrelated?

6. Analyze what Judi Marienthal did as the group leader. In what ways did those practices impede and facilitate group deliberation?

chapter 7

Revising the Social Studies Curriculum in Chester

In this chapter I portray how a group of teachers and administrators, aided occasionally by two consultants, revise the graded course of study for social studies in the Chester school system. Every five years, by Ohio state policy, each school system is to revise or redevelop their graded course of study. It is important to understand the context, namely, the policy itself. In its handout, "Guidelines to Assist School Districts in Developing Graded Courses of Study," the Ohio Department of Education says of graded courses of study:

> Section 3313,60 *Revised Code of Ohio,* requires boards of education to prescribe a graded course of study for all schools under their control. The mandate applies to boards of education of all county, exempted village and city school districts. State minimum school standards, which have the effect of law, extend the mandate to the corresponding authority in non-tax-supported schools or school systems.
>
> Under law, graded courses of study are subject to the approval of the State Board of Education. Courses of study submitted to the State Department of Education are reviewed by the Division of Elementary and Secondary Education. A follow-up letter to the superintendent indicates approval and/or suggestions for further development.
>
> Although educators often use the terms interchangeably, a graded course of study is not a curriculum guide. Rather, the course of study and the curriculum guide are separate documents which should complement one another in the same subject area. However, the course of study is prescriptive in a given subject or area of study for a particular grade or combination of grades while the curriculum guide is *suggestive.*

Although I described Chester thoroughly in chapter 4, a few other facts are particularly relevant to this case. One high school, two middle schools, and nine elementary schools comprise the Chester school system. Two administrators selected teachers for the group from lists of volunteers solicited by each school's principal. In selecting team members, George Hanley (assistant superintendent for curriculum) and Leonard Stanfield (curriculum director) say they desired to balance two matters, grade-level representation and building representation, and to include on the committee some individuals who'd developed the original graded course of study six years before. Deliberators developing the social studies graded course of study include: Holly, Jane, Bob, Molly, Janice, Jody, Susan, Alexander (elementary school); Sharon, Enid, Matt, Leslie, Paula (middle school); Dana (gifted and talented program); Kent, Marian, James (high school); and George and Leonard (administrators). Both George and Leonard have substantial experience with and interest in social studies education. Additionally, Leonard has many years of experience leading committees developing and revising graded courses of study for different disciplines in Chester. He seems to have earned great respect from Chester's teachers for his ability to do this, and teachers genuinely like him. For example, Enid says, "Leonard's a teddy bear. He's a nice man, but he also *really* knows what he's doing here!" Leonard, who facilitates the meetings, takes his concerns about the committee's large size into account when he plans the meetings by breaking them into smaller groups. Two consultants work with the committee on several occasions.

The committee begins the work in January 1991, and the board approves their graded course of study on March 9, 1992. The committee meets once a month after school in a large conference room at the central office. During the summer they continue their work, meeting at Roosevelt Middle School for one week and then at Chester High School for another. Each teacher receives a stipend of $450 for summer work. Obviously, they do not work on it every day from January 30, 1991, through March 9, 1992, for at times the document is ensnared in one bureaucracy or another. Ultimately, they develop a curriculum document containing 244 pages. It details the content, but not the instructional strategies, for each social studies course at each grade level. This exemplifies the amount of time needed for careful group curriculum development.

I've organized this chapter into four parts. I'm sensitive to Senge's caution not to separate complex wholes into parts if we want to understand them, so these four parts are not tidily separated. Moreover, the development of group agreement (subtext) and the development of the curriculum document itself (text) are not neatly separable because they occur simultaneously and interact. I describe the first section, the longest, the process teachers and administrators used to develop the subtext and texts. I next analyze and interpret the process in terms of the development of agreement. In a third section I analyze and interpret the curriculum document itself. I close with a brief summary.

This case exemplifies the theory I developed in chapter 4. Interestingly, Leonard helped the committee develop both the subtext and the text of deliberation, although he had not read chapter 4 and was not overtly aware of the theory presented there. Indeed, my involvement in this case led me to revise my prior theory of deliberation to include the important subtext of developing group agreement. This illustrates my view of the dynamic relationship between theory and observed practices in qualitative research (see Research Appendix).

A DESCRIPTION OF THE PROCESS

The first meeting to revise the social studies graded course of study is on a bitter January day. Each member enters the conference room at central office, obtains a name badge, writes his or her name on it, and then takes a seat around the large wooden table in the center of the room. In one corner, coffee is brewing, filling the room with its pungent aroma. Some teachers deposit belongings and then pour themselves coffee or get soft drinks. Others already know one another and begin catching up on recent events in their personal and professional lives. By 4:00 P.M. everyone has arrived except one teacher, so Len starts this first meeting by cordially and enthusiastically welcoming everyone:

LEN: Welcome, everyone, to the social studies revision team! It's a *large* team, but like a basketball coach, I can't cut anyone. [*Laughter*] We have representatives here from every building and every grade level except second and special education. The gifted and talented program teacher is going to be late today. We're also represented by individuals who were on the graded course of study team last time we wrote it six years ago. It's important for us to get to know one another, and I want to provide some time and occasions for that. But now I want to present a short overview of what we'll be doing. In the February meeting I'll invite Laurence Foster from the State Department [of Education]. Also, Alice Calhoun from Ohio State will be here about multiculturalism some time later. The staff development you'll get in this will be quite extensive. [*Len passes out one-and-one-half inch thick folders containing photocopied recent articles about social studies education.*] Let's take a break for sodas and coffee then get back to this.

Over refreshments they talk about their families, recent trips taken during winter break, and new practices they're using to teach social studies. A small knot of elementary school teachers gossips about Chester's new language arts graded course of study and that committee's arduous work. After the short break, Len reconvenes the committee for a while longer:

LEN: I want to ask you why you joined this committee. I've made these transparencies about some reasons other people have given in the past. One reason they gave was that it's an invaluable form of in-service and gives them a perspective on what happens at other grade levels preceding and following their own. This, they said, made it easier to plan and teach. Others said it gives them a chance to resolve conflicts among grade levels and between school levels. And others said it gave them, as master teachers, a chance to share their expertise and thereby the experience helps to provide leadership in that content area. What about you folks? Are there some to add?

Enid adds, laughingly, "A chance to get rich!" The rest join in the laughter, and a first in-group joke has been made. Leonard continues, smilingly,

LEN: One thing that'll happen is we'll definitely have some conflict here. Conflict is a very positive thing. I noted before that several of you were talking about the language arts graded course of study meetings, and there was a *lot* of conflict in that group just as there will be here. But it's important.

Many would probably agree with Enid, who told me in an interview that she had volunteered because "I could either be on the outside [and not a committee member] looking in and wondering what they would do to me in terms of what I'm supposed to teach or be on the inside helping make the best decisions we can. I chose the latter, obviously. It's a big time commitment, but it's important to do it right." While she did not voice this aloud in the meeting, she probably speaks for many who wanted to have some input into this social studies curriculum policy for the Chester system. Leonard goes on to predict some issues that will probably be contentious: how specific to be in writing objectives, how to integrate social studies with other disciplines, which grade level should be responsible for teaching Ohio history, how to prescribe social studies content yet word the document to acknowledge teachers' professionalism and their rights to select instructional strategies, how to evaluate social studies learning, and several others.

I should point out that Leonard's interest in conflict probably dates back to previous research I did in Chester, when they were revising the graded course of study for the gifted and talented program. (See McCutcheon, in Marsh et. al, 1990.) Len reassures the committee members that conflict is unavoidable and helpful even though it may not always be comfortable. He continues the meeting:

LEN: You'll be getting $450 for your work on this committee. [*Jane asks, "How much time will this involve?"*] About four committee-at-large meetings during the year, a release day, and two weeks in the summer, 8:30 to 11:30 in the morning. I usually like to have those two weeks separated so everyone has time to process it. We'll also have subcommittee meetings, like high school, elementary, and middle school, so you can interact more in smaller groups and deal with problems about those areas you're experts in.

He goes on to describe how he and George selected teachers for the committee, using three criteria: balance of grade level and building representatives and a range of teacher-professional experiences. Then he turns to describing the process they'll be using:

LEN: We'll start with a needs assessment survey of attitudes, feelings, and perspectives teachers at large have. All secondary school teachers in Chester will complete it and one person at each grade level selected by a representative on the committee will complete it. This way we'll get the feelings of all teachers throughout the district. After that we'll launch into the philosophy of the discipline. We'll take a look at the district's current one and attempt to revise it. From that philosophy all other things are derived, so it's our guiding star. Then we'll derive our program goals—some people like to call it strands. Then this summer we'll write objectives and the scope and sequence. Simultaneously, a materials search will be going on. You don't have to write PPOs (pupil performance objectives) because the state department doesn't require it for social studies. Then we'll need to talk about the proficiency test.

We need to all understand what a graded course of study *is*. It's supposed to be a broad prescription, not too specific. It defines each subject in terms of a philosophy, goals, and objectives. It's not as specific as a curriculum guide. A curriculum guide gives teachers more indication of what to do and how to do it. So we won't include activities in the graded course of study. That's something a teacher plans. The graded course of study shows the legal basis from the state department document. By force of law, daily planning is to originate in the graded course of study.

At 4:25 he asks for questions. Holly asks, "Why not develop a curriculum guide while we're developing the graded course of study?" Jody says, "We'd probably do *double* work if we did that, but if you think that's what we should do [looking at Holly], that's what we should do. The language arts committee took a *year* to write the guide! It was very wearying. I can't imagine doing that." George suggests, "We might do a materials collection throughout the year." Len emphasizes, "That's *needed* in social studies." At 4:30 he circulates a calendar and requests teachers to initial those dates they will *not* be available so he can decide when to hold future meetings. "Some of you just won't be able to make the meetings sometimes." He promises to distribute a revised schedule well in advance of the next meeting, but he adds that even the revision will be subject to change because it's difficult to anticipate all the possible scheduling problems and getting this many people together creates scheduling nightmares. "So don't think it's carved in stone," he says.

Paula briefly describes Project Business, a ten-week set of lessons about economics taught in her grade level, and asks the group to add to its deliberation the question of whether it belongs in the social studies curriculum and why. Len asks if others have questions, but they do not, so he reviews who will be completing the needs assessment. George says he'll distribute them on Monday or Tuesday and suggests asking teachers to fill them out within a week.

Although many already know each other, teachers introduce themselves, and Leonard tells everyone something about each person's work or introduces a question about the graded course of study their particular practice raises. He says of Kent, "Kent teaches some fascinating classes about the Orient. You know, he's been interested in that area for years, so he has a lot of materials and knowledge about it." He also reminds others of James's (see chapter 4) high school courses using computer simulations. "He really got us going on those here in Chester! They're absolutely fascinating," says Len. He also describes the "fine work going on in Hastings Elementary School where classes are exploring the history of the Chester community in splendid detail through speakers, field trips, and reading." These introductions and Len's flattering comments may begin to help people know each other, since they all are committed to social studies and to perceiving one another's competence. When they leave the meeting at 4:45, they seem enthusiastic about the task as they chat quietly on their way to their cars. Even at this first meeting, they have made some progress toward unifying as a group on the road to developing group agreement, although they might be unaware of it. Holly, at least, sees it. "We're starting to be a group," she says, walking me to my car.

Preceding the February meeting, teachers greet each other and talk with animation about personal and professional events. They smile as they sit casually in small, close groups around the periphery of the room, sipping coffee or sodas. A few have read some articles in the packet Len passed out last month and call one another's attention to interesting parts, but most conversations center around events they've recently experienced. Two discuss their anticipation of the upcoming "March madness" of the NCAA basketball playoffs, remarking on different teams and their coaches. Len calls the meeting to order, and people gather around the table. He starts by reminding and supporting them about the upcoming work and the conflict it will cause:

LEN: There's a need here for you to voice your opinion. It's my responsibility to be sure everyone does. At first, you may feel it's hard to do until you get to know one another. Sometimes you'll feel like nothing's happening. That's typical, and we will be making progress. It's just that at points it'll *feel* pointless. *This* curriculum is by far the most difficult. No one knows just what social studies is; the experts don't even agree. With the *espirit d' corps* that I already feel in here, we'll make these tough decisions, don't worry!

Len introduces Lawrence Foster, a consultant from the state department of education whose specialization is social studies education. Larry draws everyone's attention to a document he's photocopied and passed around, pages 1 through 7 of "Proposed Graduation Requirements," a report prepared by the Ohio Department of Education in July 1990 and delivered to the governor and members of the 118th General Assembly. Everyone reads the handout about proposed changes in graduation requirements. Then Larry begins to explain and discuss the document and its implications:

LARRY: This proposal is now in the hands of the General Assembly. Right now the battle over proficiency exams seems to be taking precedence, so action is unlikely until April [of 1991]. This proposal is seen by the state board of education as an interim step before abolishing the Carnegie units and going totally outcomes-based. We think students should acquire credit for what they actually *learn*, not just for occupying a seat for a certain amount of time, so we're moving to outcomes-based education, away from the Carnegie unit idea. [*Carnegie units represent the number of credits students earn for taking a course.*] But not all at once. The state board is interested in being on the forefront—we're usually in the rear guard—on this issue. Look for a minute at Item G, page 7. [*It reads that one proposed graduation requirement is "School and community service, 100 hours, as defined by the local school district board of education, one-half unit."*] This is seen as a lightning rod issue, and an administrative nightmare because it'll be *difficult* to administer. There's also concern about the proficiency test [for social studies] because of the positive concern about the interdisciplinary nature of the social studies. See the second item under Item H, page 7. [*It reads, "In order to move Ohio toward integrated, interdisciplinary curriculum offerings, an option for school districts to offer courses combining two or more courses that previously were discrete should be provided. Teaching teams would utilize combined time on task to provide a variety of activities to meet student learning styles and assure a level of competency in all areas utilizing various integrated forms of assessment."*] See, a move away from Carnegie units may help that.

Larry pauses, perhaps to catch his breath or reorganize his thoughts, or perhaps to decide how to recapture everyone's attention. Some teachers have wandered from page 7, the object of Larry's attention, to Item E on the facing page 6, where three required high school units in social studies are listed:

one unit of U.S. History, including the integration of U.S. Geography, with at least one-half unit devoted to the twentieth century;

one unit of world studies, including the integration of geography, history, and international studies;

one unit of American Government and Economics, including the integration of participatory citizenship, the free enterprise system, leadership development, critical decision making, and citizenship.

Like misbehaving high school students, they began chattering and speculating as a backdrop to Larry's presentation. The following dialogue takes place:

LEN: The Chester schools are sophisticated in our desire to integrate the curriculum, but we're mandated to write separate graded courses of study. You know, Larry, we seem to be doing everything we can to encourage teaching separate disciplines.

LARRY: At least we're getting school districts to meet by subject matter specialties across elementary and secondary levels. That's a victory. Even though we have discrete courses of study, *numerous* teachers across the state integrate across their graded courses of study.

LEN: Teachers here are far ahead of the state department, though. We want to integrate more, but need some guidance about how to create documents. Sometimes we're impeding [integration] through the format we have to use.

Holly raises issues about the coding form they use when planning lessons. This form, required by many Chester principals and department chairs, requires teachers to write for each lesson the number of the intended objective from the graded course of study. Holly charges it's "unwieldy." Larry agrees with the charge, but offers no solution for how to code objectives in a more practical manner. George refers to a three-page handout he's distributing about various ways to organize the curriculum. It describes design options ranging from discipline-based through multidisciplinary units and courses and the integrated day to the complete program. He wonders aloud about developing some interdisciplinary "magnet courses" and suggests looking in publishers' teacher's guides for materials to support teaching integrated units or courses. "The elementary is already doing that. Maybe secondary schools can too," he says. "The graded course of study needs to be a discrete course of study. In the curriculum guides we develop, we can push for interdisciplinarity." It is interesting to note here George's assumption the committee will develop a curriculum guide as well as a graded course of study, a point Holly and Pat had discussed with no resolution during the January meeting. Because George is an assistant superintendent, his assumption may be critical, but the group never actually develops the idea.

Larry refers the committee's attention to another handout he's distributing. This eight-page document contains six alternative suggestions about the content and organization of social studies from the National Council of Social Studies Task Force on Scope and Sequence, a Scope and Sequence Recommendation by William Kniep, one from the National Council for Geographic Education and the Association of American Geographers, another by the Ohio Council on Economic Education, one from the Bradley Commission, and two sample scope and sequence lists from nearby school systems. He gives people a few minutes to examine these alternatives and then continues:

LARRY: A common message here is that no *one* of us can teach the whole thing in one year. It's especially true when we're shifting from Western civilization to some other parts of the world as well. We have to teach one and a half years of Ohio history before eighth grade. If you conceptualize something that will cause an inspection nightmare [for the state department's evaluation], or it contradicts the state standards, but those standards interfere with what you think has to do with providing for a good education, you can apply for an exemption.

Len replies and refocuses the committee's attention, "It's the *format* that's beleaguering us." He goes on to review what by definition a graded course of study is through a dialogue with Larry. It continues:

LEN: The Chester district seems evenly divided about the amount of specificity needed in writing the graded courses of study. How to write them? The only thing some people can think of is a curriculum guide. But I have to remind myself constantly that we're developing *broad* goals for a graded course of study, *not* a how-to guide.

LARRY: Knowing how specific to be is very important—you need to write it as specifically as you think the district needs. I've heard some clues that the state is going to develop a model for people to have a look at. There's no mandate in the law *currently,* but who knows what's next? So it can only be a guideline. A helpful *guideline* would be terrific, not a prescription. There are too many knotty issues that can't be mandated statewide. For example, Chester wants to move toward being more interdisciplinary in curriculum design than other districts.

The teachers continue to chat as Len disbands the meeting until next month. People gather their belongings, notes, and handouts and leave together in small groups, escorting each other to the parking lot as they laugh and visit. On the way to our cars, Pat says, "I feel good about this now. We're *already* a group." When I ask her what she means, she continues, "Well, we're all experts in social studies—at different levels—but experts at our own levels. So we have to respect each other, but we don't have to waste a lot of time explaining things because we speak the same language. And we all truly believe in the importance of social studies in the curriculum. So I know we'll do a great job."

I miss the next meeting because of a conflict with a course I teach. Len begins the final meeting of the school year:

LEN: Today's agenda concerns the philosophy revision. We'll revisit it this summer, though. Today's just a beginning. We'll probably raise a lot of issues today for further attention this summer. But it's very important to start seeing what those issues are now, so you can reflect on them some before we get together again in another month. To start, get something to drink from up here and move around the room to form triads and work for about 15 minutes. Start by looking at the current philosophy.

Len distributes photocopies. Typically, one person in each triad quietly reads the current philosophy aloud, pausing occasionally when others remark about problems they see or significant omissions.

When they reconvene, Len asks a person from each triad to report major ideas to the whole group. Pat says her group thought "it contains too much educationese. What do you think it means 'integrates learning opportunities'? Does it mean participatory opportunities or what?" James reports, "Maybe I'm biased by the need for some mention of the movement here in the U.S. to a technological society, but it's totally missing here! We can't get it funded if it's not in the philosophy. Now, folks, we have to be able to *deal* with a technological society. I mean, it's everywhere—at the bank, in businesses, when you register at O.S.U., or even make some phone calls. I think it needs to be very prominent here. My group also wants us to talk in the philosophy more about *social* development throughout, not just individual." Rita says, "My group focused on respecting differences and want it to promote respecting contributions of both women and men." Holly jumps in and says, "If the intention here is to respect gender differences, we want to respect *everyone*. Period! Maybe we should say that right out front. Respect for people? Their contributions? Both genders? SES? Ethnic groups?" The deliberations are interrupted here by much talk about these stirring issues. Holly raises her voice a bit and says, "Isn't the point here that we want to teach respect for *people*—alike or different?" James returns to his technology issue, and Pat to the educationese problem. Len suggests a very brief break. Afterwards, he leads triads through presenting their ideas about revisions. George reads through his own, line by line. Because this is the final meeting before the close of the school year, Len wishes everyone a good summer and Paula a bon voyage for her short trip to Europe. On the way to cars, people discuss summer plans, worries about what they didn't get to teach this year, and the issue of how to state the respect for differences among people.

The summer sessions begin in mid-June in a middle school, and people seem genuinely glad to see each other. Dressed casually, they sit around a large table, and Len welcomes them back, noting how relaxed all are and the tans some are acquiring. He welcomes Margaret back from Italy, and a few women jokingly ask her if any interesting Italian men pinched her while she was there. She good-naturedly shakes her head that it didn't happen. Then Len poses today's agenda:

LEN: Today we'll start wondering whether to develop a schema, K through 12. We'll also spend considerable time examining the current graded course of study to collate existing goals with ones *you* think are important. Alice Calhoun is here from O.S.U., and Samuel, a [preservice] field experience student from O.S.U., is also here observing. Let's start by you individually reviewing Larry's materials he passed out last spring. Remember, he's the state department guy who was here. One thing he passed out was a collection he'd made of alternative patterns for scope and sequence recommended by different organizations and experts. Please find your copy. If you can't, I made a couple of extras. So get yourself a cup of coffee and find a place to review those plans. We'll review them aloud in a few minutes as a committee of the whole, not by grade level.

They find the materials in their folders or briefcases and start rereading them closely, some jotting occasional notes. They reconvene and go through each scope and sequence plan in order, taking turns around the table. Of the National Council of Social Studies (NCSS) plan, they say:

MATT: I'd like to see history broken down into parts more than this.

HOLLY: They have an obvious logical sequence.

JANE: I like the lower grade levels, and I think a schema's a good idea.

BOB: I like it for elementary, and I agree with Jane that we need to create a schema.

MARIAN: I agree about developing the schema. It's not an enormous task. Specifically, I like what they did in elementary. In elementary some things should be incorporated throughout the year, for instance, law and multicultural ed.

SHARON: I want a schema, too—not too much specificity, though—but fourth grade here [in the NCSS plan] is too loose—definitions are needed about "community" and "region."

JODY: Yes, a schema is definitely needed so we'll know what each other is going to do.

DANA: Yes to schema. Please, not too much specificity, and don't underrate the capacity of lower elementary education. We should introduce *more* in primary school.

JANICE: I want the schema for all the reasons mentioned, and I agree with Dana. We need more opportunities, I think, to develop thinking skills and get our kids to think in a critical way.

JAMES: I don't see a focus here at all on geography, which we need. I like the electives in Grade 12. The major advantage is that they'll be selecting college courses the next year [in college] so they need to learn how to make choices.

ENID: There needs to be a schema, but not so specific that we can't use our teachers' strengths to advantage. We need more specification than this [NCSS plan], though, because of the proficiency test here in Ohio.

MARIAN: I'm more predisposed to history than this [NCSS document].

SHARON: We need more multiculturalism, global studies and history in the early years than this. I like the idea of developing timelines, here, but I want more.

ALICE CALHOUN: The reason for scope and sequence is that by laying it out you can make sure you can *build* on ideas and aren't constantly repeating. Very large concepts such as global interdependence—how to start, build, and keep building the concept so as a system you know what you're building toward all leads to consistency. If themes are impregnated in courses, you can say what you're trying to do as a school system. If teachers are professionals (and I think they *are*), they'll have to make a lot of those decisions themselves.

ALEXANDER: I want to have a schema, too. [*He then refers to an article from the thick packet Len had passed out that specifies a region of the world worth teaching.*]

SAMUEL: [I see] a problem with the lack of geography in the NCSS plan [and believes twelfth grade is] too loose.

In discussing the Kniep proposal, people generally say they do not favor it, offering two basic reasons: it branches out too quickly, and it's vague. They turn their attention now to the three Bradley proposals for scope and sequence. In these deliberations they speak in no special order, building on or reacting to each other's ideas:

MOLLY: I really like Pattern C.

JANICE: So do I. Pattern C would be excellent for literature-based language arts and a whole-language approach that many of us here in Chester use. This one's my favorite! It's people-centered, new and fresh, yet it displays and organizes some important, *fundamental* things in social studies. [*Many enthusiastic yeses are heard.*]

JANE: C *is* exciting. A has a good sequence, but I don't like B at all.

BOB: I like A better than B, but C can't be the sole schema because it doesn't show the total social studies schema. We can't just adopt it.

ALEXANDER: I like A. There's more "meat" in it. No. "Meat" isn't the right word—skills. I wish A and C could be merged.

MARIAN: Yes. If A and C could come together it'd be more meaningful than either one alone.

DANA: I like A and C, too.

JAMES: C at the high school level solves many problems in terms of trying to teach too much at once. It's nicely focused. Tenth and eleventh grades could treat a lot. C's also interesting at lower levels.

ENID: A. I like the idea of C, though, although I'm really wondering if there are any materials for Grade 6. [She teaches 6].

TED: I'm in favor of C, but I'd want eighth grade changed. Much would have to be delineated; it's awfully vague. Chronology and history are very important and need to be treated in depth. Our kids need to develop a real understanding of it—a sense of time and place.

MOLLY: C would give elementary kids a rich background.

KENT: The curriculum in secondary [his level] is really intriguing for C, but elementary worries me. K to four isn't really social studies; it's too literature-based.

JANE: I like B for the most part, but I like A's Grade 2 better. Let's remember they don't have anyone on the committee.

ENID: I like their categories but not their sequence. C seems richer in elementary than A, which is more traditional by far.

Here they are examining several alternative possibilities. In the process they air their own values and start to recognize each other's. They examine other alternatives from two school systems in much the same way. Clearly, none of the examples Larry had provided can simply be adopted for use here in Chester, but the group has made important progress in examining alternatives and their own values. By having to respond in public, perhaps they have examined these alternatives more closely than they would have had they been working alone.

At 10:25 A.M. they take a doughnut and coffee break. Following that, Len welcomes them back, saying:

LEN: I have a good feeling about the notion of schema. I think everyone wants one, right? Now, to compile one, I'd like us to divide into three groups: K to 5, 6 to 8, and the high school. Your charge is this: In the grade-level cluster discuss a proposed schema, appoint a recorder to report to the committee-at-large. You have 30 minutes to develop a draft. Then as a committee-at-large we'll look at the fit through the give and take of deliberation. So develop a proposed schema and your rationale for it.

As groups work, they ask each other occasionally: "Well, let's think about that." "What's wrong with it?" "What about economics—what should *we* do about that?" "Yes, but how can we *word* it? We know what we mean, but we have to communicate!" "How does multiculturalism fit in here?" At 11:10 Len reminds people, "We need to finish up here, even if we can't totally wrap it up today. We have this room again tomorrow morning, so why don't you recorders start writing your stuff on the boards around the room?" By 11:15 all recorders have begun this task, and Len asks others to divide into triads to raise concerns about the process they're using to develop the schema. When they discuss these later, their three chief concerns are: "Elementary people have one set of assumptions and secondary another"; "Sometimes we get absolutely *lost* in the dialogue"; and "We're worried about our lack of recent up-to-date reading." Alexander adds heatedly, "Chester teachers have *outgrown* the current social studies graded course of study. We're all more sophisticated than that now." The session is over, so they disband, again escorting each other to cars and visiting. Len tells the custodians not to wash the boards.

The next day several bring the current issue of *Time* and, provoked by an article in the magazine, start spirited discussions in little groups about whether the United States is (or should be) a melting pot and whether it can become genuinely multicultural by cherishing cultural differences while simultaneously encouraging identification with the nation as a whole. As they convene more formally, James raises several other high school concerns he has:

JAMES: Do we have American studies or American humanities so we can combine literature, the arts, and social studies? Do we expand our electives? Do we offer advanced placement honors? In what courses?

LEN: Your [high school] subcommittee should be addressing those now. Your mission is to suggest a course of study including electives. Then we'll take it to the Powers that Be—mostly administrators. We'll see what you come up with.

They begin examining the schemas each subgroup has developed. Enid asks what the fourth-grade theme means and why fifth grade stops at 1800 rather than the Civil War. Alexander explains they were unhappy with so much history revolving around wars, so by thinking in terms of centuries they hoped to avoid that problem. Enid smiles at Alexander and nods her head in understanding.

Len suggests, "I think you've been doing fine in terms of thinking of your*self*. That's important. But think now in terms of Chester's *children*."

Holly talks about developing an across-disciplines grid to aid in integrated planning. At 10:55, Len says, "Tomorrow we'll revisit the program goals and begin brainstorming." When they leave, the schemas remain on the boards, and Len again reminds the custodians to leave them there.

Today, Len's secretary has typed and photocopied the social studies plans for scope and sequence developed in the small groups, and Len begins by distributing them. The original document is shown in Figure 7.1. As they receive their copy, each pours a cup of coffee or gets a soda and then moves to a comfortable spot around the room. They huddle over the paper and read, occasionally jotting notes on their copy or on a piece of paper. Len calls them together about 15 minutes later to begin their deliberations. At the beginning, few changes are suggested for the lower grade levels, but then several are suggested:

ALEXANDER: For Grade 5, what about cutting it off at 1865 instead of 1800. That's a better date historically.

SUSAN: Yes. I agree. That just makes more sense. I don't know why we did that. 1800's too arbitrary a date.

BOB: And in sixth grade, what if we change "Regions" to "Cultures"?

ENID: If we do that, it makes the whole ending in parentheses redundant, so let's drop that.

JAMES: In Grade 7, let's get that geography in there, folks! How about World History and *Geography*: Ancient to 1800?

MARIAN: Eighth grade needs some work too. I sure hope you middle schoolers don't think we're picking on you. But what about changing the American History dates to 1863–1900? And how in the world can we teach all of the twentieth century in nine weeks? I sure couldn't! Maybe you're just better teachers than I am.

PAULA: I was on that group, and I agree. But what we *wanted* there was a quick overview of it so they'd start to get a sense of its progression—obviously not a detailed study of all its events.

K	Children of Other lands and Times (Traditions, Symbols, Celebrations)
1	Families, Neighborhoods, and Communities: Local and Global
2	Urban History: How Cities Begin and Grow
3	Ohio Studies (N. American Geography)
4	World Regions and Communities
5	National History and Geography: Exploration to 1800
6	World Regions: Africa/Europe/Latin America/Middle East (Government, Geography, Current Trends, Culture)
7	World History: Ancient to 1789 (3 nine-week sessions); American Colonial Experience to 1789 (1 nine weeks); Civics
8	American History: 1763–1900 (3 nine-week sessions); 20th Century (1 nine weeks)
9	Intro I (Prof.*); Intro II (Prof.,* Geography, Economics)
10	World History: 1790–Present
11	American History (1 credit)
12	Government (1 credit)

FIGURE 7.1   Social studies grade K–12 schema: Draft: 7/15/91

*Prof. = Proficiency exam skills and content.

JAMES: One other change I see is in tenth grade. A lot happened in 1789 to 1790, and it relates to the present a great deal, so in my view it should read "1789 to Present."

Paula heatedly wonders when they'll treat immigration, and James remarks, "Paula, that's too specific a topic for the schema. That'll go in later under more specific goals for grade levels; I agree it's important for understanding American history, but it would fit in nicely in fifth, eighth, and eleventh grades."

Len has been taking notes about all the suggested changes, and he promises he'll give them to his secretary so they can see the recommendations before making any decisions about the schema. The changes to the schema are passed out the following day; they are shown in Figure 7.2.

At the close of this discussion, Len asks all to "have another look" at what they've decided and asks for reactions. Paula says vehemently,

FIGURE 7.2   Social studies grade K–12, changes

5	National History and Geography: Exploration to 1865
6	World Cultures: Africa/Europe/Latin America/Middle East
7	World History and Geography: Ancient to 1800; American Colonial Experience to 1789
8	American History: 1863–1900; Overview: 20th Century
10	World History: 1789–Present

PAULA: I hope this can hold the elementary teachers accountable. I can't depend on kids coming to the middle school knowing *anything* in social studies. Sometimes I think some teachers don't even teach social studies. It goes on the back burner, *way* behind language arts and also behind math. I'm beginning to think we should develop end-of-year proficiency tests in social studies.

No one, not even elementary school teachers, responds to this. Alexander later tells me, "Well, I didn't say anything because I think it's a bad idea that'll just die on its own. There wasn't any point in saying anything. I'll bet other elementary school teachers felt that way too." At any rate, this was one opportunity when conflict might have arisen, but it did not. Jung's research (1991) showed teachers in this school system avoided conflict when developing a different graded course of study, and perhaps this is another example of what she found. At any rate, the issue never resurfaces. The session has ended, and they leave, chatting with each other on the way to their cars.

The next day teachers have poured themselves coffee and are sitting around the table, obviously ready to begin promptly. Len passes out the edited schema, and when he asks for changes none are suggested. Len goes on to describe an evaluation of the current social studies graded course of study document that Chester solicited from a university. He reads parts of it:

This curriculum deals with the real social world from a theoretical, written perspective. The designers have made a concerted effort through the various objectives in three areas of concern and through the critical skill tasks in the secondary courses.

The high school courses help focus upon various contemporary issues and problems which face society. Exploration, analysis, and focus on alternative solutions are also noteworthy.

[The] group who designed this graded course of study did outstanding work in identifying objectives, especially in the skill development area.

The course outlines (secondary only) are very well done.

The designation of the critical skills in the course outlines is excellent.

The performance objectives come through clearly in the critical skills list and at the end of each course outline.

Then he points out major deficiencies cited in the report:

The overall structure of the program is adequate though traditional in its 1950s concentric circles approach to the program. Even though this scope and sequence was listed as an alternative by the NCSS Task Force, other structures should be examined for the elementary school.

There are no elementary course outlines in the graded course of study. This is a major concern in that social studies for the elementary student is left to happenstance even though the subject is one of the major areas in the elementary curriculum. Further, because so much time is devoted to reading/language arts and mathematics instruction, little time is devoted to social studies and science. The group needs to ensure that this curriculum does not receive such treatment by developing course outlines for each elementary grade level as soon as possible.

There is need to develop skill objectives in the K-12 curriculum which go beyond acquisition. Objectives, activities, tasks, and evaluation procedures should lend themselves into skill applications in a more direct manner.

The objectives are categorized as introductory and developmental. This is good; however, when in the program, will students be assessed at the mastery level? This category does not exist in the course of study and should at different points in the curriculum.

One of the major foci in the social studies curriculum is the emphasis upon learning the structure of each discipline: concepts and generalizations. This course of study states that this is a major purpose for Chester's curriculum. Concepts are thus listed as a focus for this program. However, what is listed does not come close to the major concepts in the social sciences. In fact, the area of "cultural diversity" is but one concept of many to teach the concept of "culture." A study of the major concepts in the social sciences needs to be undertaken in order to be consistent with the introduction and philosophy statements of this document.

There is not an economics course in the graded course of study. This should be a part of the social studies program and should not be limited to the area of business education.

Following this mixed news, the group takes a coffee break, during which members of the elementary subgroup say: "We really have our work cut out for us!" "No wonder Paula was annoyed about kids' coming to her either knowing different things or nothing at all," and "We've really got lots to do, so let's get going!"

Following their short break they reassemble, and Len passes out six sets of the current graded course of study's program goals and related objectives he's had his secretary type. Some are multipage documents. He directs everyone to read them closely for a few moments so they can begin revising them in the remaining time this morning. Ten minutes later, Len directs them to review them in their three school-level subgroups before examining them as a committee of the whole. They meet and discuss different program goals for 20 minutes, and then Len reconvenes them as a committee of the whole. They begin by examining program goal 3, which reads:

The Social Studies Curriculum enables students to develop a critical understanding of the history, geography, economic, political, and social institutions, traditions, and values of the United States as expressed in both their unity and diversity.

Three pages, with 25 more specific objectives, follow. Len requests them to look through the three pages briefly. Then he solicits suggestions:

JAMES: Anthropology plays a significant part in social studies. Then objective 12 becomes a bullet under that: Students will understand the role anthropology plays in the understanding of history and the social sciences. We also need to examine *closely* how well our objectives are in line with the ninth-grade state proficiency test.

MOLLY: We compared this to the ninth-grade citizenship goals. Objectives 2 and 4 here might be better thought of as bullets under the first one because they're all part of sociology.

HOLLY: You know what I'm hearing? I think we should really reorganize this whole thing by related sections—the components—disciplines—of social studies. It would be more usable and easier to read. I also think we should somehow flag items on the proficiency test.

For the remainder of the morning they cluster objectives around sociology, history, anthropology, political science, geography, psychology, and economics, sometimes identifying an objective under more than one discipline. They also reword program goal 3 to read:

The Social Studies Curriculum enables students to develop a critical understanding of the origin and development of the traditions, institutions, and values of the United States of America through the study of history and the social studies.

They chat with one another while on the way to their cars after the session. On the way to my car, Kent says, "I really feel we made some progress today. We did a better job of listening to each other instead of the talk wandering all over the place in terms of topics. It was more of a conversation, although it stayed focused on the tasks Len outlined for us to accomplish."

The next day is the final day of the first week of summer work, and as teachers enter, they seem enthusiastic about their work, perhaps because they thought they'd accomplished so much yesterday. They get a cup of coffee and a doughnut and then promptly sit at the table. After welcoming them, Len has teachers move into their school-level groups to examine other program goals. They do this for most of the morning. They ultimately make no changes in the program goal about international studies and only a few minor changes in program goal 5, which concerns developing traditional skills used in social studies. Here they distinguish between primary and secondary source materials and reword one objective. Just before they leave, Len speaks.

LEN: We've just reviewed different perspectives on how to organize all of this by examining those alternatives Larry gave us. Based on those and on what teachers bring to Chester—and that's a lot—it's our task to develop the *best* graded course of study we can. This is the most difficult curricular area to develop, bar none. The nature of knowledge here is different from math. There are some gray areas in social studies; it's not cut and dried. That's why it's important to have a *very* unified philosophy and strands here. We also have to focus on the proficiency exam. If anything, the state will focus on learning outcomes *more and more*, probably through outcomes-based education. We have to do more than just pass over the proficiency items and assume kids have learned them, so don't ignore it. Like it or not, I see it as the wave of the future.

Before the next session in August, I'll have Jo Ellen, my secretary, type up your rough draft of the goals. It would help if *you'd* overview again the current graded course of study. I'll be sending out a written agenda with dates, times, and assignments so we'll all be ready. I hope we can quickly put some things to bed so we can quickly move forward. And finally, I want to encourage all of you to participate very fully in this. We're doing a great job!

Then he foreshadows their work for the final week in August: "developing each course's graded course of study and critiquing one another's plans." As they leave today they talk and dream about their plans for painting their houses, completing yardwork, and taking vacations. But on the way out to our cars, Holly says, "I sort of hate to *take* this break. We're working so well right now. Maybe Len's right, though. Some time off will give us some distance on it—perspective— and maybe we'll be able to see some corrections to make. But I'll miss these people and think about them a lot."

When they reconvene in August at the high school, many greet each other fondly and quickly catch up on news. Len assembles the whole group and directs them to work in school-level groups to review the five program goals they established in July and to suggest rewording or reordering them. They're to select a recorder/reporter. They work in these groups for 25 minutes and then Len suggests they get coffee and doughnuts and return to the big table. The recorder/ reporters present their ideas. Most find little or no fault with the five goals, except for Kent:

KENT: I think we should have a conceptual progression rather than ranking. For instance, in kindergarten they could develop knowledge and skills then apply them to them*selves*. It just seems to me we ought to think about developing sets of knowledge and skills at all grade levels, but to apply them to different matters—to selves, to Ohio, to the United States, to the world.

Today's five goals, seemingly agreed upon by all, are shown in the following list:

The Social Studies Curriculum Enables Students to Develop:
1. The skills and the knowledge base of the social sciences, using critical thinking to engage in constructive problem solving.
2. Perspectives of their own life experiences so they see themselves as part of the larger human adventure in time and place.
3. A critical understanding of the origin and development of world institutions, traditions, and values through the study of history and the social sciences of anthropology, geography, psychology, economics, and political science.
4. A critical understanding of the origin and development of the institutions, traditions, and values of the United States through the study of history and the social sciences of anthropology, geography, psychology, economics, and political science.
5. Civic responsibility, cooperative skills, and active civic participation.

Following this, Len talks about materials selection. Matt and Jody, two classroom teachers on leave and assigned to work with Len for the year, will organize and facilitate this task. Len wants people to think about what to preview as primary and supplementary texts or materials.

LEN: There's the approved Ohio list, which equals the officially adopted texts. Others are listed as supplementals, and there are precedents for authoring your own text. All kinds of things are possible to pursue. The point is to nominate some things you'd like to consider to Matt or Jody so they can request examination copies for us to review later in the process.

Now we need to consider the format for the scope and sequence. This is the part that takes the most time, but it's the most meaningful to the teachers who'll use this. It's hard to sequence in social studies, because so many different disciplines enter into social studies and seem to be integrated. Take this information you've been revising, for your grade level or course, and take ideas from the list of five program goals and start to outline it all. One thing that will drive you *crazy* is the issue of specificity. Remember, the graded course of study doesn't prescribe activities, only content. So think in terms of being broad but specific enough so teachers know what to teach—the content to teach. We also need an overriding framework for this. We [in Chester] often use a matrix or a grid because it gives you an overriding picture. It's not always as easy in social studies as in other subjects because social studies changes and virtually everything is developed throughout K to 12. Also, we need to decide whether we want to note mastery-level skills and content; remember the evaluation we had done pointed out our lack of those was a weakness? We also have to take the proficiency tests into account. We *have* to give our kids the background on what's going to be on those tests.

However, the teachers get into a discussion related to academic freedom first. Holly asks, "Are we going to *require* things or *suggest* them?" Len doesn't answer

Holly's question directly, but instead goes on to give an example of how they *could* organize the curriculum through grade-level clusters. He says, though, "This is not the *only* way to organize it." Susan asks, "How do we disentangle the content and skills necessary at each grade level? They all seem so interrelated to me." Len smiles, then says, "Would it add clarity and organization to divide it up? Are there alternative ways to divide it up? What you need is a way to focus the teacher's attention on the goal and objectives." Paula wonders aloud whether teachers will be able to "select a few items from the mastery list, but still get away with emphasizing his/her own thing." Alexander reminds her that they can indicate I for introduce and M for mastery on each objective. Paula asks, "Why agonize over all of this if it can largely be ignored and we can only count on teachers to teach what's on a page that indicates what's mandated?" Alexander responds, "If people here feel it *has* to be taught, it goes on this mandated page. Holly asks, "Is there some way we can give both suggestions and academic freedom to say we should pose them as *suggestions*?" Enid maintains, "We *have* to be about specifying skills and goals but not specific content, such as China." Kent says, "We almost need some protection so if we are teaching X and someone asks why—if it's in the suggested list, we can justify it that way." Len replies, "When I think of a graded course of study, *I* think of the *whole thing* as *required*. Other things are supplementary. *How* one teaches a subject is one's academic freedom." Holly asks, "What if you're teaching something not in the graded course of study?" Kent replies, "Everyone wants academic freedom for them*selves*, and everyone else is to do it too!" At this, everyone laughs. Sharon says, "We need to decide what students are to know in each grade level." Paula asks, "What about an evaluation page?" Dana responds, "You can't put the cart before the horse!" This confusion shows they do not fully understand their task and the nature of the graded course of study document they are to develop. It also illustrates the lack of linearity in such work.

George is concerned about delineating the content below the high school level. Susan moves that they should delineate what they teach. She argues, "I see the need for each grade level to list major topics that need to get covered. Then we could get together with people below and above that level and decide whether these things *must* be taught, not merely suggested."

Today's time has expired, so people leave, again discussing animatedly some things they'd recently done.

The next day, the teachers enter ready for business. Stowing their gear rapidly, they pour cups of coffee and sit around the large table. Len starts promptly,

LEN: I managed to process your program goals, and basically I found out you wanted to reorder the goals. I hope I reflected the opinion of the committee-at-large, although you'll want to examine it closely and probably change some other things, too. And we need to deal with Sally's motion of yesterday. My secretary will be over in a few minutes with it. I'm thinking I see Sally's motion as easy for people grade 5 and above because what they're doing isn't going to change very much. K to 4 is going to have problems with this because they haven't worked with this backdrop. We have no choice in this because we have to pass the state department mandate. As of today we have five goals. From those we have to delineate program objectives. We revisited that and revised it. Much of that came from the current graded course of study. The heart of the graded course of study comes at the next level which is at elementary grade-level objectives and in those for secondary school courses. This then will become the scope and sequence. *These* grade-level and subject matter course objectives have to be written in measurable terms. And there are problems here, chiefly the problem of specificity. By definition a graded course of study is to be broad. Some of you will not get the degree of specificity you want about what to cover. You can't do any of this unless the last item is done. We need to revisit the suggested format. What I suggest is to place in columns the five goals. These are the things—no matter whether they're in kindergarten or grade 12—to appear in every grade level. Some of you need to star some of these things kids should master in each grade level. This committee needs to decide how to deal with the specificity issue. So many issues are at stake here. For one, we need to decide how to get teachers up to multiculturalism and career education.

KENT: One problem is that if we have all these lists of things teachers have to cover, the risk is that they might deal with everything superficially, and nothing in great depth.

HOLLY: Let's just do it. We're starting to talk at great length about how to do it, and we'll never really get it *done* if we keep doing that!

TED: We *can* revise. Let's experiment from now until 9:30 and see if we can do this. Let's just do it and see what happens. We can start with program goal 1, start with the objectives, and just keep going if it's going well.

For the rest of the morning, the group goes through the goal and objectives statements they have developed so far, discussing the positive and negative features of each, editing slightly for redundancies. They say they need secretarial help to clean up the lists because they've written all over them. Len sends Ted over to his secretary with the neatest lists so she can retype them for tomorrow's meeting.

Today, teachers meet again at the high school in their elementary, middle, or high school subgroups to detail what content belongs in each course at each grade level. The administrators and Alice Calhoun circulate, working with each group for a while.

At one point, for example, the high school subgroup decides they would like to increase the social studies graduation requirement from three to four units.

JAMES: Summing up, it looks like we need to propose four units. Grade 9 could be a general introduction to social studies including a review of proficiency [test] items, followed by introductions to economics, geography, psychology, sociology, and anthropology.

MARIAN: Then, according to my notes, grade 10 would be world history and geography since 1789.

KENT: Then we'd have an American focus for eleventh grade with some latitude about a beginning date, but 18 weeks of the twentieth century. If people taught that thematically (and I think they would), they could do so and probably work with the language arts folks to come up with something really interesting.

JAMES: Twelfth grade should have a mandated one-half unit of American government, then the other half unit filled out with a senior elective in things such as American politics, American foreign policy, economics . . .

MARTHA: The business department has taught that [economics] in the past.

JAMES: Yes, Maybe so, but economics taught with a *social studies* perspective is different from economics taught from a *business* perspective.

MARTHA: Fine, James. But maybe we could work with them and redesign the course? There's got to be something really interesting we could do about it!

JAMES: [*continues his list*] . . . government theory and application, psychology, sociology, and a computer simulation about the U.S. Constitution, or the Arab-Israeli conflict. In all likelihood for two years the extra one-half unit of required credit for graduation won't be required—we can't exactly grandfather it in. But 95 percent of our students go to college, so it's likely that guidance counselors will suggest this anyway, even though it's not required.

LEN: Doing this was no easy task. But there's still more to do. Two problem areas are in ninth and twelfth grades. But I think the rest of the department will agree with you because it represents the whole department. We have to pay attention to kids, but also to teachers because if it doesn't fly with them, it won't get taught no matter what.

Here Len seems to be acknowledging the important contribution of individual teachers' practical theories of action and vested interests in solo deliberation. James nods his head in agreement with Len.

JAMES: Advanced placement American history for eleventh grade is also problematic because students will want to be in A.P. for honors. It also pulls the best students out of other classes.

LEN: It constitutes tracking.

PAULA: Maybe so, Len, but it's terrific for students who are really interested in it.

LEN: We almost *have* to have honors sections because of parents' expectations and students' desires.

PAULA: If a course isn't A.P., it might be perceived to be easy. Kids here are absolutely *hyped* about math and English, but not about social studies. I'd be very concerned if we had no A.P. courses in eleventh, only in twelfth grade.

KENT: In the twelfth grade there's no place to hide with all these electives. Teachers have specialized in these and teach a very challenging course. They have *very* high expectations.

George later reminds the high school group they must take the proposal for increasing the social studies graduation requirement to four units to the principal and board of education. James reveals a vested interest when he confesses his major fear about the high school curriculum proposal.

JAMES: We're the largest user of the U.S. Constitution simulation in the world. What if this plan brings about a dramatic drop in enrollment? If we offer all these electives, some courses are bound to suffer enrollment drops. I *love* what I'm doing, so I worry about a significant drop!

KENT: I think teaching economics is more important than teaching about the U.S. Constitution. We can't afford the luxury of having just eight to ten students in classes.

JAMES: We also have a wording problem here concerning students' witnessing policy making in action.

KENT: Demonstrating a practical application of action?

They add his wording to the objective. They continue their deliberations for four days, learning from George very early of the high school principal's lack of support for their four-unit graduation requirement and that the principal has instituted a new-course moratorium. They list all required and elective courses to be offered, and each teacher begins writing its objectives. James says, "Writing these high school course descriptions is easy now because we had thorough discussions where we worked out most issues." Kent adds, "So writing them is fairly straightforward." This illustrates the contribution of conflict to deliberation.

Meanwhile, the middle school group worries about the eighth-grade curriculum. Matt asks, "What's important for us to *focus* on the twentieth century?" He proposes, "Maybe the thirties through the eighties. We can use music as a core." Leslie smiles and says, "Yes, you're thinking we have those terrific *National Geographic* filmstrips with cassettes that go decade by decade with music holding it together reflecting the society that produced it. Is that what you mean? I think everyone knows those materials, and a lot of us are using them." Here the middle school group, like James of the high school group, turns to published curriculum materials to develop the graded course of study. This illustrates the pervasive influence of such materials on the curriculum. Enid adds, "Quickly dealing with the twentieth century in nine weeks and dealing with some major themes . . ." She consults her notes, then continues, "We listed civil/minority rights, career futures, economics, peacemaking, world power and war, and the environment." Paula adds, "If we take these strands and use the decade materials it could be an exciting course. But we have a big problem here, though. *Real* historians don't even talk about anything for 50 years." Despite her reservation, they decide the idea of using those themes and the organization of the *National Geographic* materials is a good idea and begin writing objectives for their grade levels.

The elementary school group focuses on fourth grade for a while before writing their courses of study. Jody asks, "Where we're dealing with historical documents here, do we want to specify which ones?" They reply by volunteering several documents they think are crucial. Janice says, "The Northwest Ordinance of 1787." Holly argues, "The Constitution, including the Bill of Rights." Alexander adds, "Salient Supreme Court decisions and the Declaration of Independence." Then Jody refers to an earlier discussion and implies reversing it when she says, "Maybe chronological order *does* need to go into fourth grade to start giving them a concept of chronological order." "Well," retorts Alexander somewhat tentatively, "okay, as long as it doesn't turn into a memorize-this-date-this-event kind of thing." Molly agrees, "*That* I couldn't abide!" Bob also agrees as do Holly and Janice, so they adopt the idea.

Alice Calhoun has joined the group and notes "a lack of enthusiasm for economics. I would like to suggest that kids and adults need to know a great deal about economics, particularly now. When we [teachers] *know* we have a weakness we have to learn about it as professionals."

The next two days are quickly consumed as people write objectives for individual courses, then conferring briefly with each other for feedback, which consists primarily of requests for rewording to clarifying. At the end of their work on Friday they suggest going out for lunch to celebrate. Len also announces a tentative date in late September for a meeting to begin discussing materials selection.

In the autumn they meet several times, where subgroups propose texts, kits, materials, and programs to adopt for each course. The group votes to accept each.

Eventually, the 244-page document contains individual graded courses of study for the 21 courses offered in social studies in Chester. Objectives and materials are listed along with a philosophy statement for Chester's schools, a social studies philosophy, an overview of Chester's social studies scope and sequence, a statement about evaluation, and a glossary. It is approved by the state board of education on June 22, 1992.

THE SUBTEXT: REACHING
INTERSUBJECTIVE AGREEMENT

Several features of this group of teachers and administrators helped them reach agreement, as the preceding descriptions illustrate. Some features preceded their actual work. For example, many knew each other, having served on other committees and attended university courses or systemwide meetings together. Additionally, many teachers knew Len. They trusted him because of good personal contacts and his excellent reputation for facilitating curriculum development. Further, they knew of his abiding interest in the social studies. They may have been less trusting of George, who was new to the system and had virtually no reputation. George became a minor player in the deliberations, even though he outranked Len. A second prior feature was their sense of pride in the Chester school system and their commitment to social studies education. A third feature was that they were *volunteers*. To be sure, they were modestly remunerated for this work, but that was not a motive for volunteering.

Several patterns of action may have also helped them become cohesive and reach agreement during the meetings. One is the tone Len set. He was informal and positive yet businesslike. Everyone knew the agenda for each meeting, and either it was accomplished or significant progress was made on it. Len expressed his obvious respect for the teachers through his flattering introductions of them, and on several occasions he acknowledged the difficulty of their task but his faith that they could accomplish it. Additionally, Len had planned the meetings to include breaks for informal socializing. Some teachers began voluntarily bringing in homemade cookies or muffins, doughnuts, and fruit for these breaks. Len also kept moving the agenda forward, and teachers felt successful as they saw their progress. The teachers themselves worked toward group cohesion, as evidenced by unsolicited comments made to me while walking to our cars. Len had teachers put their thoughts on paper, then had his secretary type them so everyone could read them, critique them, and rewrite them if necessary. Not only did this practice let them refine their work, but it also let them see their progress. They engaged in professional discourse about a serious matter, and conflict was polite rather than hostile. On occasion they avoided conflict. Their deliberations were frequently at a high level.

As a result of these patterns and features, they actually grew in self-confidence as individuals and as a group. They respected each other's expertise; they knew what they could expect of each other and that all were dedicated and committed to social studies and to developing an outstanding graded course of study. They did not feel one person was taking advantage of others by shirking the tasks at hand. As a result of these patterns and features, they could work together effectively and efficiently. Ultimately, they developed a feeling of great group power. They seemed sad when they disbanded, but proud and glad their work was completed. This subtext set the conditions for the group to develop the curriculum, but was developed as they were developing the actual curriculum. In this following section I briefly analyze how they developed that curriculum.

THE TEXT: DEVELOPING THE CURRICULUM

This group began with *general* matters when deliberating about the social studies graded course of study. They discussed the social studies philosophy and then broad goals and their sequence. When discussing the scope and sequence, they began by examining several alternatives from well-known sources. After this general work, they became more specific, writing objectives for each course and grade level and then finally selecting curriculum materials. Had they not trusted each other and recognized their commitment to social studies in general and their task in particular, their work would probably have gone more slowly and contained more flaws. Developing the subtext permitted developing the text, but developing the text gave them pride in what they were doing. So, the text and subtext are developed simultaneously and support each other in that development.

SUMMARY

In this chapter I described how a group of teachers and two administrators developed the social studies curriculum for the Chester public schools. Then I analyzed the development of group agreement and the curriculum itself and how the two interact.

STUDY QUESTIONS

1. What practices helped this group develop agreement?
2. What did Len do to facilitate group deliberation?
3. What is one example that this case of deliberation is not tidily unidirectional?
4. What is an example of conflict in this case? What brought it about?
5. Even if increasing the social studies requirement from three to four units for graduation were an exceptionally good idea, what would interfere with doing so in Chester?
6. What is an example of the relationship between interest and conflict in this case? How did it aid the work?
7. In what ways is this group's work disorganized? Why is that the case? Does it interfere with their work? How might their work be improved so it is less disorganized?
8. With a partner, list what you believe to be four crucial pieces of advice to people developing a curriculum in a group.

chapter **8**

Discussion and Implications

I begin this final chapter by briefly summarizing characteristics of deliberation and presenting examples of these characteristics at work, as depicted in this text. Then I discuss implications of these characteristics for improving the curriculum.

DISCUSSION: CHARACTERISTICS AND CASES

Curriculum deliberation consists of careful consideration of what students would optimally have opportunities to learn; it is a process of reasoning about this practical problem. Both individuals and groups engage in deliberation. Several characteristics of deliberation are evident in both the theoretical literature and the cases I portrayed in this book.

One characteristic concerns *alternatives*. In the case of Chester (chapter 7), where teachers developed the social studies curriculum, this weighing of alternatives was an important characteristic of their work. They considered suggestions by several authorities about what to include in the curriculum, how to organize the curriculum, and the nature and therefore appropriate content of multicultural education. In deciding which reading series to adopt, Mapleton teachers (chapter 6) on the committee reviewed 15 different series of reading textbooks before narrowing their choice to the three they ultimately voted on. This consideration of alternatives is evident in both group deliberation and when teachers deliberate alone. Karen's planning (chapter 3) is made more difficult, she says, because of the enormous number of truly fine examples of children's literature. As a result, she has almost too many alternatives to use in her planning. Consideration of alternatives is less apparent in the cases of Hascal and James (chapter 4), although Jill (chapter 4) considers several options when deciding on each class art project and whether to begin a new topic with abstract, theoretical lessons or with hands-on projects. During interactive planning, teachers consider many alternatives—for example, what questions should they ask, on whom should they call, and the like.

A second characteristic concerns *envisioning potential actions and outcomes* of each possible solution. Like the first characteristic, this was present in both solo and group deliberation. Individual teachers like Iris (chapter 3) and Jill (chapter 4) claimed "[I could] virtually see myself doing this [plan], and the outcomes are important ones." Teachers also envisioned these during group deliberation, particularly in side comments as the deliberations were ensuing. For example, in Mapleton, when deliberating about a whole-language reading series, one teacher said, "This is fine for places like Chester or Potomac, but I just can't see most of our teachers using this. Not only that, their evaluation approach is just too amorphous and complicated. The teachers couldn't do it, and neither could the kids. We'd have to do some serious in-service!" Another example of envisioning actions and outcomes appeared in chapter 7, when Matt could see using the *National Geographic* materials to teach chronology and U.S. history. Jill voiced serious concerns now that her school system is starting to implement outcomes-based education, which will be mandated in Ohio in the near future. Her dilemma concerned what is meant by outcomes. On the one hand, she's aware that her art students produce desired outcomes of creating individual styles of artwork. Their competence is attested to by the large number of art awards they receive each year. On the other hand, objectifying the production of artwork as an outcome is not easy for her to do. Although Chester's administrators conceive of outcomes broadly, examples of outcomes offered in in-service courses are of concrete objectives, and she struggles about how to word art outcomes so the creative nature of art will not be negated. Jill has difficulty seeing how to do this for her major art goals.

Regarding the *moral dimension* of curriculum deliberation, teachers clearly were committed to making the best decisions guided by their responsibility to their students and to teachers who would be working with them subsequently. On occasion they even resisted administrators' policies out of this commitment. For example, Hascal (chapter 4) viewed his colleagues' expectations as too low and continues to resist conceding to them, despite pressure from his department chairman. During group deliberations, James (chapter 4) worked to include a computer simulation course as an elective because he believes it is important to teach various dimensions of computer use. Likewise, Iris (chapter 3) feels morally committed to teaching students about science because "it's what made America great and will continue to." Mark (chapter 3) sees no reason why students in his school cannot be as highly educated as students in Chester and Potomac, and he strives to educate them excellently: "Just because they aren't sons and daughters of rich people doesn't mean they can't learn. They *can*; I've proven that. This means we have to teach them well, stay in some kids' faces to make them learn it and suck others into learning it." He reorganized the mathematics he taught, because he felt it contained serious errors. In so doing, he resisted Mapleton's graded course of study, which by state policy he was to follow. Likewise, Chester's teachers developing the social studies curriculum were very diligent about their work out of a moral commitment to excellent social studies education.

Interest and *conflict*, two other characteristics of deliberation, were evident in both solo and group deliberation, too, although they manifested themselves somewhat differently. One root of conflict is probably related to the consideration of alternatives. Without the alternatives, individual teachers would not have a conflict when they conceive of or find two equally attractive ideas. In such cases, teachers speak about being "of two minds." This is also the case in group deliberation, where conflict is compounded by competing interests of various individuals. Teachers' interests during solo deliberation influenced them to include in group deliberations particular skills and ideas about which they were knowledgeable and about whose importance they were convinced. It was in their interest to do so because of the breadth and depth of their knowledge about such matters as space (in Iris's case), excellent examples of children's literature (for Karen), logic (for Hascal), computer skills (for James), logical thinking (for Hascal), mathematics (for Mark), and developing a personal artistic style (in Jill's case). Such interests are a part of each teacher's practical theory of action and as a result affect a great deal of what teachers say and do.

In group deliberation, these interests fuel conflict, forcing the group to examine alternatives closely. Conflict in solo deliberation also forces the individual to examine alternatives closely so one can decide to act.

In group deliberation, teachers' individual interests inform what they say and do, and this is one way solo and group deliberation are related. It is in each teacher's interest to have an idea adopted by the group because it is easier to use the adopted curriculum and curriculum materials if it is consistent with that practical theory of action. This is seen in chapter 6, when teachers argued for the textbook series most congruent with their own view of reading along either a whole-language or a skills (including phonics) approach. A clear case of this also appeared in chapter 7 when James argued for the inclusion of computer simulations and was worried that adding many senior electives might cause an enrollment drop in his U.S. constitution simulation course. Differences among teachers' practical theories force people to examine the alternatives more closely than they would if unanimity were present. It also affords teachers the opportunity to have the group examine and challenge parts of their practical theories. If the social environment of group deliberation is open, supportive, and fairly safe, and sufficient time is permitted, a discussion can ensue in which they can examine and perhaps defend their practical theories. Whether this can occur relates to the group processes they develop as they socially construct knowledge and to how they interact, as related in chapter 5. Conflict also unifies the group as witnessed in chapter 7 when Chester teachers ultimately understood their common interest in developing an excellent social studies curriculum and worked together to define it. Conflict is also apparent in solo deliberation when teachers conceive of two viable alternatives but must select only one. It was also present for Iris and Mark when each developed an interesting lesson but was concerned about whether a particular student could control himself during it. In these cases, the conflict centered on whether to do the interesting lesson and create conditions under which a child could misbehave or teach a more easily controlled lesson. Both teachers opted for the interesting lesson because they believed the group would benefit from it, although in both cases the miscreant had to be ejected from class.

Another important feature of curriculum deliberation concerns the three *commonplaces* of content, learners, and milieu. Iris and Karen in chapter 3 tend to focus on content and students to a large extent in their deliberations, while Mark also takes the setting into account. In Ohio teachers are to follow their school system's graded course of study, and while these three teachers did so in planning what to teach, they did not adhere rigidly to it. Iris elaborated greatly on science, Karen on language arts, and Mark on mathematics. Mark also changed the sequence in mathematics when he found errors in the graded course of study. By contrast, James and Hascal (chapter 4) focused much more on content than on any other commonplace. Perhaps this is due partly to their preservice education, which typically focuses more on the content of their teaching than is true for that provided for elementary school teachers. Also, the recent growth of the testing movement coupled with teachers' desires for their students to succeed on those tests has increased the focus on content. High school students seem to have a sense of what they want to study after high school, and perhaps that also influences these high school teachers to focus more on content.

Nurturing the development of a group in a socially supportive environment during group deliberation might allow reflection about both individuals' views and the curriculum under development, thereby leading to curriculum improvement. This is clear when comparing the content of chapters 6 and 7. In chapter 7, Len and the group took care to build and nurture the group, whereas in chapter 6 Judi followed school system policy and focused primarily on technical steps agreed upon by the teachers' union and the board of education. However, in neglecting the building of the group (other than the superficial acts of bringing snacks and worrying aloud about some teachers' health), she may have failed to facilitate the optimum decision and may not have created opportunities for teachers to make a full examination of their beliefs.

Another negative factor influencing the textbook adoption (which nonetheless was allowed for in developing the social studies curriculum) relates to the necessity of acting within a *zone of time*. In selecting a textbook for the Mapleton school system, the group *had* to reach a decision early enough to develop a ballot that teachers could vote on, according to the board of education and union agreement. They also had to allow adequate time so materials could be purchased and delivered in time for school's opening in late August. This may have caused stress for the group and Judi, which may have forced them to act more hastily and with less than full consideration. This zone of time issue also affected individual teachers—for example, when Mark Schaefer knew he had to administer standardized tests in April that he wanted his students to do well on, he realized he had to complete most of his significant teaching by then. The state-wide competency tests also influence teachers at other grade levels. In another example, because the computer simulation that James Kennedy used was interactive, he and his students had to reply to messages or take actions in a timely manner.

Deliberation is also a *social enterprise*. This is most obvious in group deliberations as portrayed in chapter 7, although it also influenced solo delib-erations because many of the teachers considered the good of society. Iris (chapter 3) held this as her chief reason for teaching about science, and Mark (chapter 3) hopes his students will be productive members of society.

Finally, *simultaneity* is apparent in both group and solo deliberation. It seems particularly characteristic of teachers who improvise, as most of the teachers portrayed in these cases do. These teachers generally do preactive planning, but interactively fill in details as they see where the lesson is proceeding, how attentive the class is, and how well behaved students are during the lesson. This is obvious in Jill Richardson's planning, for while she is teaching she is simul-taneously deciding how to treat many matters. The same is true in the cases of Iris Robole's and Karen Smith's planning. It is less true of Hascal Legupski, Mark Schaefer, and James Kennedy. James follows the notebook accompanying the computer simulation he uses, and in order to maintain the simulation's inter-activity, he cannot deviate much from its schedule.

As can be seen from this brief discussion of characteristics of deliberation evident in the cases, people are already naturally doing bits of deliberation. However, I think it can be improved upon, and I turn to that topic in this final section of the chapter.

IMPROVING THE CURRICULUM

Genuine curriculum improvement—reaching into the classrooms where teachers and students interact so the students actually have opportunities to learn—depends on teachers' deliberations and actions, not on legislators' or adminis-trators' policies. I think curriculum improvement is a slow process that occurs mostly in specific classrooms, schools, and local school systems instead of on a statewide or national level. The reason is that curriculum improvement calls for teachers continually to make sense of what they know about the content they teach and their students. They then reformulate actions when needed, improving the opportunities students have for learning. Because teachers have different theories of action, wide-scale curriculum reform policies and movements are unlikely to mesh with many teachers' theories. What can be done, then, about curriculum improvement?

This theory of curriculum development carries with it several interrelated implications for improving what is taught in schools, and I discuss several of these in this section. Since people are clearly already doing bits and pieces of deliber-ation, I think the primary problem is to enhance those efforts. One way to help with this is through preservice and in-service education, where teachers could learn about the development, reflection upon, and refinement of their own theories of action. Because teachers develop their theories of action *in* action (see Argyris and Schön, 1974), this work should be as similar to their practice as possible, and it may be best suited as a goal of in-service education. Preservice education might assign work in which interns analyze and reflect on their teaching, using videotapes of their own teaching rather than merely reading about theories of action. Another approach is to study detailed cases or video-tapes of other teachers' actions and theories and then interpret how their own theory of action differs. They would then reflect on why it differs, defending and critiquing those differences. University educators would do well to deliberate about the need for these and similar activities in the curriculum and how to enact them. In-service teachers can record lessons and reflect on what must be their theory of action in those lessons. This might be done effectively in groups, where the interaction might support teachers' considering matters they would not have had others not raised them. I think it is central and crucial for improving the curriculum. Indeed, much current education reform literature calls for the development of reflective teaching (Holmes Group, 1986; Green, 1988; Gitlin, 1990).

Teachers should reflect on how their insights into teaching, students, and the curriculum fit together with their theories of action. However, Freidus (1991:1) says few teacher education programs take into account this wealth of knowledge teachers already possess. I argue that teacher education should help teachers to examine what they know and order it into a theory of action because such examination, discussion, and writing will help them bring it into their conscious knowledge from their tacit knowledge. Once the theory is in their conscious knowledge, they possess it rather than it possessing them. They will no longer be acting on it blindly.

I also think teacher education should help teachers become conscious of the nature of deliberation in its ideal form rather than providing an objectives-first model of planning that dedicated, experienced teachers apparently rarely use for some excellent reasons. Countless studies and articles devoted to the nature of planning by professional teachers show that teachers do not write linear, objectives-driven lesson plans. I think a better way to teach about planning is to focus upon the nature of deliberation and to help teachers understand their own deliberation process.

Thirdly, teacher education needs to develop leadership skills. Teachers can then facilitate the frequent group curriculum deliberations in which they are involved during grade-level, departmental, and other decision-making forums. Understanding how to facilitate group curriculum deliberation is needed for educational administrators as well as for teachers.

In addition to reforming teacher education, schools need to become learning environments in which teachers can collegially construct and reconstruct their theories of action, redevelop the curriculum, create appropriate curriculum materials, and resolve curriculum problems. In this view, educators use their feeling of responsibility to one another and to the students they teach to actively seek to master their own work and to create an environment to make their school effective.

However, this further means that curriculum policies and materials also need to support deliberation rather than narrowly mandating highly specific outcomes that strip teachers of the responsibility of deliberating in order to create goals and instructional strategies most appropriate for their students, subject matter, and setting and also to create conditions where the most students can learn the most possible. Here the role of the school is not just to teach students, but also to become an exciting environment for educators to learn, to inquire into their own practice, and to examine and develop the curriculum through solo and group deliberation. When the developers of the curriculum also enact it, they learn from that process of development, become committed to their work, and enact better decisions than when the curriculum is developed by an outside agency and mandated for all to use.

STUDY QUESTIONS

1. What are some actions you can take to improve the curriculum? In what ways do they or do they not relate to deliberation? In what context(s) can you take these actions?
2. What research still needs to be done about deliberation and the curriculum?
3. If massive school reform through dictating top-down curriculum policies and developing teacher-proof kits is not likely to work to improve schools, what *does* have a chance? Why is it likely to work?
4. Why is it crucial for each teacher to understand her/his practical theory of action fully? Is it likely that leaders of group deliberation also have practical theories of action? What about administrators? Is it important for administrators to understand these theories as well? Why?
5. How does the set of ideas presented in this book relate to teachers' professional development?
6. Currently, the development of a national curriculum in the United States is under way. Based on this book, what advice do you have for people engaged in this?

chapter 9

Research Appendix

In this appendix I discuss the methodology I employed for my research in chapters 3, 4, 6, and 7. I begin the appendix by relating my views about qualities of my research approach to Eisner's (1991) six features of qualitative studies. Then I specify how I designed the studies, collected data, analyzed and interpreted it, and wrote about it. I include this information here so people can consider how trustworthy the research is. I used a qualitative approach to the research because it was sensitive to my research focus of describing the nature of deliberation alone and in groups. However, many kinds of qualitative research are possible, and this first section describes features of my approach. Its major sources are educational ethnography and educational criticism.

CHARACTERISTICS OF THE RESEARCH

Eisner (1991:32–40) enumerates six features of qualitative studies. Because I find his list helpful, in this section I briefly review them and discuss how my research reflected those features. Eisner (1991:39) maintains that "the character of the enterprise [of qualitative research] has a strong rational and often aesthetic spirit."

His first feature is that qualitative studies are typically *field focused*. The studies in this book occurred in natural places: classrooms, meeting rooms, and other parts of schools where I examined the educative processes, particularly the process of deliberation. They were nonmanipulative, or in Lincoln and Guba's (1978) language, "naturalistic." Further, they focused on meanings that educational practitioners constructed of phenomena as well as my own meanings. In the sense that I tried to understand participants' life-worlds and the meanings they constructed, they were phenomenological. Further, for these cases I strove to ensure participants were genuine volunteers. I scheduled my work around normal school schedules. In addition, I promised volunteers I would do what I could to assure them anonymity, and I asked them to check for that when they read their cases. Teachers made up their own names, frequently from family names. They claimed to have gotten rewards from the research. For example, perhaps because her mother had been a teacher, Karen Smith's (chapter 3) mother had persistently asked her how she taught. Karen gave her a copy of chapter 3 to answer a recent barrage of questions. Jill said I probably knew her better than she knew herself, so she understood her own practice better. Teachers further claimed they liked having me in their rooms so they could discuss their practice with someone who knew it intimately. I helped occasionally with small tasks such as supervising seatwork and assisting with making bulletin boards or study centers, but I believe the discussions and interest in their practice were much more rewarding than my assisting with lessons. Iris Robole and Mark Schaefer claimed they became more articulate about their practice.

A second feature Eisner considers is *self as instrument*. Researchers do not use an external or predetermined form for coding behaviors or interviewing participants. Rather, they use their connoisseurship—their perceptivity and knowledge—to explore topics. Eisner introduces a related idea, the *positive exploitation of one's own subjectivity,* in which one uses one's own background and knowledge to develop insights. My own experiences teaching and deliberating alone and in groups, as a facilitator of curriculum development, and as a group member were invaluable in building my knowledge of processes of curriculum development. Of course, I also read widely to enrich my perspective, as chapters 1, 2, and 5 reveal. I tried to create and maintain a balance among participants' views of phenomena (to ensure a phenomenonological and emic—insider's—stance) and my observations and insights developed from my own experiences and reading (for the etic—outsider's—stance). When I sensed imbalances I frequently shared my perceptions and interpretations with participants in member checks. Although this moved the phenomenological and emic stance to the foreground over the etic stance, my aim was to understand the nature of deliberative practices. I believed the insiders' views were a better route to this than would be possible through etic avenues.

A third feature Eisner cites is the *interpretive* nature of qualitative studies. Here he differentiates between two sorts of interpretations (see also McCutcheon, 1981). One concerns understanding why something is occurring, and for this researchers can draw on the social sciences or can begin developing new theories. As chapters 1, 2, and 5 indicate, I drew on much social science literature in reading for these studies. I applied several theories to this work and elaborated on some. This is the etic dimension of interpretation.

The other sort of interpretation concerns the meanings of phenomena for participants. Because my studies focused upon how and what people thought in developing curricula, this sort of interpretation was particularly important to me. It grew out of my observations and collaborative discussions about them, related to the emic dimension, as discussed. The studies assumed individual and social construction of knowledge and used this premise as a research tool. When selecting participants I openly discussed my research focus and asked practitioners to teach me about their experiences, views, and practices about curriculum development. In Zaharlick's (1992:119) words, this employs the "researcher as learner." Particularly at the beginning of the research process, I was in the subordinate role of learner because I was trying to acquire knowledge. As a result, I did not normally solicit information. Rather, participants raised many matters in discussions that were more than interviews since we both controlled their initiation, content, flow, and length. This meant I had to establish an open, trusting, and ethical relationship with participants, which I tried to do through both my actions and words. I believe commitment, honesty, and confidentiality are crucial dimensions. I am concerned about the degree of exploitation in research requiring collaboration with participants to understand phenomena such as curriculum development.

Geertz (1973) argues that highly interpretive research is a necessary condition to enhance understanding the human condition because people develop complex ways of interacting in their cultures. Understanding the meanings of actions is, for Geertz, at the heart of human inquiry, and I agree.

Eisner's fourth feature is the *use of expressive language and the presence of voice in the text*. I think this is important because one way readers might understand phenomena such as curriculum development is through evocative nonfictional stories. The presence of voice is due to self as instrument and the positive exploitation of subjectivity. The researcher's voice is inherent in the text, and readers evaluate that subjective voice in order to have a (mental) conversation with it while reading the text. I have tried to help readers understand what other people experienced. In these cases, the many teachers, students, and administrators were the participants in the settings. I assumed an emic stance in these studies by portraying these participants' views and life-worlds. I assumed an etic stance when I interpreted what I saw through the literature of the social sciences and deliberation.

I think virtually kidnapping readers (albeit, with their agreement) and taking them to the settings through evocative prose might enhance their opportunities to understand my experiences and those of the participants in curriculum development. This can enhance transferability, the reader's ability to generalize from what is known about the research to his or her own situation when warranted. Further, the voices in these studies are those of the participants— the students, teachers, administrators, and I—who tried to understand how curriculum development was occurring and the nature of the resultant curriculum. As a result, in places I developed a text where various participants tell their own stories.

Eisner's fifth feature concerns *close attention to details*. I tried to do this throughout my observations and discussions by using a separate set of field notes of what I saw and heard for each study. I filed field notes, documents, and other evidence in a separate folder for each case, as there was an enormous amount of evidence. Staying organized is crucial. After leaving the setting each day I reread field notes and reflected on what I was learning and what needed further scrutiny. As I drove to schools I thought about what I wanted to examine if possible that day. I tried to arrive sufficiently early to reread my field notes yet again before starting my work, and I was able to do so on most days, barring traffic jams or parking difficulties. Attention to details is obviously necessary while observing and discussing practices as well. One problem resulting from the attention to myriad details is the length of qualitative studies. However, I believe their richness outweighs this problem, for they can yield exciting and important understandings of practice. An implication of this for readers is for them to pay close attention to details, too.

Eisner's final feature of qualitative studies pertains to *criteria* for assessing them. While I can discuss each criterion and how I tried to take the criteria into account, it is up to readers to judge the studies. Eisner's criteria include coherence, insight, and instrumental utility. By coherence, Eisner means how well the argument underlying the story holds together. Does the argument make sense, support conclusions, and use multiple data sources? Are the various parts and the evidence congruent with each other? Readers wonder whether the case "rings true," and I considered this throughout the writing process. I tried to treat it in three ways. First, I checked many of the cases by returning to the setting and reading the case there, wondering, "Is this case about what happened here?" Second, I asked each participant to read her or his pertinent case in a final member check. Third, I field tested these cases in classes I taught or when I guest lectured in other classes and asked students whether the cases rang true in their experiences.

A related concern is about consensus, the degree of consistency between the researcher's interpretations and the evidence. One aspect concerns referential adequacy, the sufficiency of evidence for interpretations, its warrant (Erickson, 1986). This is related to the idea in qualitative research that interpretations require several pieces of evidence for support. Ethnographers call this "triangulation" (Webb et al., 1966), and aesthetic critics (Pepper, 1945) refer to it as "structural corroboration." This criterion is important since it permits readers to assess the credibility of interpretations and might permit them to extend or develop aspects of theory independently of the author. I attended to this issue through my method of analysis and interpretation, as I will discuss below.

Although Eisner does not say so, I think by insight he means educational significance—the importance of the studies. I tried to enhance significance by raising what I consider to be fundamental questions from the beginning and by rereading my field notes frequently to check whether I was in fact studying those important matters. I had developed some of those fundamental questions from my experiences in curriculum development and others from reading. Still others came up while I was doing the research, for some teachers saw the process differently or focused on different aspects of the inquiry. I tried to keep the studies somewhat parallel to ease comparison, but I did not want to force a study merely to maintain that parallelism. As each study progressed I wrote interpretive memos where I noted possible plausible interpretations for what I saw and heard.

I kept trying to push my interpretations to deeper levels by asking myself and participants why particular phenomena were occurring as well as what they meant.

By instrumental utility Eisner means a study's usefulness in helping readers understand otherwise confusing phenomena. This relates to the criterion of expressive language. As I designed the studies, I tried to account for this by considering what would be practically useful to know about curriculum development. I also tried to account for it as I wrote and reread my work. I also checked on this somewhat during field tests.

To Eisner's characteristics I would add that qualitative studies are *site specific,* which is related to being field focused. I chose particular sites because some of their features were likely to shed light on the research. Because I used particular settings and their people, I do not claim generalizability for the research. However, if I have been at all successful here, readers will be able to transfer and apply relevant parts of the cases and insights to their own settings and practice. This could help people to modify or develop practices or to merely understand their own and others' practices better.

Finally, in this section, I want to discuss the relationship among research, theory, and practice. I believe research about education and other human endeavors should be done about the nature of human practice (in this case, curriculum development) so we can understand our own work and improve upon it. I believe qualitative research works toward this end, as shown in Figure 9.1. That is, a researcher begins with theories and questions gleaned from reading, experience, and previous research not with a tabula rasa. This is what Eisner means by connoisseurship and what others mean by starting with a theory. By studying the interpretive interplay between that early understanding and what is seen in the field, research into practices can yield insights and new theories. This is a long and slow process, but eventually the researcher can generate new theory—interconnected sets of understandings about a phenomenon.

In the next section I discuss how I designed the studies with these views in mind.

RESEARCH DESIGN

Many qualitative studies have a somewhat fluid research design. In my research I designed parts of each case before commencing field work. The most important design aspect of any research is deciding what to study. I believe that curriculum development is a very important matter, but before I began to study it I needed to narrow my focus somewhat. Early in the process I decided to conceptualize the work around deliberation because in my experience it seemed more powerful in explaining what happened during curriculum development than other theories. I also knew I wanted to link individual teachers' planning processes to deliberation because my prior research into teacher planning and practical theories of action seemed to indicate such a relationship. Moreover, deliberation has not

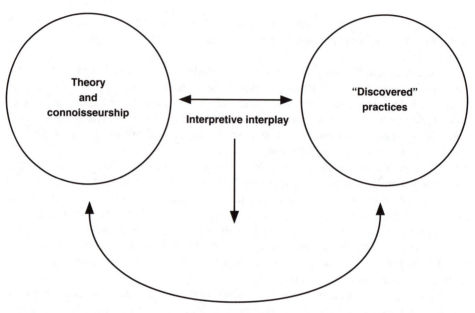

FIGURE 9.1   The growth of theory using qualitative research

recently been much studied in the curriculum literature, although it seemed powerful in helping people understand fundamental curriculum processes. I wanted to present the ideas associated with deliberation and enhance an understanding of the process. In short, I wanted to amplify ideas about deliberation to help people understand its potential for curriculum development so they could apply it to their own work. Over the years I built a set of questions about curriculum development and noted possible fertile research routes. Out of these questions I developed a set of questions for my studies of solo deliberation:

1. Who is this person? What is his or her background? Where does this teacher work?
2. How does this teacher think about her or his practice?
3. What is the nature of this teacher's practical theory of action? How does this teacher talk about it?
4. To what does this teacher attribute it?
5. How does this teacher use it?
6. What else influences this teacher's curriculum? In what ways?
7. How does this teacher plan? What constitutes planning here?
8. To what extent does this teacher consider alternatives when planning?
9. How does this teacher use the plans?
10. What roles does the graded course of study play here?

11. What is the nature of the explicit curriculum here? The implicit curriculum?
12. What is the nature of deliberation here?

These questions guided my studies of group deliberation:

1. Who are the people here? Why are they here?
2. What are purposes of this group? How does the group express them?
3. What interests are evident here? How do they surface?
4. What is the nature of conflict, its sources, and its effects on the process and resultant decisions?
5. What is this group's platform?
6. How does this group construct its knowledge?
7. To what extent does this group consider alternatives?
8. How does this group make decisions?
9. What social rules does this group develop? How? What roles do they play?
10. What role does leadership play here? Who's involved in it? How?
11. How does stress affect the process and decisions? What is its nature?
12. What is the nature of the explicit curriculum here?
13. What is the nature of deliberation here? Under what conditions does it occur?

I let other parts of these studies emerge during field work because of what was occurring in the setting. For instance, in chapter 6, conflict and interest seemed to be the richest themes, so I dwelt on them greatly, and to understand them I held discussions with three key participants in addition to observing. In chapter 4, I became interested in how other teachers made use of the simulation.

Sampling

Another crucial set of design issues in qualitative research concerns sampling, the selection of sites, and participants for the study. Many types of sampling are possible. After reviewing them I decided to do purposive sampling. I selected sites and participants where I thought chances were high that I would see excellent examples of curriculum development and where participants would be likely to help me understand what was happening. For example, for the cases in chapters 3 and 4 I wanted to locate teachers who were reflective and open to discussing their reflections with me. Otherwise, I could not study solo deliberation since it is a mental phenomenon. In cases of group deliberation, I wanted to study two situations where the processes of deliberation being used were likely to differ. Otherwise, I could have done just one study of group deliberation, where I might not even have seen deliberation occurring. I planned to do these two studies in different school systems because expertise in curriculum development varies widely in this part of the country.

In each case, I had to comply with a bureaucratic process in order to receive permission to do research in schools. I had to write a brief request to the appropriate official discussing what I wanted to study and the demands I would make on the teacher. I was denied access to one school system in a large city because in their view my study was not congruent with what they said served their interests. I looked elsewhere and was afforded access in a similar setting. Following bureaucratic approval, I contacted principals and teachers I knew in those school systems to locate teachers for studies of solo deliberation. I was gratified to receive many names of teachers whom others deemed reflective and interested in research. The process of obtaining bureaucratic approval and selection typically took two months, during which time I began studying the community where the field work would take place so I could place the study in its context. For cases of group deliberation, I selected among situations where I knew groups would be involved in curriculum development, either selecting curriculum materials or developing a graded course of study. When I located several such situations, I selected two, based on criteria of proximity, likelihood of seeing deliberation, and two different sorts of curriculum tasks. Again, I followed the process to gain access.

When I had some individual teachers others deemed reflective and articulate about their practice, I met with each for about 20 minutes to outline my work and to assess their interest in it. Because I wanted to make efficient use of my time, I made sure my travel time would not be more than one hour to the school, for qualitative research demands many visits. In the cases of group deliberation, I contacted school systems where I knew group curriculum development would be occurring and spoke to the facilitator about the schedule and the group's mission. When I selected the schools for the cases in chapters 6 and 7, I kept in mind the travel time. Because the studies focused on the participants' thinking and the meanings they made of matters, their own interest in the project was important. If they were interested, they could direct my thinking rather than me controlling the focus. This is one reason why the design was somewhat emergent. I chose key informants in group deliberations as I was involved in the studies. They shared their views with me more than others did, although I tried to represent the group's views in selecting those informants. It would have been difficult to interview all members intensively in these large groups. In other words, in the studies about group deliberation I used purposive sampling to develop a range of views representing other participants.

The Duration of Each Study

A hallmark of much qualitative research is prolonged engagement, not merely one or two observations. In each of these cases, I was involved in research for two to seven months. In the cases of solo deliberation, I typically observed and discussed teachers' practice for eight weeks. In the cases of group deliberation, I attended every meeting except two, when a family emergency occurred; on those occasions, participants collected a set of handouts for me and described what had happened. In addition to attending these meetings, I held discussions with individuals about relevant topics. In the elementary school cases of solo deliberation, I attended school every day for most of the day so I could observe the flow of the day. In secondary schools, each teacher and I selected one class for the research focus, and I attended it every day for six to ten weeks. I knew I had completed my observations and discussions when information was becoming redundant (in the solo deliberation cases) or when the group had completed its task.

Equipped with these perspectives on research and this design, and with participants selected for the research, I began my research. In this next section I discuss how I gathered evidence.

COLLECTING DATA

Because of how I conceptualized these studies I gathered two kinds of data most likely to shed light on my research problems: field notes of observations and discussions and documents.

Field Notes

Field notes consisted of what I observed in classrooms and meeting rooms and the contents of discussions I had with various participants. While some method-ologists (e.g., Bogdan and Biklen, 1992:107) suggest writing field notes after leaving the setting, I took them while there to "capture" faithfully what occurred. Instead of rewriting them, I worked directly from them while writing so they would not go through several iterations, which might destroy their immediacy and reduce their value somewhat. During the discussions, though, I was con-cerned about paying close attention and being an active participant in them, so I occasionally jotted very brief notes. After the discussion ended and I had left the setting, I used those memory joggers to reconstruct the discussion and later asked participants to check them for accuracy. I began my field notes by describ-ing the classroom or meeting room and its participants. Next, I noted changes or inconsistencies about those descriptions and focused my attention on what was occurring as well as on my research questions. I left a margin in my field notes to ease analysis. Field notes comprised my major evidence.

Documents

I collected documents participants used in making curriculum decisions. These included photocopies of pages from teacher's guides, teacher's lesson plans, the graded courses of study, memos from administrators, and a few teacher's guides I bought (for the cases in chapter 6). When doing research about settings, documents from a community's chamber of commerce were particularly helpful. Documents also played an important role in the cases of group deliberation, when I collected state and local policies and the materials they were writing.

In the following section I discuss the processes of analysis and interpretation that I used. I want to point out, though, that I analyzed my data while I was still collecting it to remind myself of what I still needed to study. In other words, analysis was ongoing primarily so I could plan research visits in light of previous ones and make efficient use of time.

ANALYZING AND INTERPRETING DATA

Analysis

I think analysis concerns rereading data and systematically locating themes linked to the research questions and other themes. My first analysis task consisted of rereading the data for each case study carefully and noting patterns. My second was to reread my data to note incidents related to my research questions. My third task was to develop ways to index the evidence so I would be able to locate it when writing. One way was first to number each page of my field notes and documents and then make a file card for each theme on which I listed relevant pages in the field notes and documents. I also coded these themes and questions by assigning each a letter, and I wrote those letters in margins of field notes. Glaser and Strauss (1967:106) provide advice about the constant comparative method of analysis, which I followed: "While coding an incident for a category, compare it with the previous incidents in the same and different groups coded within the same category." After this I wrote myself an analytic memo, which is particularly helpful in discerning the nature of a phenomenon. Since several of my research questions concerned the nature of deliberation, stress, and leadership, I found this strategy to be particularly helpful. It played a role in developing the case studies, but even a larger role in the analyses and discussions in chapter 8. At times I also developed subcategories (Strauss and Corbin, 1990) when I discerned nuances within a larger category or because the category contained so much data that it was unwieldy and not very significant. Analysis is not as exciting to me as interpretation, but it is an important aspect of making sense out of the research evidence. I recognize that computer programs are available to assist with this. While my students are making use of them, I have yet to study them sufficiently. Because I had not entered my evidence on computer disks, it did not appear to me to be useful to learn to use them, although I plan to do so in the future. Ultimately, I think they would be helpful for analysis, but not for interpretation, my next topic.

Interpretation

Interpretation consists of deepening the meanings, extending the discussion, and raising questions (Eisner, 1992:95). For Geertz (1973:60) it takes researchers to the very heart of the phenomenon being studied.

One kind of interpretation I employed consisted of describing practitioners' meanings of matters. For instance, the solo deliberators claimed they did not do formal planning, but rather had a general plan in mind. I believed this was sufficiently clear that I did not need an outside construct to explain it, so I elected to leave this interpretation as it was. Another sort of interpretation concerns the social meanings of matters. In discussing interpretation, Maquet (1964) says "social facts" are the social meanings of matters and have one or many meanings inherent in them, while physical phenomena usually have but one. He concludes that the social meanings are rarely obvious and require interpretation. Developing social meanings is one reason for prolonged engagement; otherwise, a researcher is unlikely to understand meanings of particular events and statements in the social setting. For example, consider a nod. Is it a nod of agreement, a nod of boredom, or a nod to mimic another, disliked group participant about whom the members have developed an in-joke? A second contributor to developing social meanings is literature from the social sciences. For example, it was easier to spot instances of conflict and interest while doing research for the cases in chapter 6 than it would have been had I not read the pertinent literature. At that time I did not know how conflict and interest would surface and affect deliberations, but because I was familiar with the concepts I could look for them and ask about them in discussions with three participants. Further, had I not previously done research and read about teacher planning, I would not have understood what teachers meant when they claimed they did not plan in any formal sense. Reading about teachers' practical theories of action further helped me understand what to observe and ask and how to make sense of those observations and discussions.

In short, this sort of interpretation is both an emic and an etic enterprise. One must understand the meanings insiders make of matters and know pertinent ideas from education and the social sciences. To construct these interpretations, I wrote notes about potential speculative interpretive paths and then checked my field notes to ascertain whether I had sufficient evidence to warrant the interpretation. I selected among the speculative paths I thought most significant.

WRITING ABOUT THE STUDIES

All this work goes for nought, though, without considering writing. I based my writing style for the cases on several ideas related to matters I discussed previously: use of active prose and the pronoun "I," a multi-voice text, and a speculative tone.

I employed active prose to reflect the active nature of deliberation and teaching. I wrote in first person to display my part in doing the research and because I exploited my own subjectivity. The research and interpretations did not just pop up overnight. I tried to write in an interesting, evocative, and inviting style to keep readers interested in the topic, to permit them to "see" what happened in these classrooms and meeting rooms, and to enhance the possibility of understanding and transferability. My prose is sometimes speculative since uncertainty exists about many matters in education. Primarily, though, the speculative tone invites readers to resolve some issues and challenges them to continue to think and deliberate about those uncertain ideas. Moreover, because so much uncertainty exists about many matters in education, each individual educator has to make many choices. This speculative tone may encourage readers to consider such matters in depth.

I wrote the cases from outlines where I listed major analytic and interpretive themes and from pages in field notes and documents where I could find evidence of them. While I did not use a computer for analysis, I did use it for word processing so I could reread each case many times before giving it to Linda Jones, my secretary, for her finishing touches. After member checks, I field tested each case and returned it to her again for revisions to incorporate the changes resulting from member checks and field tests.

SUMMARY

In this appendix I discussed foundations underlying my methods, how I conceived of and designed these studies, and strategies I used to gather, analyze, and interpret data. I primarily observed and engaged in discussions complemented by collecting relevant documents. My final section concerned my thoughts on writing style.

STUDY QUESTIONS

1. Assess these cases in light of Eisner's (or other) criteria for "good" qualitative research. Write to me to share your assessment.
2. Most qualitative researchers do not claim generalizability, but do claim transferability. What transfers from these cases to situations with which you are familiar? I'm beginning to think that although details differ, but some general themes and concepts may actually be generalizable—such as characteristics of deliberation, the relationship between interest and conflict, and improvisational planning. Do you agree? Why or why not?
3. How might my sampling have influenced what I found out?
4. What is grounded theory? Does this book constitute grounded theory? In what ways?
5. How did my writing style contribute to or interfere with your understanding of the nature of deliberation?
6. In what ways did my research methods fit my research problem? How did they not?

Bibliography

Anderson, C. R. (1976). Coping behaviors as intervening mechanisms in the inverted-U stress-performance relationship. *Journal of Applied Psychology* 61: 30-34.

Anderson, N. H. (1961). Group performance in an anagram task. *Journal of Social Psychology* 55: 67-75.

Annink-Lehman, C. F. (1992). Personal communication.

Apple, M. (1981). Packaged curricula control teaching. *Communications Quarterly* 4:2 (Winter): 4.

Argyris, C. (1982). *Reasoning, Learning and Action: Individual and Organizational.* San Francisco: Jossey-Bass.

Argyris, C., and Schön, D. (1974). *Theory in Practice: Increasing Professional Effectiveness.* San Francisco: Jossey-Bass.

Baddeley, A. D. (1972). "Selective attention and performance in dangerous environments." *British Journal of Psychology* 63: 537-546.

Bagley, W. C. (1931). The textbook and methods of teaching. *NSSE Yearbook* 30: 7-26.

Battison, S. (1990). *The Context of Deliberation: Case Studies in Local Curriculum Development.* Columbus: Ohio State University, Ph.D. dissertation.

Berger, P. L., and Luckmann, T. (1966). *The Social Construction of Reality.* New York: Doubleday Anchor.

Bernstein, R. (1976). *The Restructuring of Social and Political Theory.* New York: Harcourt Brace Jovanovich.

Black, H. (1967). *The American Schoolbook.* New York: William Morrow.

Bogdan, R. C., and Biklen, S. K. (1992). *Qualitative Research for Education,* 2nd ed. Boston: Allyn and Bacon.

Borko, H., and Niles, J. A. (1987). Descriptions of teacher planning: Ideas for teachers and researchers. In *Educators' Handbook: A Research Perspective,* edited by V. Richardson-Koehler, 167-187. New York: Longman.

Borko, H., Livingston, C., McCalleb, J., and Mauro, L. (1988). Student-Teachers Planning and Post-Lesson Reflection. In *Teachers Professional Learning,* edited by J. Calderhead. Philadelphia: Falmer Press.

Bowler, M. (1978). The making of a textbook. *Learning* 6 (March): 38-42.

Bromme, R., and Juhl, K. (1988). How teachers construe pupil understanding of tasks in mathematics: Relating the content to cognitive processes of the learner. *Journal of Curriculum Studies* 20: 269-275.

Bussis, A., Chittenden, E., and Amarel, M. (1976). *Beyond Surface Curriculum*. Boulder, CO: Westview Press.

Carr, W., and Kemmis, S. (1983). *Becoming Critical: Knowing Through Action Research*. Victoria, Aust.: Deakin University Press.

Carse, J. P. (1986). *Finite and Infinite Games*. New York: Ballantine.

Cartwright, D., and Zander, A. (1953). *Group Dynamics*. New York: Harper & Row.

Cattell, R. (1951). New concepts for measuring leadership in terms of group syntality. *Human Relations* 4: 161-184.

Chambers, J. H. (1983). *The Achievement of Education: An Examination of Key Concepts in Educational Practice*. New York: Harper & Row.

Cherryholmes, C. (1988). *Power and Criticism*. New York: Teachers College Press.

Clandinin, D. J. (1986). *Classroom Practice*. London: Falmer Press.

———. (1985). Personal practical knowledge: A study of teachers' classroom images. *Curriculum Inquiry* 15: 361-385.

Clark, C. M., and Peterson, P. L. (1986). Teachers' thought processes. In *Handbook of Research on Teaching,* 3rd ed., edited by M. C. Wittrock, 255-296. New York: Macmillan.

Clark, C. M., and Yinger, R. J. (1979). Research of teacher thinking. In *Conceptions of Teaching,* edited by P. L. Peterson and H. J. Walberg, 231-263. Berkeley: McCutchan.

Combs, J. R. (1984). Practical reasoning and value analysis education. Washington, D.C.: Presentation at the National Council of Social Studies, November.

Connelly, M., and Clandinin, J. (1988). *Teachers as Curriculum Planners*. New York: Teachers College Press.

Coser, L. (1956). *The Functions of Social Conflict*. New York: Free Press.

Cross, B. (1992). *Teachers' Practical Knowledge During Curriculum Planning in a Professional Development School*. Columbus: Ohio State University, Ph.D. dissertation.

Dahrendorf, R. (1959). *Class and Class Conflict in Industrial Society*. Stanford: Stanford University Press.

Davis, O. L., Frymier, J. R., and Clinefelter, D. (1977). Curriculum materials used by eleven-year-old pupils. New York: Presentation at the Annual Meeting of the American Educational Research Association. ERIC #ED 138 609.

Dewey, J. (1938). *Experience and Education*. New York: Macmillan.

———. (1922). *Human Nature and Conduct*. New York: Henry Holt.

Dinkmeyer, R. (1970). *Developing Understanding of Self and Others*. Kit #1, D1. Circle Pines, MN: American Guidance Service.

Duckworth, E. (1984). What teachers know: The best knowledge base. *Harvard Education Review* 54: 15-19.

Duffy, G. (1977). A study of conceptions of reading. New Orleans: Presentation at the National Reading Conference.

Eisner, E. (1969). Instructional and expressive educational objectives: Their formulation and use in curriculum. CERIC Document Reproduction Service No. ED028838.

Eisner, E. W. (1991). *The Enlightened Eye*. New York: Macmillan.

———. (1985). *The Educational Imagination,* 2nd ed. New York: Macmillan.

Eisner, E., and Vallance, E., eds. (1974). *Conflicting Conceptions of Curriculum*. Berkeley: McCutchan.

Elbaz, F. (1983). *Teacher Thinking: A Study of Practical Knowledge*. London: Croom Helm.
———. (1981). The teacher's practical knowledge: Report of a case study. *Curriculum Inquiry* 11: 43-71.

Englemann, S., and Bruner, E. (1962). *DISTAR Reading I: Teacher's Guide*. Chicago: Science Research Associates.

Erickson, F. (1986). Qualitative research methods in research on teaching. In *Handbook of Research on Teaching,* 3rd ed., edited by M. C. Wittrock, 119-161. New York: Macmillan.

Festinger, L. (1957). *A Theory of Cognitive Dissonance*. Evanston, IL: Row & Peterson.

Fox, D. J., and Lorge, I. (1962). The relative quality of decisions written by individuals and by groups as the available time for problem solving is increased. *Journal of Social Psychology* 57: 227-242.

Freidus, H. (1991). Critical issues in the curriculum of teacher education programs. Chicago: Presentation at the Annual Conference of the American Educational Research Association.

Gadamer, H., ed. (1977). *Philosophical Hermeneutics*. Berkeley: University of California Press.

Geertz, C. (1973). *The Interpretation of Cultures*. New York: Basic Books.

Gitlin, A. (1990). Educative research voice and school change. *Teachers College Record* 60: 443-466.

Glaser, B. G., and Strauss, A. L. (1967). *The Discovery of Grounded Theory*. Chicago: Aldine.

Green, M. (1988). *The Dialect of Learning*. New York: Teachers College Press.

Habermas, J. (1971). *Knowledge and Human Interests*. London: Heinemann.

Hammersley, M. (1977). *Teacher Perspectives, Units 9 and 10 in Open University Schooling and Society Course*. London: Milton Keynes.

Hollingsworth, S. (1989). Prior beliefs and cognitive change in learning to teach. *American Educational Research Journal* 26: 160-189.

Holly, M. (1989). *Writing to Grow: Keeping a Personal-Professional Journal*. Portsmouth, NH: Heinemann.

Holmes Group (1986). *Tomorrow's Teachers*. East Lansing, MI: Holmes Group.

Interactive Computer Simulations Laboratory (1993). *Arab-Israeli Simulation*. Ann Arbor: University of Michigan School of Education.

Jackson, P. (1990). *Life in Classrooms,* 2nd ed. New York: Teachers College Press.
———. (1968). *Life in Classrooms*. Chicago: University of Chicago Press.

Janis, I., and Mann, L. (1977). *Decision Making*. New York: Free Press.

Jenkins, D., and Shipman, M. (1976). *Curriculum: An Introduction*. London: Open Books.

Jung, B. (1991). *Curriculum Decision Making and Stakeholder Interests: A Case Study*. Columbus: Ohio State University, unpublished Ph.D. dissertation.

Kagan, D. M., and Tippins, D. J. (1992). The evolution of functional lesson plans among twelve elementary and secondary student teachers. *Elementary School Journal* 92: 477-489.

Kauchak, D., and Eggen, P. D. (1989). *Learning and Teaching: Research-Based Methods*. Boston: Allyn and Bacon.

Keinan, G. (1987). Decision making under stress: Scanning of alternatives under con-trollable and uncontrollable threats. *Journal of Personality and Social Psychology* 52: 639-644.

Kelly, G. A. (1955). *The Psychology of Personal Constructs*. New York: Norton.

Kolb, D. A. (1983). Problem management: Learning from experience. In *The Executive Mind,* edited by Suresh Srivastva et al., 109-143. San Francisco: Jossey-Bass.

Lakoff, G., and Johnson, M. (1980). *Metaphors We Live By*. Chicago: University of Chicago Press.

Larson, S. (1984). Describing teachers' conceptions of their professional world. In *Teachers Thinking: A New Perspective on Persisting Problems in Education,* edited by R. Halkes and J. K. Olson, 123–133. Lisse, Switzerland: Swets-Zeitlinger, B.V.

Leinhardt, G. (1982). Expert and novice knowledge of individual student's achievement. Paper presented at the American Educational Research Association Conference, New York.

Lewis, C. S. (1955). *Surprised by Joy*. New York: Harcourt Brace Jovanovich.

Lincoln, Y., and Guba, E. (1985). *Naturalistic Inquiry*. Beverly Hills, CA: Sage.

Mansbridge, J. (1980). *Beyond Adversary Democracy*. Chicago: University of Chicago Press.

Maquet, J. J. (1964). Objectivity in anthropology. *Current Anthropology* 5: 47–55.

Marland, P. (1977). *A Study of Teachers' Interactive Thoughts*. Edmonton: University of Alberta, unpublished Ph.D. dissertation.

Marsh, C., Day, C., Hannay, L., and McCutcheon, G. (1990). *Reconceptualizing School-Based Curriculum Development*. London: Falmer Press.

McCutcheon, G. (1993). Curriculum implementation: A misnomer? *Education Research and Perspectives* 19 (June): 78–87.

———. (1982). What in the world is curriculum theory? *Theory into Practice XXI* 1 (Winter): 18–22.

———. (1981). On the interpretation of classroom observations. *Educational Researcher* 10: 5–10.

———. (1980). How do elementary school teachers plan? The nature of planning and influences on it. *Elementary School Journal* 81: 5–23.

McGrath, J. E., and Altman, I. (1966). *Small Group Research*. New York: Holt, Rinehart and Winston.

Milburn, T. W., Schuler, R. S., and Watman, K. H. (1983). Organizational crisis Part II: Strategies and responses. *Human Relations* 12: 1161–1180.

Morine-Dersheimer, G. (1979). Planning in classroom reality, an in-depth look. *Educational Research Quarterly* 3: 59–65.

Morine-Dersheimer, G., and Vallance, E. (1976). A study of teacher and pupil perceptions of classroom interaction. San Francisco: BTES, Far West Laboratory, Report 75-11-6.

Nye, R. (1973). *Conflict among Humans*. New York: Springer.

Oberg, A. (1987). Using construct theory as a basis for research into teacher professional development. *Journal of Curriculum Studies* 19: 55–65.

Park, R. (1941). The social function of war. *American Journal of Sociology* 46: 551–570.

Peck, M. S. (1987). *The Different Drum: Community Making and Peace*. New York: Simon and Schuster.

Pepper, S. (1945). *The Basis of Criticism in the Arts*. Cambridge: Harvard University Press.

Pereira, P. (1984). Deliberation and the art of perception. *Journal of Curriculum Studies* 16: 346–366.

Peterson, P. L., Marx, R. W., and Clark, C. M. (1978). Teacher planning, teacher behavior and student achievement. *American Educational Research Journal* 15: 416–432.

Pope, M., and Scott, E. (1984). Teacher's epistemology and practice. In *Teacher Thinking: A New Perspective on Problems in Education,* edited by R. Halkes and J. K. Olson, 112–133. Lisse, Switzerland: Swets and Zeitlinger, B.V.

Pratte, R. (1977). *Ideology and Education*. New York: David McKay.

Puglielli, L. (1994). *Experiential Cooperative Inquiry as a Methodology for Effective Change*. Columbus: Ohio State University, Ph.D. dissertation.

Reason, P., ed. (1988). *Human Inquiry in Action: Developments in New Paradigm Research*. Beverly Hills, CA: Sage.

Reid, W. (1978). *Thinking about the Curriculum*. London: Routledge and Kegan Paul.

Ridgeway, C. (1983). *The Dynamics of Small Groups*. New York: St. Martin's.

Roby, T. (1985). Habits impeding deliberation. *Journal of Curriculum Studies* 17: 17-36.

Ross, E. W., Cornett, J., and McCutcheon, G., eds. (1992). *Teacher Personal Theorizing: Connecting Curriculum Practice, Theory and Research*. Albany, NY: SUNY Press.

Sackmann, S. A. (1992). Culture and subcultures: An analysis of organizational knowledge. *Administrative Science Quarterly* 37: 140-161.

Sanders, D., and McCutcheon, G. (1986). The development of practical theories of teaching. *Journal of Curriculum and Supervision* 2: 50-67.

Sardo-Brown, D. (1988). Twelve middle school teachers' planning. *Elementary School Journal* 89: 69-87.

Schön, D. (1983). *The Reflective Practitioner: How Professionals Think in Action*. New York: Basic Books.

Schutz, A., and Luckmann, T. (1989). *The Structures of the Life-World*, vol. II. Evanston, IL: Northwestern University Press.

———. (1973). *The Structures of the Life-World*, vol. I. Evanston, IL: Northwestern University Press.

Schwab, J. (1978). *Science, Curriculum and Liberal Education: Selected Essays*, edited by I. Westbury and N. D. Willkof. Chicago: University of Chicago Press.

Scieszka, J. (1989). *The True Story of the Three Little Pigs!* New York: Viking Kestrel.

Senge, P. (1990). *The Fifth Discipline*. New York: Doubleday.

Simmel, G. (1955). *Conflict and the Web of Group Affiliations*. New York: Free Press.

Simon, H. (1976). *Administrative Behavior: A Study of Decision-Making Processes in Administrative Organization*, 3rd ed. New York: Free Press.

Sizer, T. (1984). *Horace's Compromise*. Boston: Houghton Mifflin.

Small, A. W. (1920). *General Sociology*. New York: Century Company.

Smart, C., and Verlinsky, I. (1977). Decisions for crisis decision units. *Administrative Sciences Quarterly* 22: 640-657.

Smith, K. K., and Berg, D. N. (1987). *Paradoxes of Group Life*. San Francisco: Jossey-Bass.

Stake, R. E., and Easley, J. A., co-directors (1979). *Case Studies in Science Education*. Washington, D.C.: U.S. Government Printing Office.

Sternberg, R., and Wagner, R. (1980). *Practical Intelligence*. Cambridge, MA: Cambridge University Press.

Strauss, A. L., and Corbin, J. (1990). *Basics of Qualitative Research: Grounded Theory Procedures and Techniques*. Newbury Park, CA: Sage.

Talmage, H. (1972). The textbook as arbiter of curriculum and instruction. *Elementary School Journal* 73: 20-25.

Taylor, P. H. (1970). *How Teachers Plan Their Courses*. Slough, Eng.: National Foundation for Educational Research in England and Wales.

Thorndike, E. (1938). The effect of discussion upon the correctness of group decisions when the factor of majority of influence is allowed for. *Journal of Social Psychology* 9: 343-362.

Valtman, A. (1991). Planning a unit for fifth graders. Columbus: Ohio State University, M.A. general examination.

Wagner, H. R., ed. (1970). *Alfred Schutz on Phenomenology and Social Relations*. Chicago: University of Chicago Press.

Walker, D. (1990). *Fundamentals of Curriculum.* New York: Harcourt Brace Jovanovich.
———. (1971). A naturalistic model of curriculum development. *School Review* 80: 51–65.
Watzlawick, P., ed. (1984). *The Invented Reality: How Do We Know What We Believe We Know?* New York: Norton.
Webb, E. J., et al. (1966). *Unobtrusive Measures.* Chicago: Rand McNally.
Yinger, R. J. (1990). The conversation of practice. In *Encouraging Reflective Practice in Education: An Analysis of Issues and Programs,* edited by R. Clift et al., 73–94. New York: Teachers College Press.
———. (1980). A study of teacher planning. *Elementary School Journal* 80: 107–127.
Zaharlik, A. (1992). Ethnography in anthropology and its value for education. *Theory into Practice* 31 (Summer): 116–125.
Zahorik, J. A. (1975). Teachers' planning models. *Educational Leadership* 33: 134–139.

Index